PORTUGAL

PORTUGAL

INTRODUCTION AND

NOTES ON THE PLATES BY FRANK TUOHY

PHOTOGRAPHS BY GRAHAM FINLAYSON

with 106 photogravure plates, 11 color plates and a map

A STUDIO BOOK

THE VIKING PRESS · NEW YORK

TEXT © 1970 FRANK TUOHY
PHOTOGRAPHS © 1970 GRAHAM FINLAYSON

PUBLISHED IN 1970 BY THE VIKING PRESS INC
625 MADISON AVENUE, NEW YORK, NY 10022

ALL RIGHTS RESERVED

SBN 670-56755-8

LIBRARY OF CONGRESS CATALOG CARD NUMBER 79-84006

TEXT FILMSET IN GREAT BRITAIN BY KEYSPOOLS LTD GOLBORNE AND
PRINTED IN GERMANY BY ENSSLIN AND LAIBLIN KG REUTLINGEN
COLOR BLOCKS ENGRAVED IN GERMANY BY KLISCHEEWERKSTATTEN
DER INDUSTRIEDIENST, WIESBADEN AND
THE PLATES PRINTED IN GERMANY BY J FINK STUTTGART
PHOTOGRAVURE PLATES PRINTED IN FRANCE BY ETS BRAUN ET CIE MULHOUSE
BOUND IN GERMANY BY GROSSBUCHBINDEREI SIGLOCH KUNZELSAU

CONTENTS

	MAP OF PORTUGAL	*page* 6
	INTRODUCTION	7
Part One	OPORTO AND THE NORTH	
	Plates 1–34	53
	Notes on the Plates	81
Part Two	LISBON AND ITS SURROUNDINGS	
	Plates 35–80	101
	Notes on the Plates	141
Part Three	THE ALGARVE AND THE SOUTH	
	Plates 81–106	165
	Notes on the Plates	193
	INDEX	201

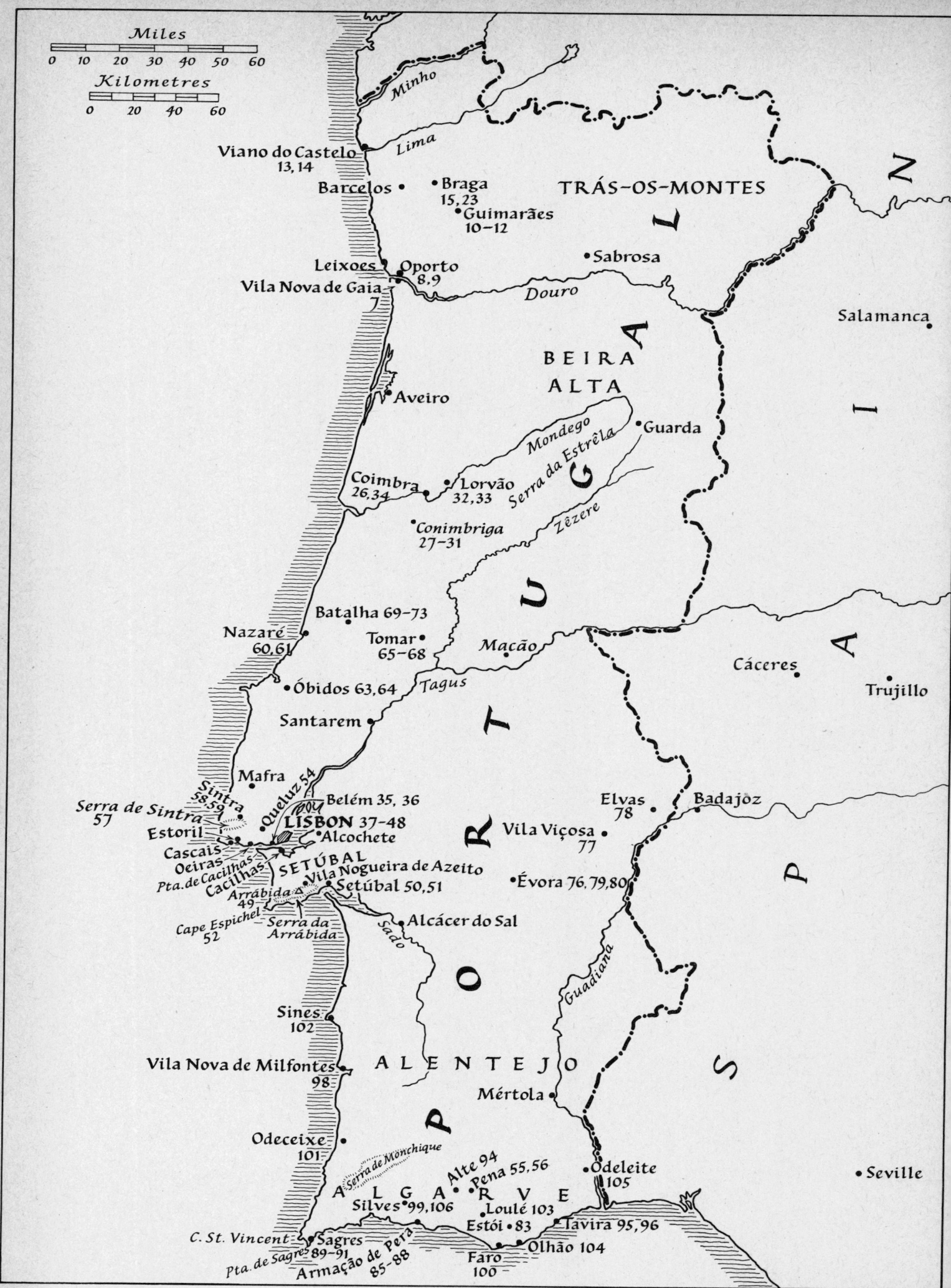

The numbers on the map refer to the Plates and corresponding Notes

PORTUGAL is the oldest country in Europe: her frontiers have remained unchanged for nearly eight centuries. One of these frontiers is the Atlantic Ocean, violent and ice-cold, the accident of eternity. The other frontier is the accident of history. A winding line which follows several rivers and the tops of several mountain ranges, it has remained unaltered (except in one small area) since long before France or Spain or Great Britain were united as nation-states.

For most of Portuguese history the open frontier has been the Atlantic one: far more has come to Portugal from overseas than ever came from Spain. The closed frontier has been the one with Spain, in spite of polite meetings between elderly despots and communiqués protesting united aims, so that the unprepared traveller is continually surprised when he moves from the one country to the other. Everything, given the similarities of climate and landscape, ought to be the same and almost nothing is. As for the foreigner who is already familiar with Portugal, he is left each time with a stronger, more heightened and more agreeable sense of Portuguese idiosyncrasy and individuality.

In fact, whenever the frequent visitor re-enters the country, he has a feeling that here he will perforce become a different person. For one thing, his manners will hardly come up to scratch; a voice raised, or signs of impatience and urgency, will have far-reaching but luckily not long-lasting effects. He is constantly encountering goodwill, but it is not the sort of all-embracing populist goodwill that takes no account of national and cultural differences. It takes account of everything. 'Foreigners!' I once heard an elderly gentleman exclaim with tolerant distaste, as a party of them left a restaurant. 'Oh yes', the waiter agreed, 'they have a mentality completely different from ours.'

The Portuguese guard their national individuality fiercely. Once at the police station on the frontier between Elvas and Badajoz, a Spanish gentleman was having a long argument with a Portuguese Customs official about what appeared to be a small packet of coffee. They were both of them scrupulously courteous and their conversation was fluent and prolonged: neither of them was at a loss for the vocabulary to express exactly what he wished to say. Then you realized (being afflicted by the sort of stagnant *angst* created by crossing any border) that all this was going on so long because each man was able to understand less than half of what the other was saying. Because one of them was Spanish and the other Portuguese, concessions were inconceivable. If both had been foreigners who happened to know Spanish and Portuguese, communication would have been easy: after all the two languages have thousands of words in common. In the end the antagonists could only stare at each other over the packet of coffee, like the two castles which face each other on either bank of the river outside the Customs House. Their conversation merely trailed away. The easiest thing that could have happened was nothing, and it did. Or rather, the impatient foreigner broke in, the two Iberians agreed in their astonishment at his lack of education, he got his passport stamped and never learned what became of the packet of coffee (if it was coffee). He drove off into Portugal, the comfortable land where everything would be different.

In Portugal there is a difference in the scale of everything: the persistence of one type of landscape, the range of human experience. Spain is like a novel with half a dozen chapters; Portugal is a short story. A compact country, with variety in a limited space, one small village church will commemorate six centuries of history and three golden ages of architecture.

Portugal's connection with Spain, then, is more distant than that of Austria with Germany. It more resembles the relationship between Japan and China. Sharing the inheritance of a civilization, the two countries differ in the ways in which they have put it into operation, either by usage or by neglect. Spain, like China, has constructed a great central capital: whenever she looks for her identity, she must always be looking inwards into her own heart, trying to resolve the differences between Catalonian, Castilian, Basque and Andalusian: foreigners are unimportant in this debate. Alone among the Iberians, the Portuguese have contracted out, and their capital is a port, a giant natural harbour, an outpost on the Atlantic frontier.

When you see the ships moored at the end of a Lisbon street, you seem to feel the trade routes to the world outside dragging like threads, pulling at the hearts of the inhabitants as they have done since the twelfth century and even before that (if one can believe all that is said about Phoenician settlements). Since the very beginning of her national existence, Portugal has been like a spider, spinning an infinite web which was to link Japan and Calicut, Timor and Mozambique, Luanda and Mazagan and the Brazils, until it connected the entire known world. No wonder that the centre could not hold and exhaustion followed.

The Portuguese are always repeating that their country is a poor one. But there are far poorer countries (not, it is true, in Europe) which strike us as abundantly vital. It is a part of the charm of this country, its gentleness and lyricism, to seem always a little tired. Tired people are ready with certain debilitating emotions, and *saudade*, the Portuguese national favourite, literally meaning 'yearning', is a nostalgia for something lost that perhaps was never really there.

This inward-looking character damps down Portuguese day-to-day life and quietens the life of the streets. If you could – if only you could – cut out the noise of cars and trams, Lisbon would be one of Europe's quieter cities, with its morning street cries and the plaintive whistle of the knife-grinders. Though social activities, as elsewhere in the South, centre on the public place rather than the private house, they are carried on quietly. Each table in a Lisbon café is isolated from its neighbour, a temporary room. One table has become a study for a student of mathematics, at another a professor is coaching a plain girl for an examination, at another serious men with brief-cases discuss legal matters.

The inward-looking Portuguese have, with a few exceptions, proved ungifted at the visual arts and their craftsmen have relied on inspiration from abroad. But they possess a large number of poets – perhaps too many, for the language lends itself readily to facility in rhyming, as anyone who has ever listened to the words of the *fado*, the traditional song of the Lisbon cafés, will discover. And they have at least one great novelist in Eça de Queiroz, whose novels give as candid a picture of nineteenth-century life as any outside French or Russian literature. It is tempting to use Eça, as he is always known, as a reference for every aspect of national life, for his range is wide and he has a perfect eye for detail. He even possesses the precisely gauged kind of sexual frankness which says to the reader: you know exactly what I am talking about, so I need not explain further.

As with all old countries, the Portugal you drive through today is mostly the creation of man. Good King Dinis started planting his forests of imported pine trees in the thirteenth century, and under Dr Salazar the plantations have reached almost to the very mountain tops. On the lower slopes they have been joined by the horrible eucalyptus, which exhausts the soil, smells like a chemist's shop and drives away insects and thus birds and animals as well. In March, whole woodlands of mimosa turn to clouds of gold, and throughout the winter months the roadsides are thickly covered by the yellow flowers and green trefoils of the Cape sorrel *(Oxalis pes-caprae)*, which has appeared from South Africa within living memory. A friend of mine in Cascais has found that the freesias which flourish in her garden have escaped to the surrounding countryside and have even been listed among the indigenous plants of Portugal.

But the greatest and most decisive mutation that man has wrought in the bare bones of this country is his importation of the vine. In the Douro, the region of schist, that curious form of rock that looks like flaky biscuits, the Romans are supposed to have first terraced the mountain walls and grown the grapes that much later were to be used for port.

Within the three hundred and fifty miles between the Minho river on the Spanish frontier and the warm coast of the Algarve, there is an immense variety of landscape. On the granite mountains of the north-east and between the Douro and Mondego valleys, nothing much will grow and there the shepherds guard their flocks with the help of huge wolf-dogs. The mountains gradually diminish in size as you go southward, the coastal plain grows broader and belts of pine-trees keep back the shifting sands.

A few miles before Lisbon there is a last little, almost suburban, range of hills, the Serra de Sintra, a landscape garden in the picturesque style much favoured by the English visitors of the Romantic movement and after. Unhappily, since a disastrous fire a few years ago, many of the vistas admired by Beckford, Southey and Byron have been permanently damaged, and now housing estates are being laid out among the blackened pine trunks that remain. Enough survives, however, to enable the visitor to recapture the romantic dream of a lost Eden: there is the garden of Monserrate with its tree ferns; there are strange villas, products of fantasy often untrammelled by good taste, peering out of the thickets of Portugal laurel, which grows here to an immense height, and the dozen or so varieties of mimosa tree. And in the early spring there are the flowers: the romulea, like a small violet crocus, asphodels, wild daffodils of the 'hoop-petticoat' type, buglosses that carpet the tilled fields, little irises and blue squills, and clumps of yellow crown daisies.

South of Lisbon and the valley of the Tagus is the area of earthquakes. Nearby, the Outra Banda is one of the corners of Portugal that jut out into the Atlantic. Since the construction of the giant bridge across the Tagus at Lisbon, the whole of this area has become much more accessible, to its detriment. But the great limestone range of Arrábida remains almost untouched, and there the road runs through a natural arboretum of indigenous plants – arbutus, tree-heather, lentiscus, phillyrea and cistus – until it emerges on to a ridge, where you can see, as if from a swooping aeroplane, the inhabited plain on one side and, on the other, the marbled sea which hides a drowned city called Troia. The Outra Banda to me is more beautiful than the Serra de Sintra, but it is too near Lisbon, the town-planners are on their way and its charm is unlikely to last.

To the east of Lisbon the vast area known as 'Alentejo' (beyond the Tagus) stretches almost to the Spanish frontier. Cork forests alternate with large fields of grain; herds of fighting bulls look tame and uninteresting on the far-off horizon. In scale this is perhaps the area of Portugal which most reminds one of Spain. However, it contains Évora, one of the most splendid and individual of Portuguese cities.

South of this, the Serra de Monchique is a sudden return to the spectacular mountain landscape of the north. But on its southern side the land slopes gently down through orchards of almond, apricot and fig, until it reaches the warmest of the country's chill, fish-swarming coasts. This is the Algarve, the last part of the kingdom to have been wrested from the Moors.

The Portuguese countryside has suffered not only from the usual problem experienced by agricultural countries, the flow of the more intelligent men to the towns, but also from economic upheavals caused by mismanagement of the wealth coming in from overseas. Its story carries the sadness of ambitions frustrated, bankruptcies and wasted lives. Yet one can still find in it all the natural beauty which is typical of the Mediterranean region, varied by the fresh, boisterous influence of the ever-present Atlantic.

In a few places still, the original vegetation has built up into what botanists call a 'climax' plant community, the optimum for the vegetable world given the climatic conditions of the region. In Portugal this is represented by the type of evergreen forest which covers the mountain side at the Bom Jesus outside Braga, a forest of ilex, cork oak and various pine-trees. Further south, at Bussaco, exotic trees have been added, including the so-called Mexican cedar trees (*Cupressus glauca*) believed to have been introduced by returning missionaries in the sixteenth century. In spite of such imports, however, botanists have described Bussaco as 'the most perfect specimen of the old forests of primitive Lusitania'. On the Serra de Sintra much more is artificial, for mimosa and eucalyptus are to be found flourishing among the Portugal laurels and evergreen oaks. But, for an Englishman at any rate, the texture and the very smell of these woodlands are like a return to the past, for they recreate on an adult scale the shrubberies known in childhood, planted round the Victorian and Edwardian villas of southern England in places like Folkestone and Tunbridge Wells.

One feels more at ease perhaps in the second of the types of wild vegetation, that of the limestone range of Arrábida. Here the trees are of lower growth: it is *mato*, or maquis, but a maquis which has formed naturally through the inability of limestone to support a more luxuriant vegetation. In other districts where conditions are poorer, this maquis is taken over by the various types of cistus – the white-flowered, sage-leaved type, the big gum cistus with its papery-white petals stained with black round a golden heart – and various types of lavender and sage. Such areas look uninteresting save in the early months of the year, when the cistus is in flower and is joined by the various tuberous and bulbous plants, iris, narcissus, asphodel and daffodil, which can also flourish in the drought-ridden soil.

Finally, there is the sort of wild landscape which supports the minimum of vegetation:

on the slopes of the mountains approaching the great shrine at Fatima, and on the headlands that jut out towards the sunset at Cape St Vincent and Sagres. Here one stumbles over small, thorny shrubs, clipped smooth by the Atlantic gales, and finds many well-known aromatic plants, rosemary and thyme, whose stunted growth seems to make them smell all the stronger.

The visitor to present-day Portugal is bound to see it as an enclave of the past, a country where a pre-industrial, pre-enlightenment civilization is still intermittently functioning. With a selective eye on the look-out for good value, he rejects whatever is familiar and seeks out whatever is strange. He notices, for instance, the oxen that drag the fishing boats up the shore at Nazaré, but excludes the tractors that perform this function almost everywhere else. He grieves for the Douro wine-presses where the bare feet no longer tread, and is glad about the squat, whitewashed windmills, whose sails still keep busily spinning.

Half-consciously, too, he looks for a country which is complete, its history over, its problems solved. Of course, he never finds it, but in Portugal it will often seem that he has done so. This impression is reinforced by the obligatory calm of the past forty years, the long convalescence after a period of financial and social upheaval. As I am writing this, this period is coming to an end. But any move into the future depends on an interpretation or a reinterpretation of the past.

The noise of the past is everywhere: its echo reverberates from the granite walls of fortresses, in the long lists of imperial possessions, in the allegorical ladies – Europe, Africa, Asia, America – leaning against the pediments of public statues. Here history was a series of shattering explosions which belong to a time outside the memory of living men. Palaces, castles and monasteries look harassed by the efforts of restorers who, in the interests of the national heritage and the Tourist Association, try to keep them with us still. We decide that the economic miracles of Portuguese history belong to the age before the machine, and a small country has no contribution to make to a post-industrial world. But the strange fact persists that it was the Portuguese themselves who started the whole process of world discovery and tied the continents together.

I The former Throne Room, Queluz
The Palace of Queluz was built between 1758 and 1794 for King José's brother Dom Pedro, who later, by marrying his niece Maria I, became King-Consort. The throne-room, with its wonderfully delicate rococo decoration in white and gold, is the result of a collaboration between the Lisbon woodcarver Silvestre de Faria Lobo (d. 1769) and the French decorator Antoine Collin. Today, during state visits by foreign notables, it is used as a ball-room.

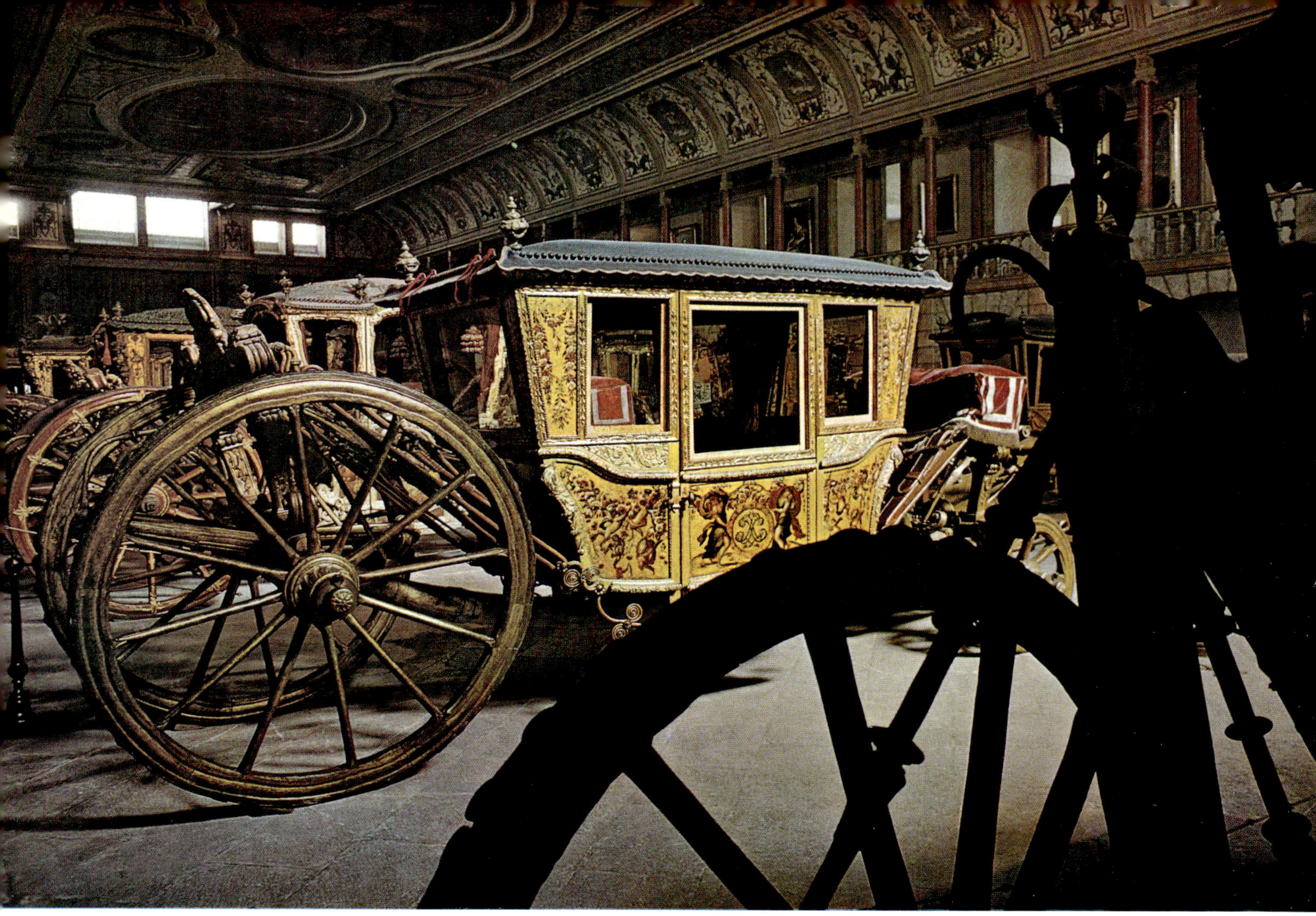

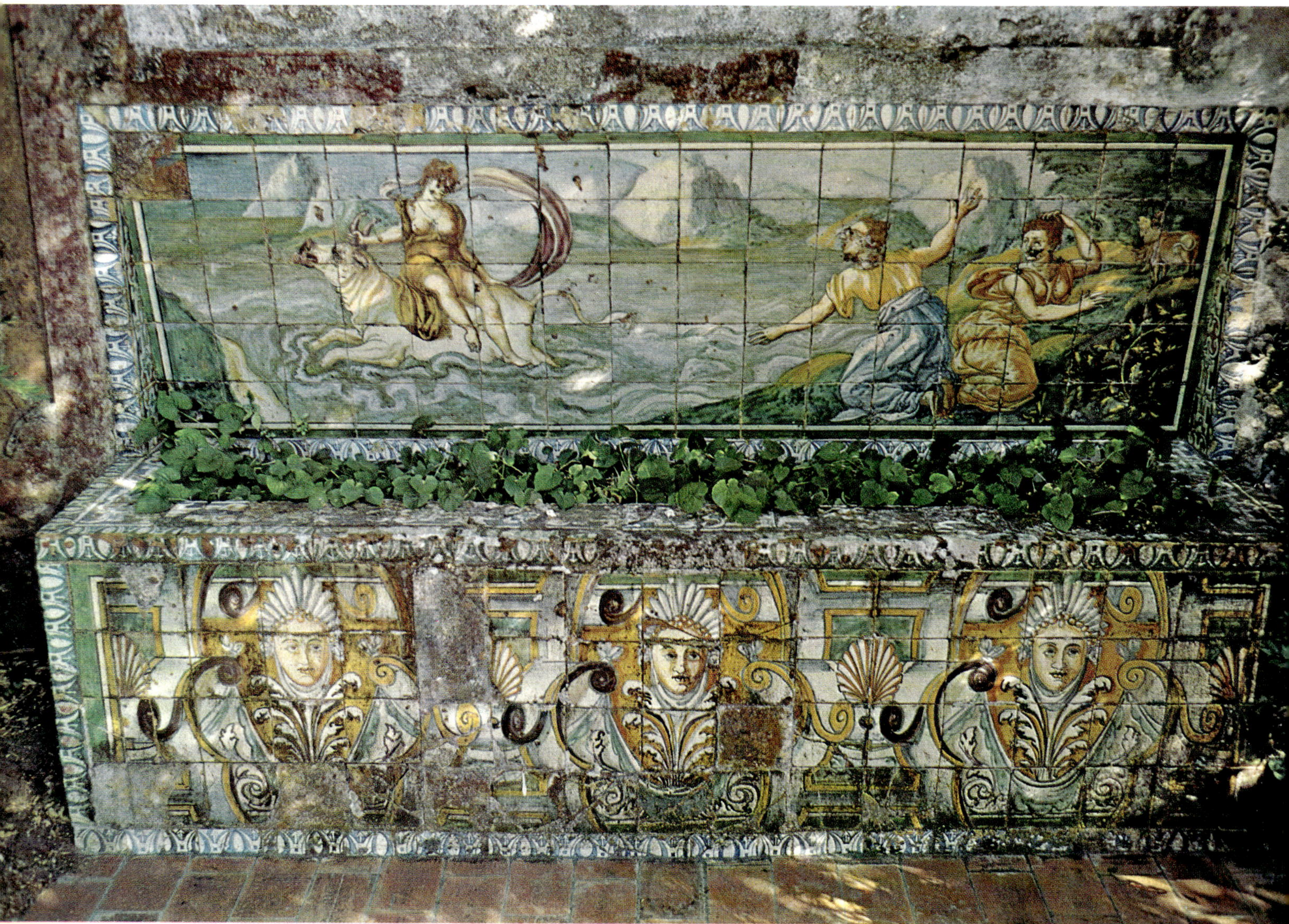

By an early assertion of independence, the Portuguese threw the Iberian peninsula off balance. They won early what Basques and Catalonians are still struggling for, and surrendered Spain to the domination of Castile. Portuguese independence was at first only a dynastic accident, caused by the arrival of the Burgundians, the master race of their age, in Leon and Galicia. Count Henry of Burgundy made a judicious marriage and received as dowry what is now northern Portugal, the land between the Minho and the Douro. His son Afonso Henriques, born in 1111, was to become the first king of Portugal.

A land blessed by nature, it was already old, with abundant traces of neolithic and Iron Age civilization. The hill-towns of the Celt–Iberians are known as *citânias*. The largest of them, Citânia de Briteiros (pl. 18), overlooks a vast valley to the east of Braga. Today you can stand in the middle of a maze of stone walls and round houses, where goats pasture and the blue squill grows in springtime. Everywhere in the north are strange stone relics, like the Pig of Murça, a blunt monster from a comic-strip, the guardian figures in the museum at Viana do Castelo, and the large image, phallic and mysterious, which waves a crippled paw in the garden of the museum at Guimarães.

The people who made these succeeded in establishing a settled agriculture around their fortified townships, and the Celtic towns continued to be in use during the Roman period: at Conimbriga, near Coimbra, inscriptions have been found in an unknown language mixed with Latin. But Conimbriga is a typical Roman town, with its mosaic floors, bath houses and underfloor heating systems, set in a classical landscape of tilled fields and olive groves (pls. 27–31).

II THE MUSEUM OF ROYAL COACHES, LISBON
In the riding school of the Palace of Belém (now the residence of the President of the Republic) a magnificent collection of the royal coaches is on display, showing the evolution of applied decorative art throughout the seventeenth, eighteenth and nineteenth centuries.

III AZULEJOS AT BACALHOA
Azulejos, or coloured tiles, a favourite Portuguese form of decoration, first became popular at the end of the fifteenth century. The earliest ones are in the Moorish style; later, however, pictorial tiles painted by the Majolica method were introduced from Italy. Some of the earliest of this latter type (dated 1565) are to be found in the garden pavilion at the Quinta da Bacalhoa, near Setúbal (*see* plate 53). This one shows Europa and the bull, and also some of the Renaissance-style decoration introduced to Portugal in the reign of João III (1521–57).

The Romans arrived very early in Portugal, in the third century BC, during the Punic Wars. For them it was the extreme limit of the known world: on what is now Cape St Vincent you could witness the sun entering the netherworld and hear the sizzling noise it made when it struck the ocean. Faced by such a spectacle, they retreated from the edge and left the Islands of the Blest unvisited. They founded cities all over southern Portugal – at Beja (Pax Julia), Mértola (Myrtilis), Évora (Liberalitas Julia). This is still Roman country: the roads that link some of these cities run straight as rulers through the cork forests. Driving along them, one sees nobody for miles except for an occasional shepherd, wearing a cape made of a whole sheepskin, watching his miscellaneous herd of sheep and goats, black and white, ring-straked, spotted and pied.

The Portugal of today has little surviving Roman architecture: the small temple at Évora, Conimbriga, one or two bridges. Yet in various ways it remains the most recognizably Roman of Latin countries. The language, which has changed very little since the foundation of the kingdom, is said to bear the closest resemblance to Latin: *filhos* for sons, instead of the Castilian *hijos*; *ovos* instead of *huevos*. Whole paragraphs can be written which are equally comprehensible as Latin or Portuguese. There is something very Roman, too, about Portugal's sense of an 'imperial mission', epitomized in her national epic *The Lusiads*, in which Vasco da Gama takes the place of Aeneas.

Most of all we are reminded of Rome by the quintessential classical landscape: the vineyards where the vine, instead of being staked, is married to other trees; the long-horned oxen which pull the heavy plough and harrow (both Roman introductions) or drag the laden carts along the dusty roads. The axles of the carts (axles were also a Roman innovation) are still left unoiled, and the weird atonal music they make in the countryside is supposed to keep off devils as well as frighten wolves.

All these, the long-horned oxen, the heavy ploughs and carts, belong to the lands between the Douro and the Minho in the north. It was here, according to Livy, that Decimus Brutus's legionaries, stunned by the beauty of the landscape, thought that they were passing through the Elysian fields; taking the River Lima for the waters of Lethe, they refused to cross it in case they would forget the temporal world for ever.

An odd result of the Roman inheritance is that the Portuguese Empire has lasted longer than that of Rome. In the fifth century, when the Roman administration crumbled, there were the usual barbarian invaders: the Suevi, who probably never settled but lived as freebooters and outlaws, and the Visigoths, who, we are told, 'rebuilt roughly with Roman materials'. Apart from importing the Germanic word for goose – *ganso* – they are known to have introduced wooden casks for storing wine, to replace the earthenware jars caulked with resin, and with this innovation at least the prospects for civilization in the Peninsula were brightened. They also introduced the persecution of the Jews, and the prospect darkened again.

The Visigoths were followers of the Arian heresy until they were converted by St Martin of Braga. In the fifth and sixth centuries the northern city of Braga was the centre of church government and of civilization. São Frutuoso, one of the few very old churches in Portugal, survives there, dark and mysterious like a tabernacle in a cave, beside a ruined baroque monastery. But little else is left from this period, except a few carved pilasters of barbaric design.

Nobody who has travelled long or far can have failed to observe that some peoples seem to arouse a peculiar resistance in the physical objects they encounter. The most famous, if mythological, example of this state of affairs is the Old Man of Thermopylae, who never did anything properly. He has his descendants everywhere, but in the Iberian peninsula they have flourished exceedingly. Under their influence, irrigation systems fall into decay, green vegetables cease to be grown, the plumbing clogs up and bills present everything but the exact total.

It must be frankly admitted that the Portuguese on occasion appear to be Thermopyleans. There is that vaguely embarrassing catch-phrase 'para o inglês ver' – for the Englishman to see – which is used for a job botched up to pass alien standards of judgment. But on the whole there are few Thermopyleans in Portugal compared with the uncounted multitudes who run the hotels and do the cooking across her only frontier. The reason for this seems to be an outside influence, but an influence from far too long ago to be called foreign, that of the Arab and Jewish populations.

Our grandparents who first encountered the world of Islam decaying in the grip of the Turkish Empire, and passed through the Suez Canal with averted eyes, found it hard to imagine that they had come in at the end of something, that there once had been an Arab civilization which was much more advanced than the Western European civilization which supplanted it. In the Islamic world there was, together with religious tolerance for 'the People of the Book', a racial tolerance which extended to the then-known world. There was a concern for learning which was moribund elsewhere, and a special interest in mathematics (algebra) and geography. Most important, there was skill in making the desert places flourish, which was shared by the humblest. The Old Man of Thermopylae who never did anything properly was to return again and again in Portuguese history and make one blade of grass grow where two had grown before. But his effect was never final, thanks, no doubt, to the fact that the Portuguese Inquisition was milder than the Spanish and intermittent in its persecutions, and that the Portuguese assimilated and intermarried with their Jewish and Arabian neighbours, so much so that many travellers have noticed the markedly Eastern look of the more prosperous members of the population. In southern Portugal, too, there are still signs of Arab influences on agriculture. Crossing the Serra you descend into a tamed landscape, with orchards of almond, fig and apricot, prickly pear fences and waterwheels, in which mules instead of oxen are used for ploughing and the women still muffle their faces from the direct gaze.

By their persecution of the Jews, the Visigoths ensured that the invaders would have allies. In the end, a three-sided community evolved, with the Moors, as they were known (though they had come from as far off as the Yemen), the Sephardic Jews and the Mozarabes (the Christians who, accepting Arab rule, continued to build their own churches and obey their own laws). All three races spoke the Latin patois which was soon to become Portuguese, and wrote it in one another's alphabets. Politically they were united against Viking raiders and built towns like Alcácer do Sal, Coimbra and Santarém at some distance up the estuaries of the rivers.

The Christian conquest in the eleventh and twelfth centuries was too violent for much to remain of Moorish architecture. The Royal Palace at Sintra, much rebuilt, retains a few Arab grace notes among its cacophony of styles (pl. 58). There are Moorish influences on some later architecture, notably the Tower at Belém. And there is Mértola, a strange little hill-town on the Guadiana river near the Spanish frontier; it was captured by the Suevi from the Romans in 459, by the Moslems from the Christians in 712, and by the Portuguese king in 1238. The Castle of Mértola is of the Moorish type: an outer rampart within whose perimeter the whole population could gather for protection and listen to the town being looted down below. But the parish church has no less than five naves: it is a little thicket of columns. Here alone in present-day Portugal you can imagine the prayer mats, the believers bowed towards Mecca.

Arabic words in profusion remain in Portuguese and they describe a whole culture for us in swift outline: *azulejo* (the coloured wall-tile which was to become a Portuguese fad); *nora* (waterwheel); *algodão* (cotton); *alecrim* (rosemary); *alface* (lettuce); *almofada* (cushion); *alfaiate* (tailor); *almoxarifado* (storehouse). And civilized life in Portugal has retained its Moorish elements. William Beckford, travelling at the end of the eighteenth century, found 'a group of senhoras seated on the ground *à la façon de Barbarie*'. The sweet cakes with peculiar names like 'soft eggs' and 'bacon of Heaven', which such ladies still prefer, are said to have been handed down in recipes from convents; but their cloying stickiness also reminds us that the Portuguese convent was sometimes a descendant of the harem.

Indeed, the matter-of-fact approach to sexuality, surprising us in a nineteenth-century novelist like Eça de Queiroz, is reminiscent of other countries, such as Greece, which have had close contacts with Islam. Lastly, it is perhaps possible to see the influence of Islam in the notable sobriety of the Portuguese. Inhabitants of a wine-producing country, they are curiously abstemious and compare themselves favourably with the English in this respect. And of course they almost never drink port.

*

Throughout the Middle Ages the Christian conquest of Moorish Portugal continued with heavy-footed steps. The last city to fall was Faro, on the southern coast, in 1249. To the north stretched a land which, as the national historian Alexandre Herculano wrote, was 'devastated by wars of religion and embittered by racial hatred'.

Why did this happen? Another Portuguese writer has said that 'there was no ethnographic reason for the foundation of the Portuguese monarchy.' The same could be said of most European countries: nationalism came much later. But wherever there was a frontier with the Infidel, a challenge existed to make the world safe for Christianity, and to enrich yourself at the same time. Already in the tenth century the country as far south as the Douro, with its estuary town known as Portucale (hence Portugal), had been colonized by the Galicians. Henry of Burgundy ruled over an area as far south as Coimbra. His son, Afonso Henriques, declared himself king and pushed as far as Lisbon. After a miraculous vision of the 'Labarum', the Roman standard with Christ on the Cross, similar to that of the Emperor Constantine, Afonso Henriques won the legendary Battle of Ourique, at a place and date which remain imprecise.

More is known about the band of English crusaders who stopped off at Oporto in 1139. The king immediately hired them for the assault on Lisbon: they were to keep all enemy property and to possess the city until it had been plundered. As later at Byzantium, the Crusaders were regrettably ill-informed about the spread of the Faith: they murdered the Catholic Bishop of Lisbon, whom they took for a Moor telling a good story. In his place they put somebody called Gilbert of Hastings, and had him consecrated by the Archbishop of Braga. He is the first of a long line of Englishmen in Portuguese history.

As was to happen in the future, the new conquests led to economic breakdown. In the central part of the country the farming methods introduced by the Moors, the irrigation system and crop rotation were forgotten and the land fell into disuse. The Mozarabes, who had been free Christians under Moslem rule, now became the serfs of their liberators.

Enriched by loot, the feudal conquerors hardly needed to make use of the lands they had captured: the spectacle of others in misery merely promotes one's own sense of wellbeing. The king himself made some efforts to restore agriculture, and even pronounced it a capital offence to cut down a pine-tree. But what he needed was expert knowledge and this arrived only by good luck. The Royal family was Burgundian, and Burgundy contained the great monastery of Clairvaux, founded by St Bernard. In thanksgiving for the miraculous victory over the Moors, the king established a monastery for the Cistercians at Alcobaça, in territory still raided from time to time by the infidels. Probably without knowing it, he had brought civilization back to Portugal.

In the monastery's great years, the Abbot of Alcobaça held the titles of Lord of Winds and Waters, Lord of the Woodlands, Donator of the Crown, Chief Almoner, King's Counsellor and Governor-General; he was also lord of thirteen villages and three seaports. But the monastery owed its importance not to his titles but to the agricultural skills that the monks reintroduced: they procured seeds and plants from Rome, they taught shepherds to become landworkers and redeemed landworkers from slavery and serf-dom. Today the monastery buildings, already ravaged by the looting of Napoleon's soldiers, have been further damaged by the type of over-restoration which has stripped off all later ornamentation, the accumulated craftsmanship produced by centuries of wealth, in order to arrive at the bleak and chilly Gothic skeleton. But perhaps one can still guess at the Cistercian feeling for priorities from the giant kitchens, with their marble slabs as long as cricket pitches, chimneys which ascend like cooling towers and, through the middle of it all, a living stream of water which once long ago swarmed with trout, salmon, shad and lampreys for monastic fast days. When William Beckford visited Alcobaça in 1787, the cooking had acquired a Chinese aspect: the monks were thrilled by the novelty of his French chef. Beckford's description of his stay was written up for publication after the abolition of the Portuguese monasteries in 1834 and he evokes a vanished world in languorous post-Romantic cadences. The Abbey was filled with his own special version of 'la douceur de vivre': a place of cosy dinner parties, naughty clerical giggles and charming acolytes dancing minuets together.

The monastery church at Alcobaça contains the celebrated memorial to the event which hastened the fall of the Burgundian dynasty of Portuguese Kings: the magnificent carved tombs of Pedro I and his Spanish mistress, Inês de Castro, who was murdered by rivals fearing Castilian influence and the loss of Portuguese independence. This event, in spite of its anti-nationalist bias, has become famous as a tragic love story with a macabre sequel. On ascending the throne, Pedro had the exhumed corpse of Inês crowned beside him and ordered his grandees to kiss the bones of her hand. The story is the subject of much Portuguese writing, and foreign writers have treated it as well.

Pedro and his successor, Fernão, were bent on uniting Portugal to Castile. But economic interests were already working against them. Portugal was already turned to her sea frontier. Once the Viking threat had ended, trade and shipping benefited from the Crusades. There were then twice as many ports as there are today; some, like Obidos, are stranded far inland, and others have completely disappeared under the sand-dunes. (The port which gave its name to Oporto and to Portugal herself is today almost blocked by a bar of sand.) But in 1348 nearly a third of the population died of the Black Death, the countryside became depopulated and people sought the cities, which were all near the sea. Here a new merchant class sprang up; here were opportunities for the talents of Mozarabes and Jews. The Portuguese, like the Catalonians and the Galicians of the same period, were ready to expand. The efforts of the Catalonians and Galicians were brought to nothing by the unification of Spain under Aragon and Castile; that Portugal survived was at least partly due to the alliance with England.

The Portuguese wanted codfish, the English wanted wine: on this basis trade relations between the two countries had already begun. The Portuguese took advantage of the Hundred Years War to increase their exports of wine, cork, oil and other goods to England. An English merchant colony established itself in Lisbon, with a special magistrate to deal with disputes with Portuguese traders. With the help of these English merchants, a band of archers was hired from England and assisted at the rout of the Castilians at the Battle of Aljubarrota in 1385. The following year, João I, former Master of Aviz and illegitimate son of Pedro, concluded the alliance with England at Guimarães and married John of Gaunt's daughter, Philippa of Lancaster. With these events the long, stagey, fretful and at times purely hypothetical alliance between the two countries had begun.

At the beginning, the balance was all in favour of Portugal, her ally being involved in the French Wars and then the Wars of the Roses. The reigns of the first five kings of the House of Aviz, from 1385 to 1521, mark an astonishing efflorescence of ambition, talent and renown. Wherever one goes in Portugal, one is confronted by the question: why did all this happen? Why were the Portuguese the first race truly to break through the frontiers of Christian Europe, not only through the silk curtain of Islam, where the Venetians had preceded them, but also into the jungles of South America and the courts of China and Japan?

The official view was that Portugal was especially beloved of Our Lady (it was said to be Her privilege and not that of the Royal line to wear the Crown of Portugal) and thus had a peculiar mission to propagate Christianity among the heathen. This view is the ancestor of the 'civilizing mission' which is still spoken of today. It would be too simple to dismiss it as mere hypocrisy, but it could hardly have been a sufficient motive in itself.

The first sortie overseas was the attack on Ceuta in 1415, the year of Agincourt. This was to be a new crusade, under the patronage of the dying Queen Philippa. Ceuta, by no coincidence, was the headquarters of the spice trade in that part of the world; in addition, the coasts were infested by Barbary pirates who were reducing Lisbon to a state of commercial asphyxia. For the first and not the last time, commerce and Christianity went together. The Portuguese were the first Imperialists whose trademark was the Cross. After the capture of Ceuta, came further explorations down the west coast of Africa. In the Portuguese language, the verb *explorar* in itself carries the meaning of 'to exploit'.

Other countries had religions and mercantile ambitions. The Portuguese by chance had the talents available as well. The family of João I and Philippa was a remarkable one. In the Founder's Chapel at Batalha (pl. 70), the effigies of the royal couple lie hand in hand and their sons, the 'marvellous generation' Camões called them, lie in niches in the walls. Philippa herself appears to have been intelligent and high-minded and her court was noted for its abstemiousness and chastity. The first was less remarkable than the second, for the Portuguese are still a sober race. The 'influxo glacial' of English blood was what surprised them. The most distinguished of Philippa's five illustrious sons was Dom Henrique, Prince Henry the Navigator; he was also the most 'glacial' of the group, going to his grave, his chroniclers record with astonishment, 'as virginal as on the day he was born'.

The talents, then, were there in the person of the Anglo–Portuguese Prince Henry who, surrounded by geographers and scholars as yet unpersecuted by the Inquisition, settled in his headquarters on the promontory of Sagres to plan the assault on the unknown world. With the talent went the technical advances: the Portuguese caravels had axled, hinged rudders and a secret weapon, hidden perhaps from Spanish and Genoese rivals, the mariner's compass. Nevertheless, the whole enterprise was surrounded with real and imaginary hazards. Madeira, the island of woods, was reached in 1420, but beyond it the strong tides that raced parallel to the coast of Africa had led to the belief that the world ended here: further than this, a ship would fall over the edge. 'Quem quer passar alem do Bojador', the modern poet Fernando Pessoa has written, 'Tem que passar alem da dor.' 'He who wishes to go beyond Cape Bojador must go beyond grief and pain.'

Yet the Cape was passed in 1434: the mythological barrier was broken and the world was open to the caravels. Seven years later the first convoy of black slaves reached the Algarve. The explorers had already discovered the Azores and reached São Tomé in the Gulf of Guinea. Mozambique and Mombasa came next, then Muscat and Ormuz in the Persian Gulf. By the end of the century they had established outposts in Goa and Colombo, and soon were to pass through the East Indies on the way to China and Japan. Álvares Cabral officially reached Brazil in 1500, but since the 'Pope's Line', promulgated in 1494, divided the New World to the west of this area, it seems likely that the Portuguese knew earlier of the existence of what was to be their largest colony. For the same reasons of secrecy, expeditions to Labrador and Greenland may have gone unpublicized.

IV DECORATED WALL AT BACALHOA
Further examples of the *azulejos* which are to be found in the garden pavilion at the Quinta da Bacalhoa, near Setúbal (*also see* pl. 53). In this photograph both forms of *azulejos* can be seen: the early Moorish type, with its abstract carpet-like patterns, and the later pictorial type, in this case a representation of Susanna and the Elders.

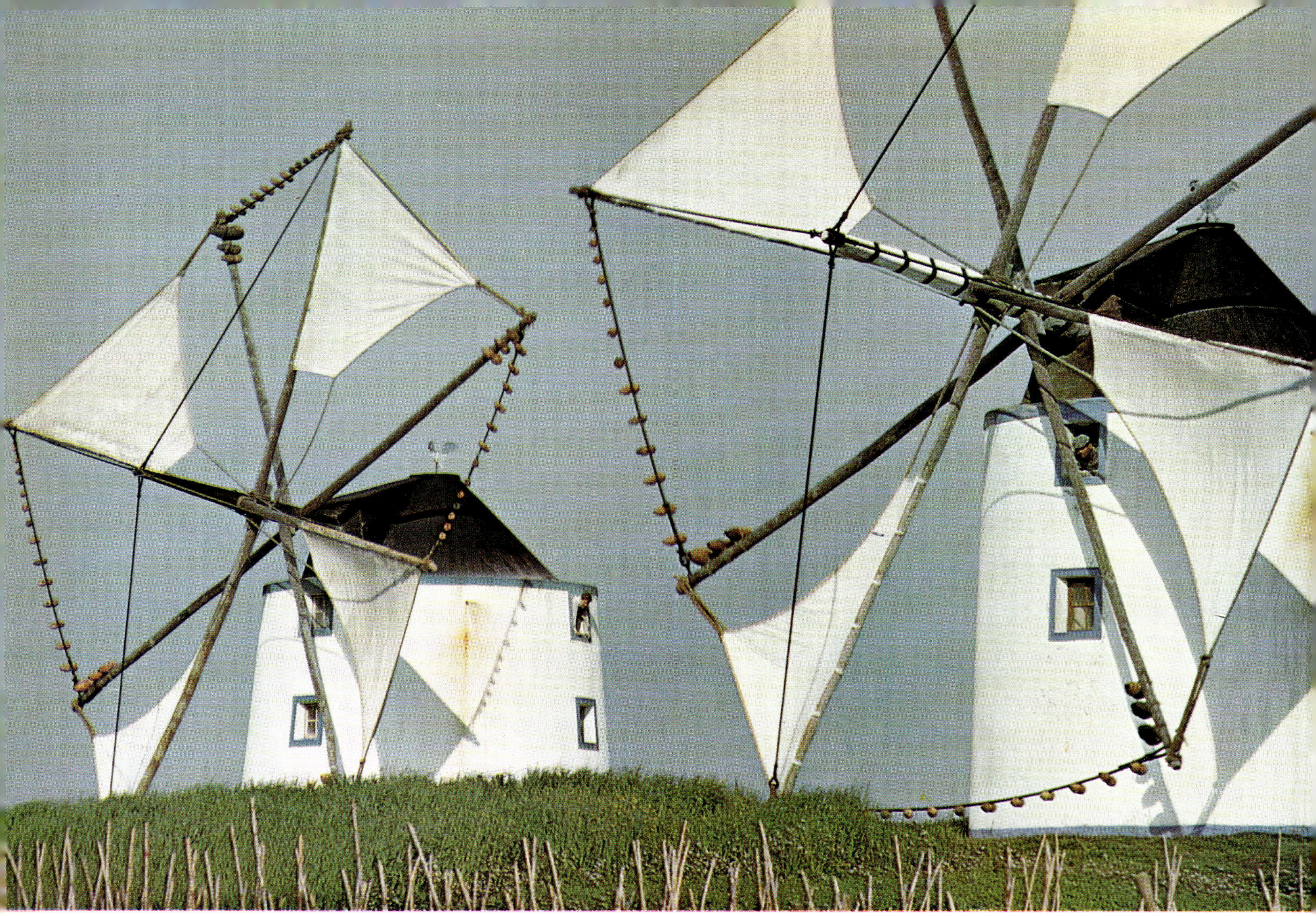
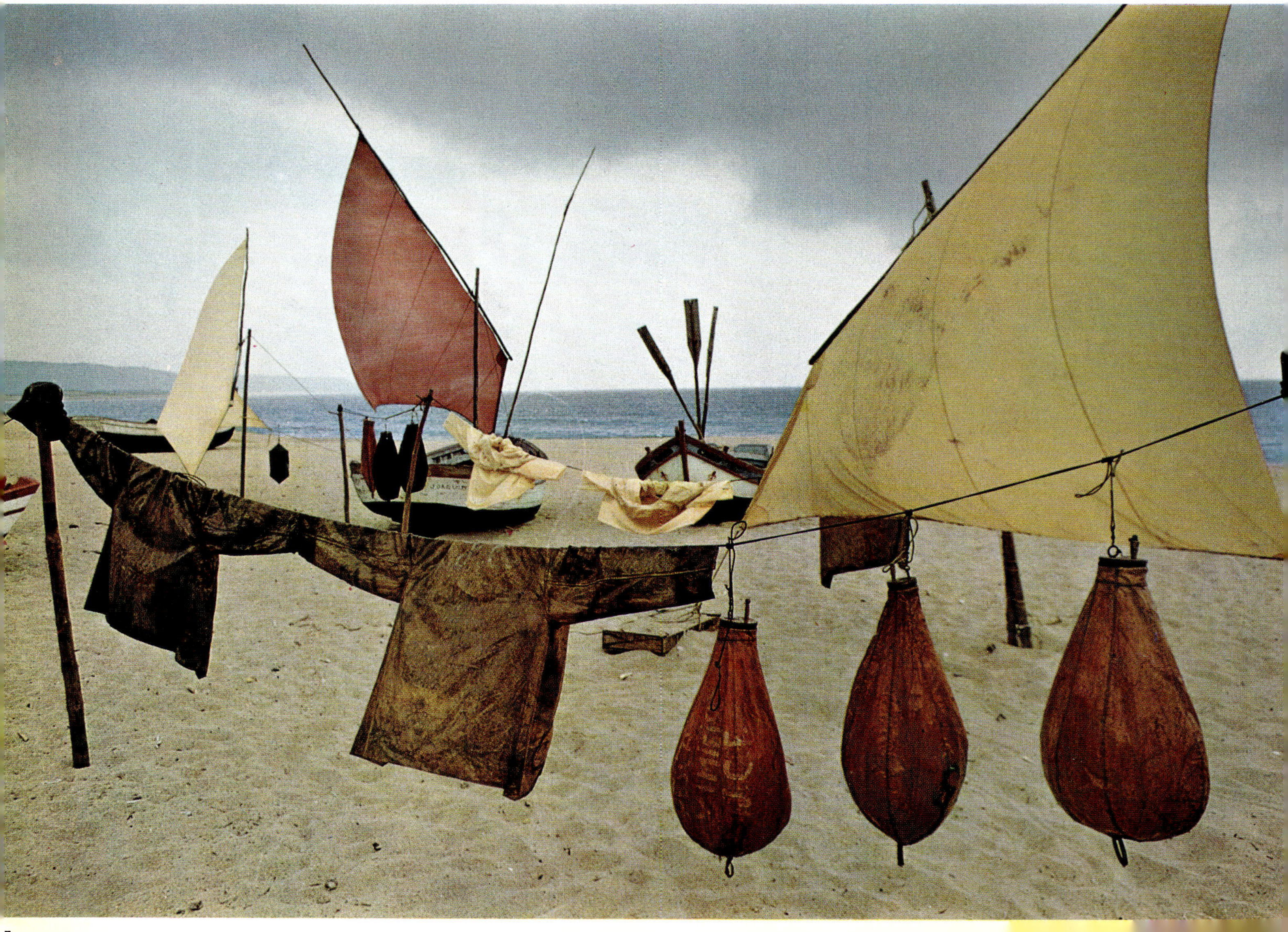

The cost of such expeditions in manpower was enormously high. Prince Henry was wise: except for the Ceuta campaign, he never accompanied his seamen on any of their missions. But if the losses were devastating, the rewards were also great: in 1499 Vasco da Gama's first cargo of spices from the East was sold for sixty times the cost of the expedition.

Vasco da Gama was a soldier and a nobleman, capable of acting as official ambassador to barbarian kings. His greatest predecessor, Bartolomeo Dias, had been merely a professional seaman. Empire was beginning to mean prestige as well as wealth, but we are still far from the nineteenth-century version. Afonso de Albuquerque, viceroy and conqueror in India, arriving in Goa in 1510, forbade the practice of trade by his men; he also encouraged them to marry Indian women. When he died he became a local deity, a great fish who swam up and down the Indian Ocean, and the Goanese went to his shrine to pray.

The Jesuit missionaries soon put a stop to this. The greatest of them, St Francis Xavier, lies embalmed at Goa, and he in his turn was to become a goal of pilgrimage.

Much of the wealth that came from overseas was handed over by the Sovereign to the Church or to one or other of the religious orders. Portugal is a country of monasteries founded by kings, of palace-monasteries and finally, after the expulsion of the monastic orders, of palaces that are built round monasteries, like the Pena Castle at Sintra, and the last palace of all, never to be occupied by the Royal family, at Bussaco.

From the first period of empire, the reign of Manuel I (1495–1521) was the most splendid, and the style of architecture named after it is the only one indigenous to Portugal. In Manueline architecture some writers have found an oriental influence,

V WINDMILLS NEAR SETÚBAL
Windmills, placed in groups on the tops of hills, are still used throughout the southern and central regions of Portugal. On the struts between the sails, hollow gourds are attached. These make a weird humming sound as the sails rotate. By listening for any alteration in the sound, the miller can immediately tell if the wind has changed direction.

VI THE SHORE, NAZARÉ
Nazaré is the fishing village where old traditions are most closely guarded. The fishing boats land on the open shore and are hauled in and out of the waves by oxen. Here sails and other equipment are stretched out to dry.

but the general view is that it is late Gothic, or 'decorated', flourishing in isolation after the style had been given up elsewhere. Anchors, ropes, armillary spheres and other maritime objects are entangled in decoration very similar to that found in English churches of an earlier period, such as St Mary Redcliffe at Bristol. What seems new in the Manueline style is a certain coarse exuberance, an extravagance which at times is more reminiscent of the Victorian Gothic revival, and thus connects one self-confident empire with another. This is surely true of the great west window at Tomar (pls. 65, 66). This extraordinary piece of fantastication is the last fling of a national style, and only a few years separate it from the Cloister of João III which lies immediately beside it, an immaculately classical example of Renaissance architecture.

The change of style reflected a change in the country itself. The influx of wealth had brought economic upheaval and, in a very few years, national bankruptcy. Lavish expenditure on religious festivals continued, but, as a Portuguese writer has put it, in the midst of what seemed a perpetual carnival the nation was begging for its bread. Mercantilism, the belief that money alone represents wealth, is a theory of economics appropriate to the plays of Christopher Marlowe and Ben Jonson, but hardly elsewhere. Yet a strong faith in it persists in Portugal today. 'Fazendo economias' is a national pastime: let us get rich quick, and then retire.

By the end of the Manueline period, in any case, the Portuguese had lost the monopoly of the spice trade. Furthermore, religious policy led to the renewed persecution of many of the most enterprising of her people. The expulsion of the unconverted, whether Jewish or Moorish, had been ordered in 1496. Later João III (1521–57) insisted, against the counsel of his religious advisers, on introducing the Inquisition. Renaissance humanism had hardly touched Portugal before the Counter-Reformation was in full swing. The University was transferred back from Lisbon to Coimbra, and by an ordinance of 1555 'the College of Arts and the Government thereof in its entirety' was delivered to the Provincial of the Company of Jesus. Henceforward any move towards intellectual progress was likely to be anti-clerical in tone.

The foreigner accustomed to other Catholic countries is surprised at the virulent manifestations of anti-clericalism that recur throughout Portuguese history: Pombal's campaign in the 1750s which led directly to the suppression of the Jesuits by Pope Clement XIV; the dissolution of the monasteries in the anti-Miguelite reaction of 1834; the atmosphere of atheist hysteria which surrounded the apparitions of Fatima in 1917. Even today Portuguese priests are obliged to wear civilian clothes in the street. Churches remain locked; one waits hours while a small boy goes to look for somebody who has the key. *O Crime do Padre Amaro* by Eça de Queiroz, written in the 1870s, still has a certain power to shock with its wholesale attack on the sexual morality of the priesthood. Yet it is an acknowledged literary classic which 'everybody' reads.

'Everybody', of course, means a rather smaller number than it usually does. Behind the scenes the Church has usually had considerable power – enough to permit it to carry the blame for widespread illiteracy. Thanks to strong religious censorship, the country missed not only Renaissance humanism but also the eighteenth-century Enlightenment, and has been unsuccessful in its dealings with such foreign ideas as democracy in recent years.

To call illiteracy a problem would be imprecise: it is a matter of acceptance, a minor difficulty easily smoothed over by natural good manners. At the counter of a bank in Faro, in the Algarve, a tweed-suited British resident is doing some sort of currency fiddle with a cheque drawn on Canada. The bank clerk treats her with the utmost courtesy and patience. As she goes out, her place is taken by an old country woman. In her brown, wrinkled fist she clutches a money order, presumably sent by a son who is working abroad. The clerk shows her where to sign. 'Oh no, I can't write', she states firmly, in the tones of someone saying she never touches alcohol. In the end she is persuaded to make a wavering cross, like the foot-print of a parrot. The clerk treats her exactly as he treated the English woman, with the courtesy that is so characteristic of everyday existence in Portugal.

I have sometimes wondered whether this formal courtesy might not owe something to Portugal's contacts with the Orient, to the influence of those elaborate codes of conduct to be found in China and Japan. But this is hardly possible, for Portuguese good manners are classless, and the vast majority of the population knew nothing of the civilization overseas and benefited from its riches not at all. *The Lusiads*, the epic of exploration, is addressed to the official point of view, and there is no popular literature about the great voyages and no folklore concerning the Portuguese Empire. (The British Empire, too, was a largely middle-class affair and produced only the pseudo-popular ballads of Kipling and Newbolt.) The Portuguese peasant who emigrates to Brazil has always had to rely on rumour and messages by word of mouth. He rarely returned to tell his friends what it was all like. How often, when you mention that you have lived in Brazil, you will be told of a father, brother or uncle who left eighteen years ago and has not been heard of since. Today Portuguese emigrants to the Common Market countries can come back with their opinions (usually unfavourable – 'Foreigners are very different from us!'). In the past the ticket across the Atlantic was usually one way only. Any return was as improbable as that of Dom Sebastião.

In the Lisbon Museum there is a strange portrait of this obviously unbalanced young man. How did the painter get away with it? (a question later to be asked about Goya's portraits of the Spanish Royal family). Dom Sebastião was the last king of the Royal House of Aviz. Like the first of his line, but with more idealistic motives, he launched a crusade against the Moroccan infidels. The expedition was supported by the Pope and, for his own reasons, by Philip II of Spain. The Portuguese Army was disastrously defeated at Alcazar Quibir in 1578; Sebastião disappeared in a mêlée of fighting warriors and was never seen again. Philip became King of Portugal.

But a strange cult flourished for many years: *Sebastianismo*, the belief that the young king would return again and save his people, like Jesus Christ, or King Arthur (or, for that matter, the Emperor Nero). The idea of a hidden saviour, whose secret existence would one day be revealed, was much favoured by the 'New Christians', the converted Jews. Through the sixty years that followed Alcazar Quibir, while Portugal in default of an heir to the throne was occupied by the Spaniards, *Sebastianismo* played its part in keeping alive the idea of Portuguese independence. Much later, madmen occasionally collected followers by announcing themselves to be Dom Sebastião, who had returned to lead his country to salvation. I have heard children in the streets of Lisbon singing a rhyme about El-Rei Dom Sebastião: thin and eery, telling of battles long ago.

During the Spanish occupation of Lisbon, the Portuguese Empire fell to pieces and the pieces were mostly snapped up by the new expanding nation, the Dutch. But the Brazilians rose in rebellion, turned out Maurice of Nassau from Recife and sent expeditions to re-establish the Portuguese trading posts in Africa.

Now that the monopoly of eastern trade was over, the mines of Brazil were to produce the wealth of Portugal. The Duke of Braganza, who became king when the Spaniards were driven out in 1640, already owned the Azores, and Grão Pará and Maranhão in Brazil. He looked on the throne as a business proposition and at one moment was ready to sell the country back to Spain. By remaining king, however, he was entitled to 'the Royal fifth', a fifth part of all wealth from overseas. Like several of his descendants, João IV had good taste, and the wealth from the Empire was to be used in transforming the country with palaces, churches and monasteries. He also founded the great music library, destroyed in the Lisbon earthquake; the Braganza taste favoured music more than painting, with the result that Portugal is deficient in pictures of value. Instead, the wealth of Brazil ascended to heaven in the incense burned in the churches and the endless warblings of *castrati*, the very tone of whose voices is now entirely forgotten.

Yet nobody can spend a week here without recognizing that this has been and still is an imperial country. Every museum or palace has its store of artefacts in the 'Indian' style, and it must be remembered that, for the explorers, 'India' was a name likely to be given to anywhere newly discovered. Porcelain from the 'India Company' was made in the factories of Canton and adorned with the crests of noble families. Portuguese ceramics were imitated in China, and *chinoiserie* decoration appeared on vases made at Coimbra as well as on the woodwork of the baroque University Library there (pl. 34). In general, the most extravagant luxuries were imported from outside, though Portuguese craftsmanship, especially in wood, was always of a high standard. At the time of the earthquake of 1755, Lisbon with its fantastic riches, its hordes of priests and beggars and its coloured population, which must then have been the largest in Europe, suggested an oriental kingdom.

How was it that a country with a tiny population, ill-equipped with soldiers and administrators, could secure, first, trading posts and, later, large areas of foreign soil? Even now, when the empires of the Age of Expansion have come to an end, Portugal still holds on to large parts of the globe.

The protection of the British Navy was obviously all-important. Other possible clues can be found in the rules set out by Albuquerque in 1510: the encouragement to marry native women and the prohibition placed on business activities.

Lack of racial prejudice has always been a boast of Portuguese civilization. Yet in Brazil, at any rate, the average Negro will tell you that he would far prefer to live in the United States. For him there is hardly any escape from the lowest stratum of society, except through football or show business. Brazil is not a multiracial society: there are two races, the Rich and the Poor, and the Rich do not mind who travels on the buses, since they never use them themselves. What has always been tolerated in the present and former Portuguese empires is mixed blood. 'Eu vou limpar a raça' a Negro says when he marries a girl lighter than himself: 'I am cleaning up the race'. Well into this century, Lisbon was reported to have a large coloured population. There are few signs of this today: assimilation is not merely a possibility but a fact.

The almost Moorish seclusion of women meant that comparatively few can have emigrated in earlier times. By the time conditions had improved, a new and ambitious mulatto class already existed. Thus there was no equivalent of Kipling's Mrs Hawksbee; E. M. Forster's 'Turtons and Burtons' were unknown and a 'fishing fleet' of young white ladies would have been definitely unwelcome.

Equally important was the discouragement of business activities, which naturally followed from the policy of the Church. There were no 'box-wallahs': commerce in the East stayed in the hands of the native population, while in colonial Brazil it came to be the province of those Jews who, whether baptized or not, preferred to keep the Atlantic between themselves and the Inquisition. I have been told that those surnames which are the names of trees, such as Nogueira, Silveira, Pereira and Oliveira, indicate Jewish origin and these names are among those most commonly found overseas. But, in any case, surnames are often avoided in favour of Christian names or nicknames, whether among one's own acquaintances or the famous people of the day. Thus the footballers Eusébio (a Christian name) and Pele (a nickname meaning 'skin') are perhaps the two best-known figures in the Portuguese-speaking world today.

Two memories of the Portuguese presence overseas: first, Macão a few years ago, just before the Chinese 'Cultural Revolution'. 'Não hà cidade mais leal' was inscribed in large Roman capitals over the portico of the Town Hall. Macão has been a Portuguese possession since 1557; now that Goa has gone, it must be the world's oldest colony. 'There is no city more loyal.' But loyal to what? An atmosphere perhaps. The Praia, which is not a beach but an embankment, has huge trees and a line of old Portuguese houses; it faces the yellow waves of the Pearl River estuary, ticketed with the sails of junks. There is the façade of the ruined cathedral, classical in style, yet closer inspection reveals a decoration of pine-trees and Chinese pictographs: the work of exiled Japanese Christians. What else is there of the mother country? Soldiers in the streets; administrators in the public buildings, intelligent, cheerful and disabused; one café for this band of exiles, at the end of the main street, wine to drink. Apart from this, all is China, commerce, gambling, brothels, everything; the China of the diaspora, which flourishes like a parasitic orchid on the branches of dead empires. In the shops the Chinese refuse to speak Portuguese, preferring English, the language of business. 'There is no city more loyal': loyal to *saudade*, the most Portuguese of feelings.

The other memory: this time of the great ex-colony, Brazil, closer to the mother country than the North American equivalent, if only because Latin society presents far fewer options. In any case, the coffee planters of North Paraná have certainly followed up Albuquerque's two recommendations: they have taken native women (or slaves), but so long ago that one can now pretend it never really happened; and they have always seen themselves as landowners not traders. Their large, rambling houses nowadays have aeroplane hangars beside them. They own horses but drive station-wagons. And in the town, dusty and expensive, even the Japanese farmers are dressed as cowboys. The whole place is pulsing with speculation: anecdotes of booms, of slumps, of annihilating frosts. This is the last Eldorado, where, if all goes well in one season, you will never have to work again.

The Spanish and Portuguese Empires came about as the result of this pursuit of Eldorado, the place of gold, whereas the Pilgrim Fathers went to found the New Jerusalem. This is true, however, only of the original impulse. The discoverers, who slaughtered and terrorized, were followed in the sixteenth and seventeenth centuries by Jesuit and Franciscan missionaries who were a good deal more effective than the saints of New England. The Franciscans, with their love and admiration of external nature, may have caused the initial change of sensibility, the whole idea of the excitement of discovery. The writings of the Jesuits in Japan show a respect, sometimes verging on tolerance, for alien systems of ethics. After less than seventy years of missionary work, about 35,000 Japanese were sufficiently convinced to die in terrible martyrdom. In the Grão Paraguay, the Society of Jesus developed a new society which looked much like a New Jerusalem. It is ironic that it was the resistance of this ideal society to being absorbed in the Portuguese Empire (the so-called 'Reductions of Paraguay') – and not Jesuit political intrigue in the courts of Europe – which caused the Order to be persecuted by the Marquis of Pombal.

The great Lisbon earthquake of 1755 is believed to have caused thirty or forty thousand deaths. The epicentre of the earthquake was out at sea: a tidal wave bursting into the Tagus engulfed the waterfront. Later there were further shocks, and fierce fires broke out. The whole of the lower part of the city was destroyed.

There seems to be something about earthquakes which undermines accepted metaphysical systems and causes men to question the whole meaning of existence. The self-confident men of the eighteenth century found in the Lisbon earthquake something demanding a philosophical explanation, a disaster which must somehow be accounted for on a teleological basis. What, they kept asking, was the earthquake for?

For Protestant divines in England the reasons for the Lisbon earthquake were quite unmistakable. God had punished Lisbon because of its unusual wickedness. Papacy and idolatry were more outrageous there than anywhere else, and even British businessmen could not remain immune. (The father of Alexander Pope is said to have been converted during a stay in Lisbon.) There were plenty of businessmen about, for, since the restoration of independence in 1640, relations with Britain had grown closer. The chance of an Anglo–Portuguese royal dynasty was lost when Charles II's wife, Catherine of Braganza, proved, as Dryden expressed it, 'a soil ungrateful to the tiller's care'. But the British Navy was bound to defend the Portuguese possessions overseas against the Dutch, and the alliance was reinforced by the treaty negotiated by John Methuen in 1703. The Methuen Treaty established the duty on wine from Oporto at two-thirds of that on French wines in return for concessions on British imports such as woollen cloth. (Methuen's brother, the Portuguese noted, had interests in the wool trade.) The result was that Portugal, herself owning an empire, had become something like a commercial colony of Britain. Probably this was inevitable, given her limited resources of talent, which the Inquisition had recently further depleted by new expulsions of the Jews and Moriscos who had fled there from Spain. Education was long to remain a luxury. Pedro II, who reigned in the last years of the seventeenth century, could neither read nor write, and during the Napoleonic Wars, we hear of a Minister of the Navy who could do addition and subtraction, but not division or multiplication.

And so in Lisbon and Oporto developed the first of those English commercial communities abroad, to a pattern that was to be repeated in Buenos Aires and Kobe, in Shanghai and Canton and São Paulo, based on club life and a rigid pecking order and a barely concealed contempt for 'these people', the natives of the country.

The remarkable reign of João V, which lasted from 1706 to 1750, was calculated to offend the Protestant ethic on almost every count. The King himself, who possessed to the full the Braganza delight in the arts, combined it with a strange, perverted religiosity: ecclesiastical ceremonies, it was said, were grand opera to him, and his preferred mistresses were nuns. With his share of the wealth from the mines in Minhas Gerais in Brazil, he built the enormous Palace Monastery at Mafra, in imitation of the Escurial. Its façade is 240 yards long; it has 4,500 doors and windows, but its corridors are cold and unvisited by the sun. 'They don't even have electric light now', the guide told me. 'How much more they didn't have it then!' His point was indisputable as one hurried through the dead rooms to the open air.

In pre-earthquake Lisbon, religious feasts took up roughly one-third of the year, and had the effect of general strikes. Holy processions held up the traffic in the streets, while the population slumped down on their knees in the mud. The spectacle was stage-managed by the Jesuits and lit by the fires of the Inquisition. Henry Fielding, who in 1754 arrived in Lisbon to die, called it 'the most horrible city in the world'.

Unfortunately for the preachers of sermons in London, the earthquake spared the Royal family and the famous monastery at Belém, while killing off quite a number of the British colony. God's punishment, if such it was, appears to have been clumsily administered. With more justification, Voltaire, in his poem 'On the Disaster of Lisbon', used the disaster to attack the popular version of the theory, based on Leibniz's philosophy, that 'all is for the best in the best of all possible worlds'. Three years later, he makes Candide and Dr Pangloss arrive in Lisbon at the hour of the earthquake. 'All this', remarks Pangloss, 'is a manifestation of the rightness of things, since if there is a volcano at Lisbon, it could not be anywhere else. For it is impossible for things not to be where they are, because everything is for the best.' Against the glib cruelty of this

VII Torre de Belém (Tower of Belém), Lisbon
    For centuries the Tower of Belém at Restelo, outside Lisbon, was a landmark pointed out to all who arrived at Lisbon by sea. Today it is dwarfed not only by the huge bridge across the Tagus, but also by a pompous new memorial to the Great Discoverers.
    The tower, of white limestone, was built between 1515 and 1519 by Francisco de Arruda. Arruda had been to Morocco and helped in the reconstruction of the fortifications of the Portuguese enclaves at Mazagan and Safim. This building, with its balconies and two-arched windows, shows a strong Moorish influence, but the stone cables, which seem to tie the building neatly together, are notable features of the Manueline style.

optimism, Voltaire's answer is that Evil in fact exists, but human beings are resilient and, in spite of everything, in love with life. 'Let us work without arguing; that's the only way to make life bearable.'

Voltaire's argument was given substance by the famous statement attributed to the Marquis of Pombal at the time: 'Bury the dead, look after the living, and shut the doors.'

The most resilient of men, Sebastião José de Carvalho e Mello, later Marquis of Pombal, was one of the rare Portuguese statesmen whose message has been not of endurance and survival, but of hope. He identified his enemies from the first: they were the Jesuits, the aristocracy and the English. His true friend was his king, José I (1750–77), who was uninterested in the business of government and gave him a free hand. Pombal, like Peter the Great and Catherine the Great, was a Westernizer. He had been Ambassador in London and had been influenced by what he had seen there, but his desire to expand native industries brought him up against the English in Portugal. The cruelty of his campaign against the aristocracy may have been due to some personal spite, yet he knew they would oppose his efforts at modernizing the country. He came in conflict with the Jesuits in Brazil, yet his campaign was directed against their influence in the courts of Europe, and led to the abolition of the Order. He admitted to having Jewish blood, and abolished the distinction between 'old' and 'new' Christians; he saw to it that every slave on the soil of Portugal automatically became free. But in the end even his left-wing admirers, led by Voltaire, turned against him, after the execution of the aged and mad Jesuit Father Malagrida.

Pombal was a premature bourgeois revolutionary. His educational and administrative reforms found nobody capable of carrying them out. In a country noticeably lacking in members of the Third Estate, he was bound to see his work come to nothing. The next reign, that of Maria I, saw him in exile in his native town and the Jesuit confessors back in the royal palaces.

To Pombal, at any rate, we owe much of what Lisbon is today: a city which architecturally very nearly lives up to the demands of its magnificent situation on the shores of the Tagus. From the waterfront, the Baixa or lower city extends from the Praça do

VIII FISHING BOATS AT ALCOCHETE
Alcochete is a small fishing port situated inside the great natural harbour of the Tagus. Here the fishing boats, which go great distances into the Atlantic, are decorated, like the barges on English canals, with naive patterns of fruit and flowers. Alcochete, which is on the edge of the great bull-breeding estates of the Alentejo, also has a well-known bull-ring.

Comércio, formerly the Terreiro do Paço, with its famous statue of José I on horseback (pl. 41), through the three parallel streets, Rua Augusta, Rua Aurea and Rua da Prata, originally destined for the activities of bankers and goldsmiths and silversmiths, to the Rossio, which today reverberates with traffic noise, and beyond to the beginning of the broad Avenida da Liberdade. All this is Pombaline, post-earthquake Lisbon and it represents perhaps the largest grouping of eighteenth-century domestic architecture in Europe. It has its faults. Except for the Praça do Comércio itself, there is little of the spaciousness of the grand style: the streets of the Baixa are cramped and dark, and the broad *praças* have all of necessity become car-parks. Yet for the passer-by, Lisbon provides innumerable pleasures: the vistas from the hills which face each other across the lower city; the Tagus glittering at the end of the street; drinking fountains or *chafarizes*, all of which date from this period; the decaying palaces which look over garden walls; the subtropical vegetation in the parks. In spite of enormous housing estates on its margins, Lisbon is a city which has hardly lost its feeling of unity. Viewed at night from Cacilhas on the opposite side of the Tagus, between its illuminated guardians, the Church of the Estrêla on the left and the Castle of St George on the right, it seems once again the perfect small capital city that Pombal must have imagined, the jewel at the centre of an empire.

In an effort to avoid foreign dynastic entanglements, the Braganzas were given to incestuous marriages. Two of the children of José I submitted to this: a son who married his aunt and died young; and Maria I who married her elderly uncle Pedro. Maria spent many years of her life insane, a condition said to have been brought on by guilt at her father's connivance in Pombal's persecution of the Jesuits. 'She kept crying out for mercy, imagining that, in the midst of a raging flame which enveloped the whole chamber, she beheld her father's image a calcined mass of cinder – a statue in form like that in the Terreiro do Paço, but in colour black and horrible – erected on a pedestal of molten iron, which a crowd of ghastly phantoms... were in the act of dragging down.'

Our informant in these matters is that most loquacious of English visitors, William Beckford, who during these years spent much of his time in Portugal. His obsession, as revealed in his private diaries of the year 1787, was to be presented to Her Majesty, but by court etiquette this presentation could be effected only by the British Ambassador. Unfortunately, Beckford had left England in disgrace owing to his scandalous relationship with William Courtenay, later ninth Earl of Devon, and was not received at the Embassy. Though he was on familiar terms with other members of the Royal family, his ambitions were to remain frustrated. The nearest he got to the Royal presence was at Queluz during a conversation with the Marquis of Angeja, which was interrupted by 'the most terrible and agonizing shrieks.... The Queen herself, whose apartment was only two rooms off from the chamber in which we were sitting, uttered those dreadful sounds: Ai Jesús! Ai Jesús!'

At Mafra a large and rather ludicrous canvas shows the Queen's son, the Regent, being offered back his future kingdom by the Duke of Wellington: Prince João, resplendent in Renaissance armour, receives the homage of the Duke, who is unpretentiously dressed in the style made fashionable by Beau Brummel; various supernumeraries, royal princesses, sea-beasts, tritons and great Neptune himself attend this awkward scene. The allegory has a remote connection with what actually happened. When the French armies were marching into the peninsula, the British had the greatest difficulty in persuading the Royal family to go into exile in Brazil. Later, when the wars were over, further difficulties were found in persuading them to return to Portugal. On reaching Rio de Janeiro, Prince João found that he liked it very much: he could indulge the Braganza passion for church music and public religious ceremonials, which were, if anything, more splendid here than in Lisbon. The only difference was that the crowds who joined in enthusiastically were black instead of white.

Back in Lisbon, Marshal Junot and his wife introduced French manners and French fashion. After this, the upper classes were to look to Paris for guidance in matters of taste: it was the end of the 'façon de Barbarie'. But Napoleon's armies, in their various campaigns against the British and the Portuguese, left a trail of destruction and looting. Wellington, with his usual bluntness, admitted that his own armies had caused an equal amount of damage. Worse, however, was to come later, with the abolition of the monastic orders; and worse still, with more recent efforts at 'restoration'.

After the war, British visitors returned to view the beauties of Sintra, and to re-establish commercial relationships as well. The Anglican cemetery in Lisbon is filled with Grecian urns and artificially broken columns in the Regency taste, and in 1833 the English community collected enough money to adorn the grave of Henry Fielding with an elegant memorial. Many of the visitors, and many of those who remain here for ever, must have come to love the country which typified all that the taste of the day considered beautiful. There is such variety in Portuguese scenery even today (and there was more in those days, before the planting of pine and eucalyptus) and such a range of architectural styles, that the country has never lacked admirers. The British army returned to England with its battle honours of Vimeiro and Bussaco, and a handful of slang phrases. (A horse called 'Filho da Puta' won the St Leger in 1815.)

For the Portuguese, however, the war in the peninsula was to have disastrous consequences. When João VI (as he now was, his mother having died in exile) returned to Portugal in 1822, he found himself obliged to respect a liberal constitution. Meanwhile, his son Pedro stayed behind in Rio and soon declared himself independent Emperor of Brazil. The loss of Brazil was to mean economic disaster, which lasted throughout the nineteenth century. In the next few years, the country was divided in the civil war known as 'the War of the Two Brothers'. On his father's death, Pedro returned to support his own daughter, Maria da Gloria, as Liberal candidate to the throne. However, his brother, Dom Miguel, was proclaimed king in 1827 and refused to adopt the usual Braganza solution of marrying his niece.

Miguel, the favourite son of his crook-backed, intriguing Spanish mother, Carlota Joaquina, was handsome, stupid and courageous. He bore no resemblance to the dull-featured Braganzas, and little to his mother, a daughter of the Spanish Royal family so unflatteringly portrayed by Goya. Strong rumours and his mother's reputation, however, connected him with a certain good-looking gardener at Carlota Joaquina's palace of Ramalhão, outside Sintra. Whatever his origins, the champion of absolute monarchy was a popular hero, with something of the romantic charisma of the lost Dom Sebastião. 'Dom Miguel's Lisbon', Eça de Queiroz tells us, 'was as disorderly as barbarian Tunis: a motley of monks and coachmen filling the taverns and the chapels with their shouting; the pious multitude, wild and dirty, surging from church to bullring, and clamouring after the prince who so perfectly personified their own vices and passions.'

Dom Miguel was defeated with British assistance, the absolutist king becoming a cherished memory among the poor of Portugal. The monasteries were destroyed in the anti-clerical reaction. Throughout the following years the consequences of the loss of Brazil began to be felt. As in Spain, there was a succession of civil wars, popular uprisings and military conspiracies. The African colonies remained unexploited and the finances of the country were salvaged by loans from abroad.

As happens in a country with a very small upper class and a large working population, there was no lack of splendour of a meretricious sort. The King Consort Ferdinand of Coburg built his Castelo da Pena on the very summit of the Serra de Sintra, like an Arthur Rackham castle from a children's book (pls. 56, 57). Much later a Manueline-revival palace was constructed, once again around the nucleus of an old monastery, at Bussaco, where Wellington had stayed before one of his victories in the Peninsular War. This strange edifice, crouched among the magnificent forest-trees, was never to be occupied. By the time it was completed, assassination and revolt had brought the rule of the House of Braganza to an end. Today the Palace of Bussaco is a hotel, inhabited by gaudy old ladies, looking like parakeets with their blue or scarlet hair, and quiet parchment-coloured old men.

But more and more the rich lived abroad – we read about their goings on in the novels of Eça de Queiroz, *The Maias* and *The City and the Mountains* – while their estates fell gently to pieces at home. Towards the end of the century there came a sudden burst of energy, a recrudescence of imperial ambitions. Angola had been occupied by the Portuguese since 1482 and Mozambique since 1498. Whether this in fact was 'effective occupation' was a point much canvassed among the European powers, not excluding the Ancient Ally, even though Britain was committed to defending the Portuguese Empire as it stood. In 1877 two explorers, Ivens and Capelo, crossed the continent from Angola to Mozambique. Further exploration was carried out under Serpa Pinto. But now the Portuguese ran up against tougher opponents than those they had encountered among the African chiefs: men like Cecil Rhodes. Britain protested against Serpa Pinto's expedition: it was recalled. The Anglo–Portuguese crisis produced a republican uprising and a national sense of betrayal, which was to be revived when India invaded Goa in 1961.

In the 1890s relations were patched up by the Ambassador in London, the Marquis of Soveral, known as 'the Blue Monkey' and a great friend of the Prince of Wales. But to outsiders the point remained established: the Portuguese were holding on to an empire which fatally overstretched the resources of a small country. Today 40 per cent of the national budget goes on defending the African possessions, and the term of compulsory military service has been put up to four years. And today, too, emigration remains the resource of many with ambition. At the last count, the number of emigrants each year exceeded the number of births.

The peculiar rhythm of Portuguese history, its periods of splendour and of decline, are in some way responsible for the special charm the country holds today. With a prosperous, mercantile nineteenth century, Lisbon today would look perhaps like Oporto, a city it resembles as little as Dublin does Belfast; or perhaps like Liverpool, a city it resembles not at all. Even the fecklessness and the extravagance of the Braganza kings have their compensations in the eyes of the present. James Lees-Milne, in his book *Baroque in Spain and Portugal* (London, 1960), says of João V, who by 1750 had brought the richest country in Europe to the verge of bankruptcy: 'Of what advantage would it have been to anyone two hundred years later, had this monarch hoarded his treasure or lavished it upon ephemeral good works or, worse still, on warfare?'

Pombal, of course, would not have agreed. And if we can forgive the Braganzas for their good taste, it is harder to forgive Ferdinand of Coburg for the equivalent amounts of money that must have been spent on the Castelo da Pena, Portugal's

Balmoral. And so far there have been no conspicuous signs that the Republic will bequeath anything as durable as the extravagances of the Houses of Aviz or Braganza. A new glory, recently arrived, is the result of an historical, and legal, accident: the magnificent museum at Oeiras, Pombal's old residence, which contains the Calouste Gulbenkian collection, some pictures of which are almost painfully recognizable after their years in the National Gallery in London.

To the past in Portugal, however, belong not only works of art and architecture, but also certain aspects of society. For better or worse, war is the great begetter of social change, and Portugal has been non-belligerent for longer than any European country save Switzerland and Sweden. It is the world of the 1920s and 1930s which is constantly being evoked – and, in the country, perhaps also the world of Chekhov's Russia. It is a place where ladies kiss their servants and soon afterwards yell at them, and where the gaps between the classes are so evident that sumptuary laws seem still to be in operation. Once a man in a dark suit, always a man in a dark suit.

And take the position of women. Where else is chaperonage as strictly enforced? A restaurant in Oporto at lunch time. All the people there seem to be regular customers, eating alone or in pairs. They wear dark suits and black ties, and have mourning bands round their arms. Like the court of Queen Victoria, a well-off Portuguese family must be almost continuously manifesting its grief at the passing of close or distant relatives. ('It is for my aunt.' 'I never knew you had an aunt.' 'She rarely came downstairs.') A funereal appearance does not restrict the appetite, however. The regional cuisine is good, if distinctly heavy; warm, thick vegetable soup, casseroles of tripe with white beans, purple slices of lamprey in a sauce of blood and wine. What is odd, however, about this restaurant is the presence of outsiders. There are ourselves, exotic in holiday clothes. But there are two others even more out of place: women, Portuguese women.

One of these is holding the attention of eight or so males. They are arranged in what appears to be a hierarchical order: at the top of the long table sits the boss, an elderly magnate in pince-nez. At the other end there is somebody who hasn't even got a tie: the driver? And next to him sits the woman, lively, attractive. From all the patronizing attention she is getting, we think she must be a foreigner. But she is not. Under all that masculine pressure, she is overcompensating a lot. She joins in; she laughs loudly. She smokes a cigarette almost as a dare, like a boy taking part in a school play. Everyone seems pleased that she is there: it makes quite a change.

The other woman, younger, prettier, creeps in alone and takes a table in the corner. She fidgets nervously with her handbag, speaks to the waiter in whispers.

It would seem that she is asking for a special diet, or a doggy-bag, but she is only ordering the soup. Because of all of us, she dare not look up. It is as though the masculine will of the whole restaurant is forcing her to be, not just a possibility, but something more picturesque and Victorian, a fallen sister, a lady of the night, a daughter of the game. In the end she finds what she was searching for in her handbag; a large pair of tinted spectacles. Now, with her own eyes shielded, she can look us in the eye.

At the end of the eighteenth century, when William Beckford found his 'group of senhoras seated on the ground *à la façon de Barbarie*', there in the midst of them was 'the newly consecrated and very young-looking Bishop of Algarve, whose small, black, sleek schoolboyish head and sallow countenance was overshadowed by an enormous pair of green spectacles.'

Those spectacles. They decorate the features of the bourgeois, giving him the blank stare of a praying mantis. For his wife, her spectacles are a descendant of the yashmak, quite as much as those head-scarves which peasant women wear in the Algarve. Through them she makes her still uncertain contacts with the outside world.

Not very long ago all secondary education had to be paid for, and its possessor is still a figure of respect. You can still tell the difference between penpusher and manual labourer by a handshake.

Watch some respected gentleman in his barber's shop. Everybody's faces are turned to the Senhor Doutor, like coltsfoots to the sun. This isn't a distant respect, for people keep touching him, replacing the blue spectacles over his crinkled brown-paper ears, helping him into his woolly muffler and his overcoat and patting him gently when the operation is completed. And when he speaks, they listen attentively so that not a word of his extensive vocabulary is lost. How orotund and well-sounding his sentences! His very platitudes have the familiar resonance of dinner-gongs. Never were elegant variations more elegant, genteelisms more genteel. But one is quite wrong to make fun of him for what is only a cultural difference. In England and America (perhaps because we have so many comic novelists) an elegant vocabulary often hides a deficient education. As a result we don't bejewel our prose, any more than we bejewel our fingers.

On the other hand, to leave Portugal for England is to leave a country where people talk in complete sentences, where imperfect subjunctives and personal infinitives slip easily from people's tongues (this is much rarer in Brazil, so that one notices) and to return once more to the land of Um and Er.

George Borrow, otherwise a disapproving witness, observed this in 1835: 'Nothing surprised me more than the free and unembarrassed manner in which the Portuguese peasantry sustain a conversation, and the purity of the language in which they express their thoughts, and yet few of them can read or write; whereas the peasantry of England, whose education is in general much superior, are in their conversation coarse and dull almost to brutality, and absurdly ungrammatical in their language.'

This fluency is surprising still, and perhaps after all it is only the Latinism of the language which causes the impression to be so persistent. For though people speak fluently and to the point, it cannot be concealed that there is often not very much to talk about. The newspapers are all as reticent as parish magazines. Television, as everywhere, deprives one of society without giving back one's solitude: the people watching it in cafés still seem to be amazed that it works at all, rather than expecting anything interesting to come out of it.

Yet the high level of civility gives to chance encounters a curiously complete and satisfying quality. Buying a fish in the market, watching it expertly dissected by one of those straight-backed, handsome fish-women with Grecian noses, whom romantics have long considered to be descendants of the Phoenicians; asking the

IX PORTUGUESE BULL FIGHTS
Since the eighteenth century, the bulls have been *embolados*: that is, their horns have been encased in leather sheaths. This has made it possible for them to be fought on horseback by *cavaleiros* riding valuable horses, as well as by *espadas* who fight on foot in the Spanish style.

Here a *cavaleiro*, dressed in traditional eighteenth-century costume, plants a *farpa,* or banderilla, in the shoulders of a bull, while his horse swerves out of reach. Later he will hand the bull over to the *moços de forcado,* and finally to a simulated kill by a matador using a banderilla instead of a sword. At some periods in the history of Portuguese bull-fighting, bulls have been killed in the ring, but this is illegal today, though members of the crowd often demand it. Instead, the exhausted animal is hurried out by a group of steers and, in most cases, is slaughtered soon afterwards.

X The *moços de forcado* are a team of sturdy young men, dressed in peasant costume of the Alentejo, whose task is to capture the bull and pull it down with their bare hands. In heroic isolation, the team leader challenges the bull until it charges, at which point he throws himself over its head while the other *moços* grab hold of its flanks and tail. Usually the bull throws them off and breaks clear, causing a good deal of damage. The *muleteiros* with capes run forward to distract the bull, while the battered team re-forms and the challenge is repeated until the bull is finally brought to the ground.

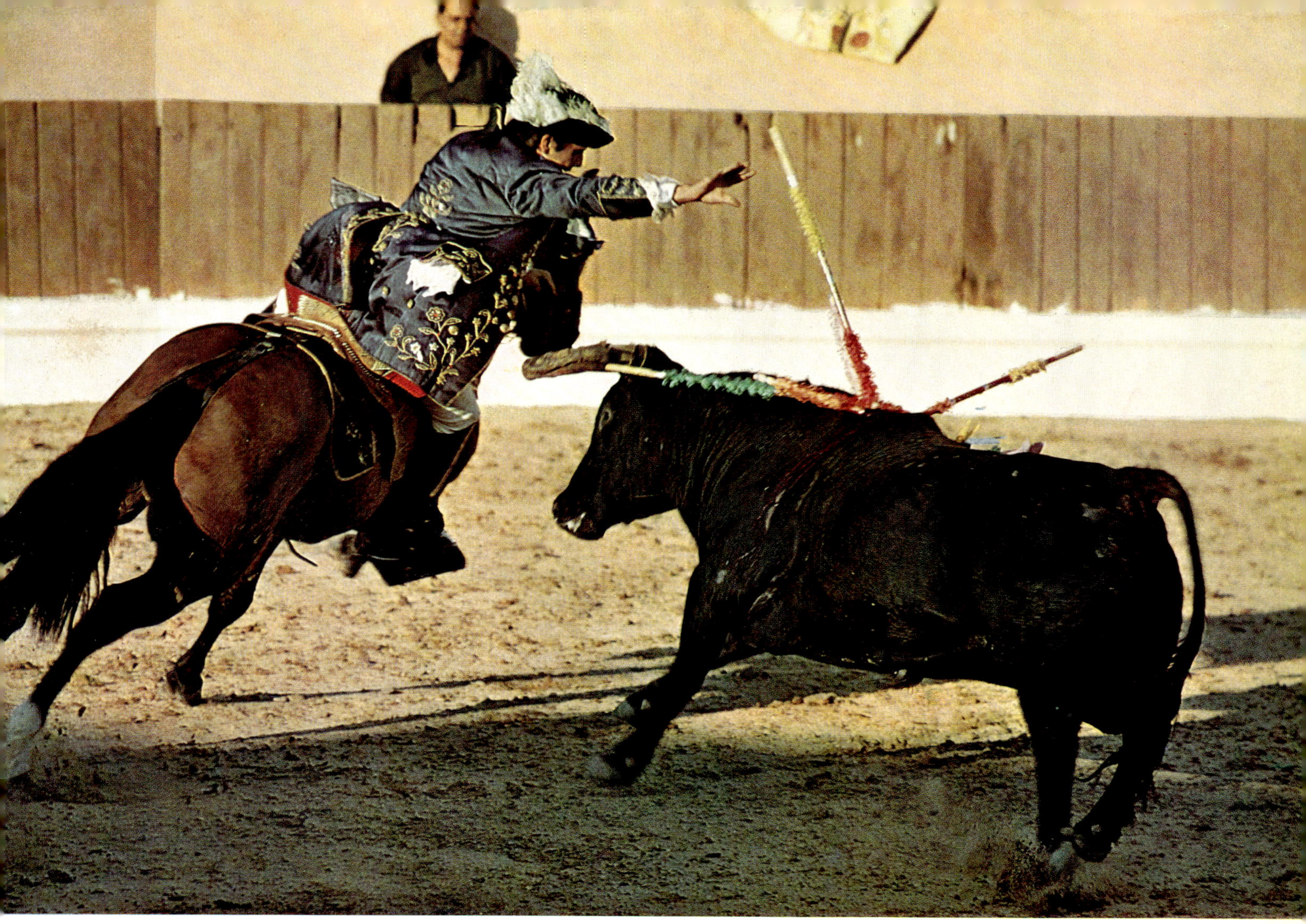

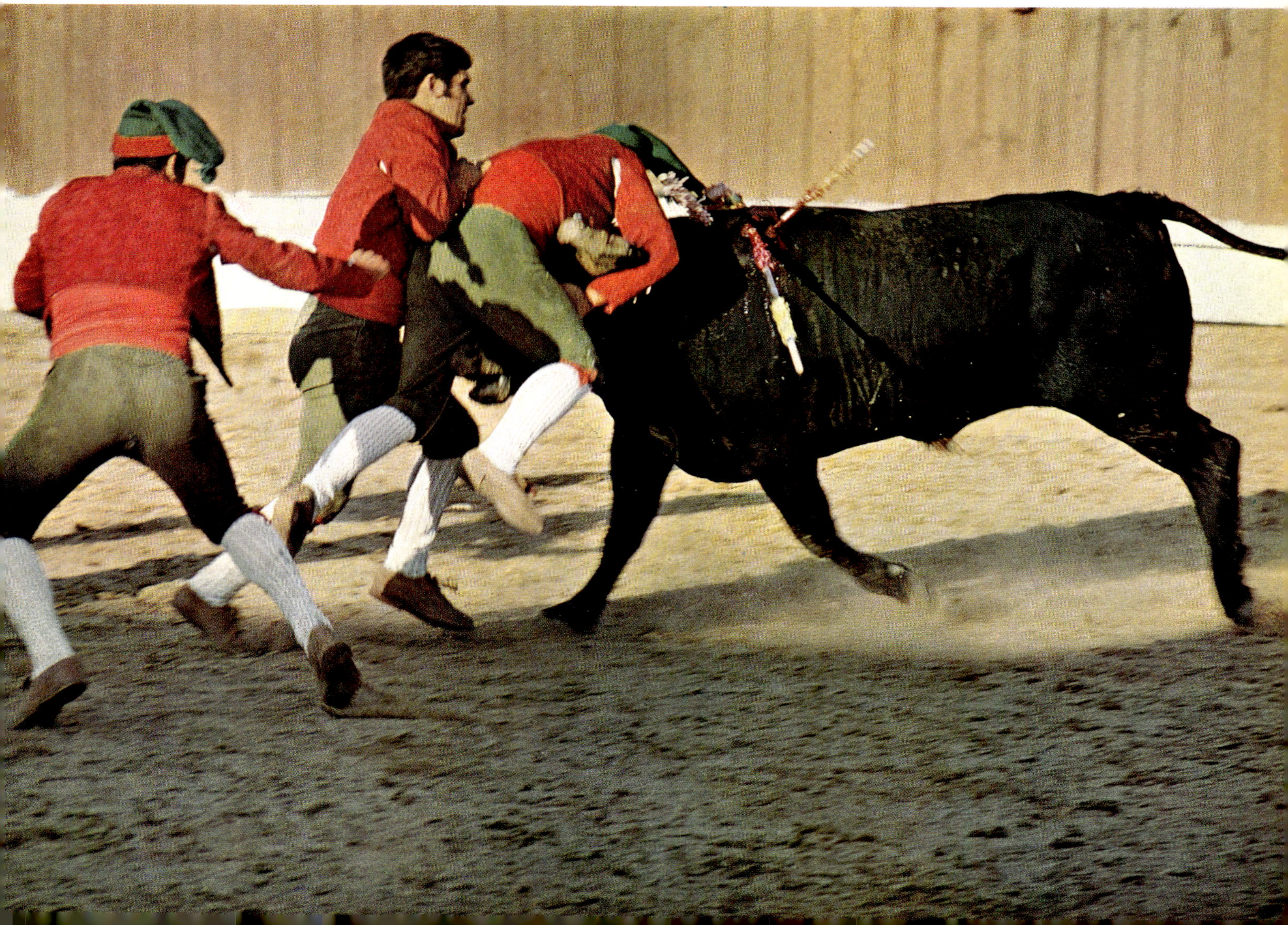

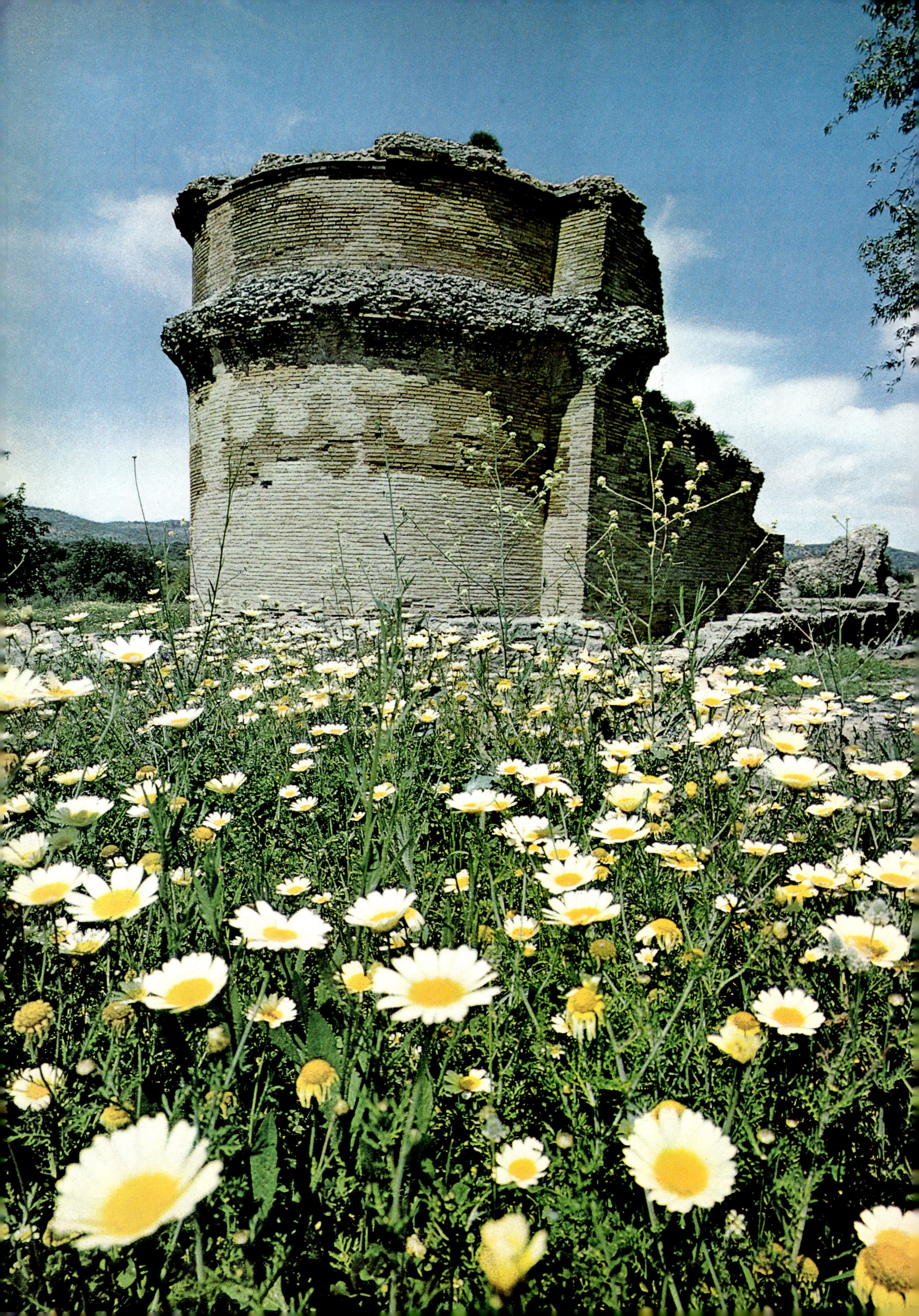

way in a country town and arousing a wave of concern in the whole immediate neighbourhood; sitting in a café and realizing that individualistic northerners can probably never appreciate the art of living in the present. For in every café, tonight is always different from last night. Small talk, masculine gossip, the whereabouts of somebody who is not there. 'Where is the João?' Theories are proposed and refuted, the mystery deepening in its intricacies until the João finally appears and then it is forgotten about. Sometimes one is reminded of a Jane Austen novel in which it became a matter of importance whether or not Emma and Harriet took their afternoon walk. (The connection is emphasized, too, by the constant arguments that go on about whether somebody has been ill-mannered or not.) In such surroundings one must tread cautiously: a foreigner will sometimes appear disconcertingly over-bright merely because he has introduced a new topic into the conversation.

In the countryside there are still few cars except on the main roads between the big cities, and those you see look important, urgent. They nearly always contain four male passengers, wearing black suits and dark, wide-brimmed hats. A somewhat disturbing sight, with its suggestion of clerical, political menace. Otherwise men ride bicycles, and women jog along on donkeys or walk with firm, heavy footsteps, while a pottery jar or a plastic bucket wavers in peaceful equilibrium on their heads. On the bigger roads there are often young men asking for lifts: students from the University of Coimbra, with their long, black, elaborately tattered gowns – each rent in the hem is supposed to represent an amatory conquest, in which case, there appear to be no beginners at the game. Frequently there are soldiers, sailors or airmen, doing their compulsory military service. In Spain, hardly anyone

XI ROMAN RUINS AT MILREU, NEAR ESTÓI, ALGARVE
Ossonoba or Sossuba, the Roman settlement near Faro, is believed to have been destroyed by an earthquake. The large brick construction which remains may have been a basilica. In ancient times, Ossonoba was famous for its persecuting bishop, Ithacius, who in AD 385 denounced Priscillian, the first person known to have been sentenced to death and executed for heresy. Priscillian, who wandered about the world in the company of his disciples, known as the Priscillianists, was accused of praying stark-naked; but, according to Gibbon, 'if the Priscillianists violated the laws of nature, it was not by the licentiousness, but by the severity of their lives.' In the spring, the Algarve is covered with an immense variety of wild flowers. Those in the photograph are yellow crown daisies of the two-coloured variety (*Chrysanthemum coronarium dicolor*).

thumbs a lift: national pride precludes the asking of favours. But the Portuguese hitch-hiker cozens his self-esteem by his efforts at conversation. He sits beside you, like a well-done-up parcel, and radiates polite concern. You sense his testing of his own identity against the strangeness of the foreigner and, with it, the unexpressed sentiment that your world is not and cannot be for him. Foreigners oblige one to make generalizations and generalizations make one feel sad: we are back at the sense of fate, and remember that the word for fate is *fado*.

In the *fado* cafés of Lisbon, the solid women in black shawls, whose voices are as curiously haunting as the call of a mullah in a Moorish city, offer in song the sort of problems which in other countries are dealt with in columns of advice in women's magazines. Here there are no solutions, however. One lady has a husband who is an invalid, in various detrimental ways, and a rich friend who wants to take her away. Her problem is obviously acute. What shall she do, she wonders for several verses. She decides to stay with her husband, because, as she sings, 'Da sua honra, sou a sentinela.' 'I am the sentinel of his honour.' She flourishes her shawl, we applaud clamorously and order another jug of wine.

This resignation, sometimes rueful and sometimes half-joking, is a constant attitude. How much, one wonders, does it depend on traditional faith? Ferreira de Castro, Portugal's most distinguished living novelist, has written: 'When we start taking a deep interest in man's destiny here on earth, and feeling concerned about injustices suffered here, then it means that our certainty that misery in this world is payment for happiness in the next has been shaken.' But has this certainty been shaken?

When one visits the shrine of Fátima, probably the most famous place in present-day Portugal, one is quickly convinced that it has not. The whole precinct, the raw new buildings on the barren impoverished upland, testifies at least to a tremendous need for belief. Through the crowds of weeping pilgrims, it is as though a civilization is crying out for comfort. Perhaps the miracles themselves, and the reckless presentation of the original evidence, were also an indication of this need – it is not for an outsider to say.

On much more mundane levels, most people act as though they expected things to go on as they are. The foreigners who in recent years have decided to settle in Portugal certainly seem to think so. The British who buy villa properties in the Algarve choose to live there not only because of the benevolent climate, but also 'because you can still get all the servants you want'; and they add (in accordance with the Law of Retrospective Gentility among exiles), 'Like in the old days.' The same considerations influence the former Royal families of Europe who have settled in Estoril. In this least Portuguese of towns, in large, ugly villas among the pinewoods not far from the Casino, they have found a haven denied them elsewhere. 'There is one book you need to understand this place', a friend in Estoril said to me, and produced the Almanach de Gotha. It is only a temporary stopping place, however. In the Pantheon of the Royal House of Braganza, the old cloisters of the church of S. Vicente de Fóra in Lisbon, there are niches for all the Portuguese Royal family, including the much-respected Ex-Queen Amélia, who died in 1951. But there is no space for the latest comer, Carol of Rumania: his coffin lies in the middle of the floor, waiting for some miracle of genealogical table-turning, or for history to run backwards.

Unlike the exiled kings, the average Portuguese still has no doubt where he belongs. He lives in a city which has probably existed for the best part of two thousand years. He speaks a language which, unlike our own, has remained largely unaltered since the Middle Ages. The fisherman who drops his lines from the extreme edge of the cliffs of Cape St Vincent, with nothing in front of him but the whole Atlantic ocean, is gazing on seas which his ancestors conquered six hundred years ago. Not far away, ploughing and tilling goes on much as it did under Roman and Arab conquerors. Perhaps, therefore, it is not remarkable that he still surprises us by his lack of envy and his unadventurous self-respect. Yet he himself can still be surprised by his fellow countrymen. I have been told by poor people in Lisbon that during the great floods in the autumn of 1967, they were astonished and overwhelmed by the generosity of their neighbours and of people who lived far off and were unknown to them.

Sometimes one is given an image which sums up a whole feeling about a place or about a part of one's life. This happened on Passion Sunday at a small village on the outskirts of Braga. We had walked down a rutted, unpaved road to reach the church of São Frutuoso, perhaps the oldest in Portugal, with its adjoining monastery. The open space in front of the church, walled on one side, was brightly lit by the afternoon sun. Children were clambering over a marble baroque fountain in the wall, which was overgrown with wisteria in full blossom. In front of them the procession was assembling, ready to start off. The firemen shone with their gleaming Roman helmets and bright axes, their faces held up into half smiles by the tight straps under their chins. The strong men of the parish eased themselves into position to hoist the images of Our Lady and of Our Lord bearing the Cross. In front of them, small children, dressed as angels and wearing bright red wigs, held up the small cushions which bore the Instruments of the Passion, the crown of thorns, the hammer and nails, the pincers, the spear and the sponge. The bishop, surrounded by priests and acolytes, gave a blessing and a dozen or so local dignitaries stood hatless, with bowed heads and the sunlight glinting from their pince-nez. Then the town band struck up with snorting music, and the whole procession moved off to the next church.

It was one of those processions for which there are hardly any spectators, for the simple reason that practically the whole population seems to be taking part. There was one exception, however, a tall old countrywoman, who followed at a little distance, walking upright with the easy swaying of someone who is used to carrying heavy burdens. On her head was a large laundry basket and in it she carried the emblems of power: a dozen or so black brief-cases, a dozen or so black homburg hats.

THE KINGS AND QUEENS OF PORTUGAL

BURGUNDIAN DYNASTY

Regency of Countess Teresa	1114–1128
Afonso I	1128–1185
Sancho I	1185–1211
Afonso II	1211–1223
Sancho II	1223–1248
Afonso III	1248–1279
Dinis I	1279–1325
Afonso IV	1325–1357
Pedro I	1357–1367
Fernando I	1367–1383
Interregnum of Leonor Teles	1383–1385

AVIZ DYNASTY

João I	1385–1433
Duarte I	1433–1438
Regency of Leonor	1438–1440
Regency of the Infante Pedro	1440–1448
Afonso V	1448–1481
João II	1481–1495
Manuel I	1495–1521
João III	1521–1557
Regency of Catarina	1557–1562
Regency of Cardinal Henriques	1562–1568
Sebastião I	1568–1578
Cardinal-King Henriques	1578–1580

SPANISH DOMINATION

Philip II	1580–1598
Philip III	1598–1621
Philip IV	1621–1640

BRAGANZA DYNASTY

João IV	1640–1656
Regency of Luisa de Guzman	1656–1662
Afonso VI	1662–1667
Pedro II	1667–1706
João V	1706–1750
José I	1750–1777
Maria I	1777–1792
Regency of Prince João	1792–1816
João VI	1816–1826
Regency of Princess Isabel-Maria	1826–1828
Miguel I	1828–1834
Maria II	1834–1853
Regency of Fernando	1853–1855
Pedro V	1855–1861
Luis I	1861–1889
Carlos I	1889–1908
Manuel II	1908–1910

Part One   OPORTO AND THE NORTH

1

2

4

3

5

6

7

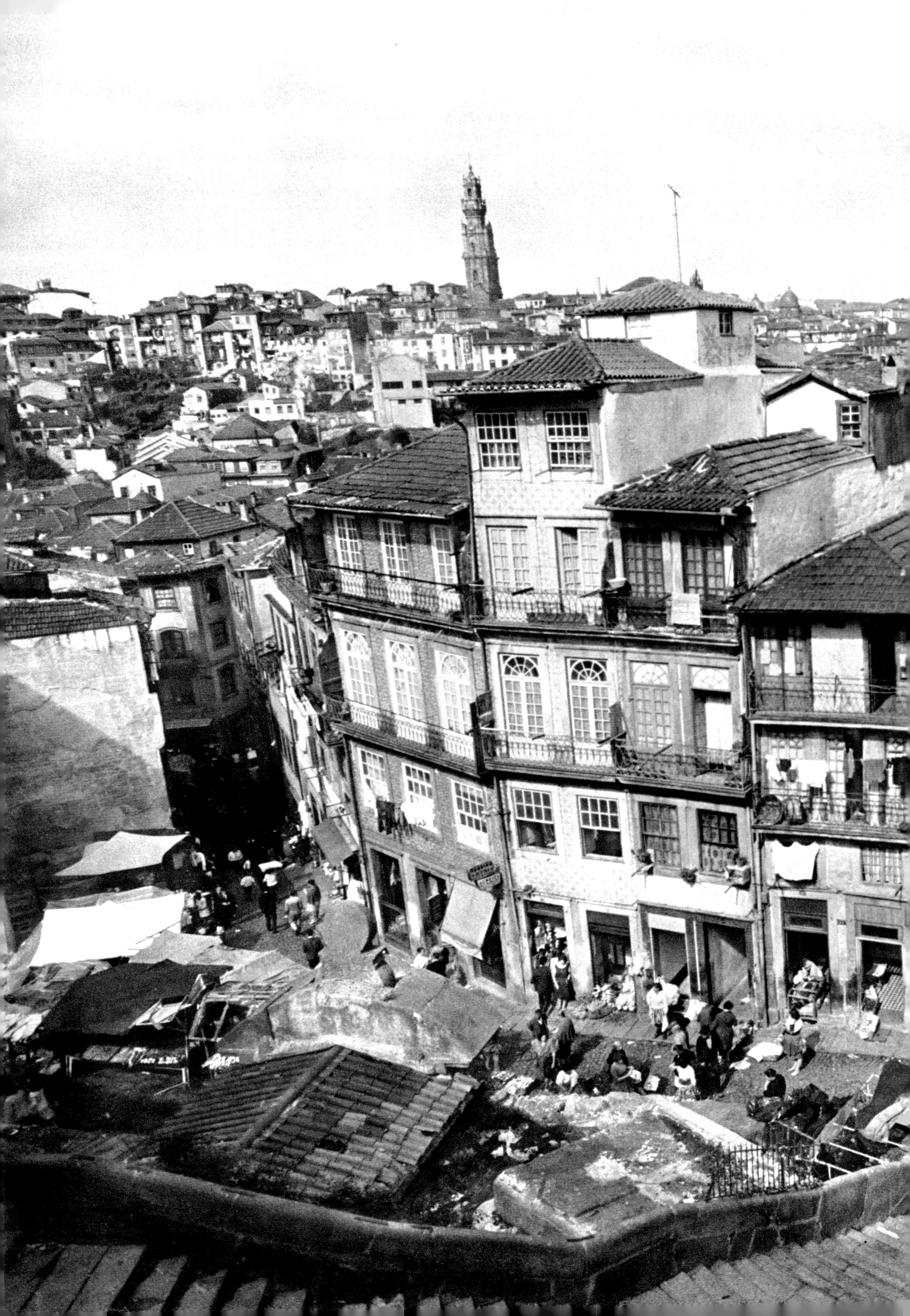

8

9

10

11

12

13

14

15

16

18

19

20

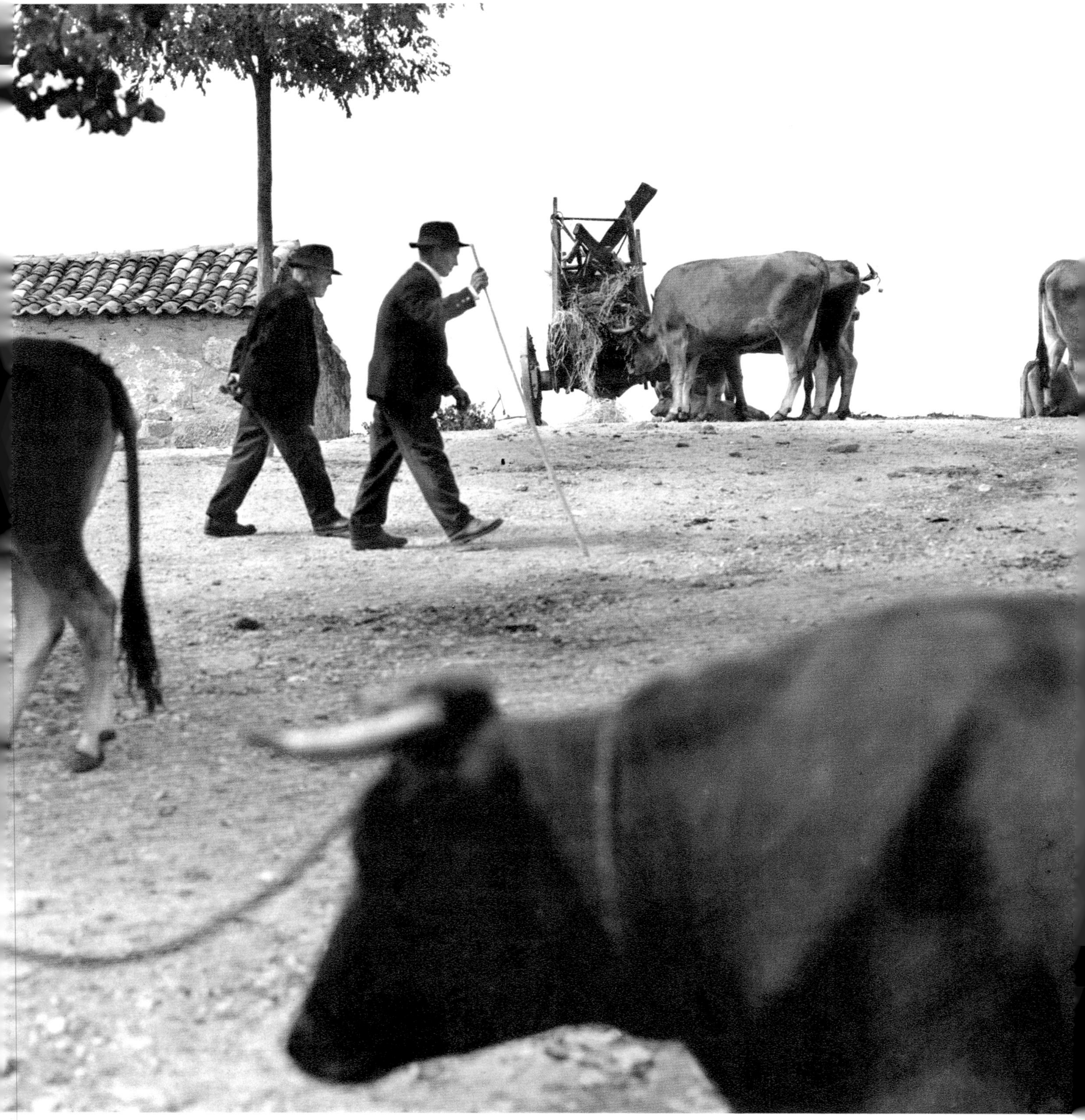

22

23

24

25

26

27

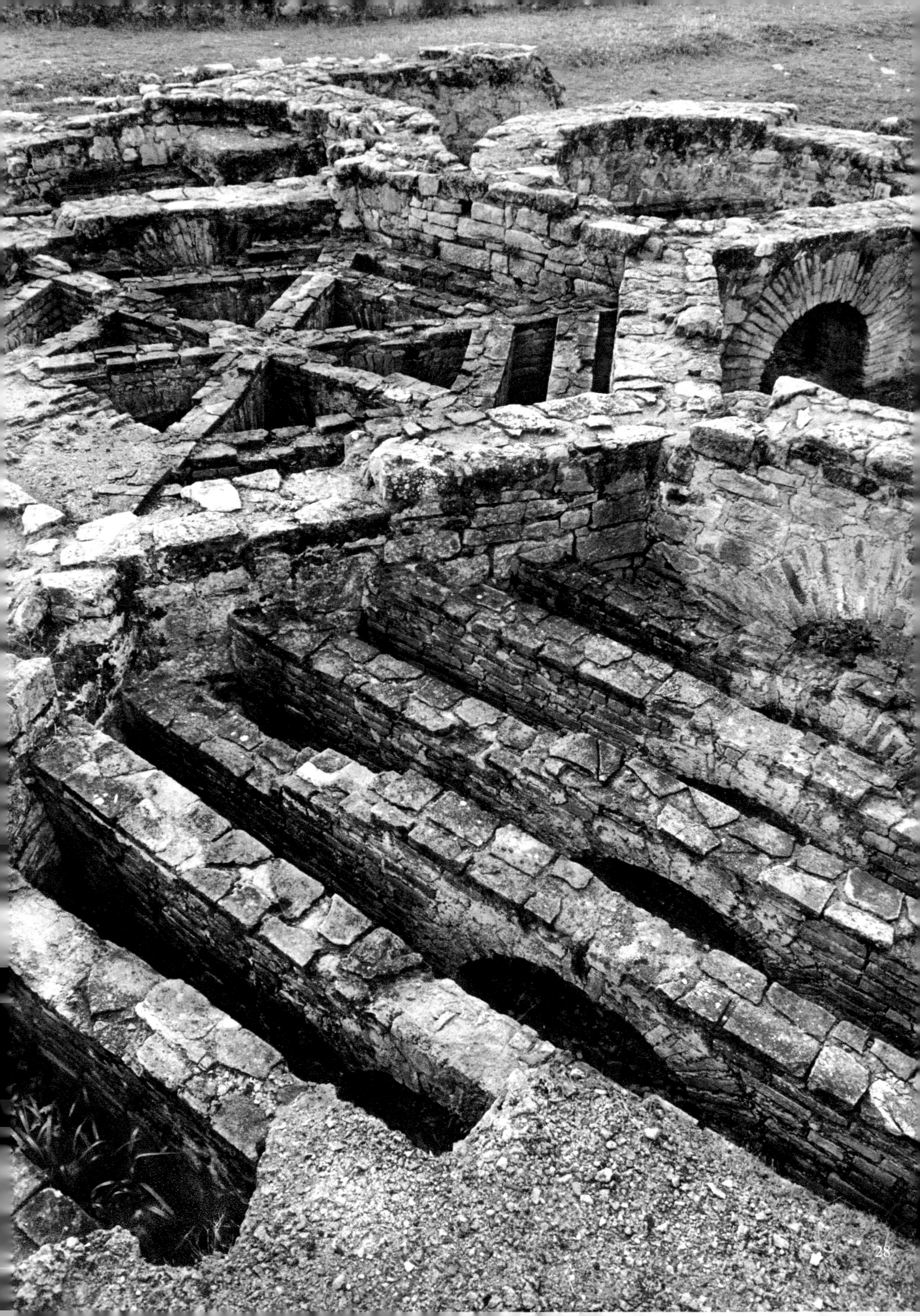

29

30

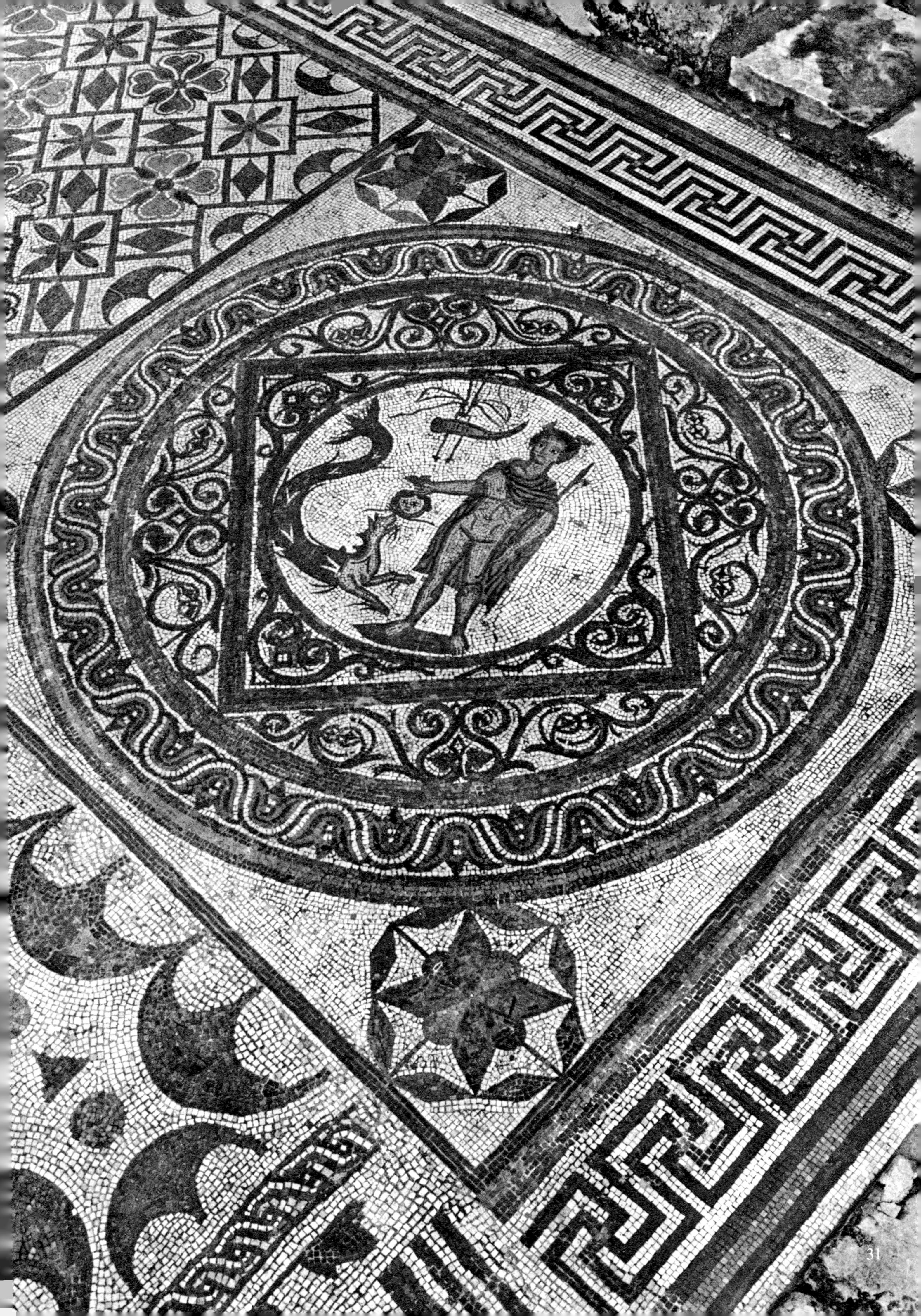

32

33

34

NOTES ON PLATES 1–34

1 THE UPPER DOURO, NEAR RAIVA

The Douro, which rises in the *meseta*, or plateau, of Spain, forms the frontier between the two countries for fifty miles. Two hundred miles of the river lie within the Portuguese frontier, and, of these, 124 are navigable with the special boats *(rabelos)* that are still used for bringing down the wine harvests. It is the Upper Douro that is famous as the country of port wine: the area officially delimited for the growth of wine-grapes occupies only a part of the total length of the river, the region of schistous rock between Barca d'Alva and Régua. Here the summer temperatures are extremely high (over 100° F.), and the winters are often bitterly cold. Elsewhere the mountainsides along the river are planted with pinetrees and eucalyptus, which are used in the manufacture of wood-pulp.

2 THE VINTAGE

During the vintage, the harvesters come from remote villages in the mountain country, where they cultivate their own pieces of land. The women, who are sometimes helped by children and old men, cut the grape bunches. This is merely the climax of the year's work on the vines – work which has included hoeing, staking, grafting, pruning, and spraying, often three or four times, with Bordeaux mixture. But it is a time of festivity and celebration, when, for a month or more, work, sleep, dancing and drinking will alternate until the last grape has been picked.

The men carry the grapes in baskets, which are designed to take the weight on their heads and shoulders. They walk rapidly, almost trotting. In the background can be seen the terraces which since the Roman era have lined the hillsides overlooking the Douro.

3 FESTIVITIES AT THE VINTAGE
The harvesters bring their own musicians with them from the villages of Trás-os-Montes and Beira Alta. Music accompanies them to the vineyards and back again, and during their dancing and drinking parties at night. It is a time when the traditional sobriety of the Portuguese is forgotten.

4 MIXING BRANDY INTO THE NEW WINE
The farms, known as *quintas*, are owned either by individual farmers or by the shippers themselves. Today many farmers sell the grapes direct to the shippers; the old custom of trampling the wine-press belongs to the past. When the grapes are brought to the *quinta*, they are poured into a *lagar*, in which they are crushed by machinery. Later, brandy is added to stop the process of fermentation. Here, the mixing with brandy is done on the *quinta* itself, immediately after the fermenting juice leaves the *lagar*.

5 WINE LEAVING THE QUINTA
Around 1678 two Englishmen are said to have mixed brandy into Portuguese wine in order to help it resist the hazards of the sea voyage to England. From this experiment was derived the fortified wine known as 'port'. The Methuen Treaty (1703) guaranteed trade with Great Britain, and the British shippers set up their establishments at Vila Nova de Gaia. A whole complicated system of commercial relationships had begun. Here wine leaves a *quinta* belonging to the shippers themselves, ready for the river journey to Vila Nova de Gaia.

6 A QUINTA IN THE UPPER DOURO
In 1868 the destructive insect known as *Phylloxera vastatrix* appeared in the valley of the Douro, and for the next ten or fifteen years the whole future of the port industry was in jeopardy: it was then discovered, however, that there are certain types of American vine which are immune to its ravages. Since the insect attacks the roots of the vine, European varieties which are grafted on to American root-stocks also remain undamaged.

In many parts of the Douro, abandoned terraces can be seen, some of them dating from this period. Others may have fallen into disuse because the American vines needed less space than the old type. Here, through the branches of a cork oaktree, a small *quinta* is seen surrounded by vineyards, with some terraces still in cultivation and others falling into ruin.

7 BARRELS AT VILA NOVA DE GAIA
At Vila Nova de Gaia are situated all the 'lodges', or warehouses, of the port-exporting companies. The city of Oporto lies across the Douro, which is no longer navigable to

large ships. (A new port has been constructed at Leixões.) The bridge on the right was begun in 1865 and has two roadways at different levels.

The large building in the centre is the former Bishop's palace, designed by Niccolò Nasoni (1691–1773), a Tuscan painter and architect who settled at Oporto in 1725. Nasoni was paid for his design in 1734, but construction progressed slowly, reaching a state of near-completion only over the next fifty years, and the great palace was not entirely finished until 1877. After the establishment of the Republic in 1910, it was used for a time as municipal offices, but reverted to ecclesiastical use in 1956.

The episcopal palace conceals the Cathedral, a Romanesque-Gothic structure which was much modernized in the seventeenth and eighteenth centuries; Nasoni, in particular, brought it up to date, both by illusionist frescoes and by structural additions. In the present century, considerable efforts have been concentrated on reversing the process: that is, restoring the building to its presumed original state. Neither of these activities can be said to have been altogether happy.

To the left of the episcopal palace is the former Jesuit College, dominated by the twin towers of its church, São Lourenço (built in 1614–22; presumed architect Baltasar Álvares). At the far left stands the baroque tower of the Clérigos church, Niccolò Nasoni's masterpiece, built in 1757–63. Nasoni's architectural contributions to Oporto and its environs may be compared, *mutatis mutandis*, to those of his contemporary, Rastrelli, at St Petersburg.

8 A View of Oporto

The city enjoys the title of *Antiga, muito nobre e sempre leal e invicta cidade do Porto* ('Ancient, most noble and ever loyal and unvanquished city of Oporto'). The phrase 'ever loyal' is not, however, easily reconcilable with the long history of radicalism for which Oporto is celebrated.

The independent spirit of the citizens of Oporto may be traced back to the Middle Ages, when they waged a long, eventually successful, struggle to set up their own elective municipal institutions; limited the autocratic jurisdiction of the Bishop and prevented the local territorial magnates from residing in the city. In 1474 they violently expelled Rui Pereira, constable of Vila da Feira, lord of the Terras de Santa Maria and a member of the Royal Council, because he outstayed the three days' residence in Oporto which was all they allowed. Although this restriction was subsequently relaxed, when the power of the feudal nobility was reduced by centralized royal government, nevertheless Oporto has few *casas brasonadas* (town houses of noble families on which their coats of arms are displayed).

Oporto is the second city of Portugal and capital of the north. Its relationship with Lisbon (including a certain semi-humorous mutual contempt) may be compared to that between São Paulo and Rio de Janeiro, or (formerly) Manchester and London.

The tower in the distance on the left of the photograph is the 75-metre *campanile* of the church of the Clérigos, built in the mid-eighteenth century by Niccolò Nasoni. The 70-metre tower silhouetted on the right (originally intended to be higher, but 'inconsiderately diminished' according to the *Guia de Portugal*) belongs to the new Town Hall, which was begun in 1920 to a design intended, it seems, to recall the *beffroi* of a late medieval Flemish *hôtel de ville*.

9 Market Scene, Oporto

A fishwife calling for customers in Oporto just below the Cathedral. The largest fish on the table are shad (*sável*), a migratory fish like the salmon which is caught in quantities near the mouth of the Douro. There are also octopus, horse-mackerel and sprats – the cheaper varieties of fish which form a basic part of everyone's diet.

10 Modern Transport at Guimarães

Guimarães, a town of some twenty thousand inhabitants, was the first capital of the kingdom of Portugal. The early twentieth century is represented by this vintage Austin Seven, looking almost as good as new in its garage in the middle of the town.

11 Arcades under the Town Hall, Guimarães

Guimarães is surrounded by a large number of factories, which provide work for the inhabitants of the Minho, one of the most densely populated areas of Europe. The town itself, however, is largely unspoilt and contains architectural relics from all periods of Portuguese history.

These fourteenth-century Gothic arches form the substructure of the old Town Hall (Paço do Concelho) of Guimarães. They provide an open arcade connecting two small squares – the Largo da Oliveira to the south and the Largo de São Tiago to the north – in the medieval heart of the town: a sheltered meeting place for transacting business or for social purposes like the *loggie* of Italian towns. The Town Hall was eventually completed in the fifteenth century, but it was considerably modernized in the seventeenth century by João Lopes de Amorim, who regularized the fenestration and modified the pillars of the arcades.

12 The Castle, Guimarães

The castle stands on a hill to the north of the town, commanding the surrounding country. Its walls, fortified by eight square towers, are built on and among huge granite boulders, enclosing a roughly triangular space within which stands the high keep (reached by a drawbridge from the parapet along the top of the western wall). The pointed tops of the merlons are a *mudéjar* architectural legacy inherited from the Moors.

The fortification owes its origin to Lady Mumadona, widow of a Count of Tuy and Porto, who founded a monastery in the mid-eleventh century at her Vila of Vimaranes (as Guimarães was then called) and built a castle to protect it from the raids of Moors and Vikings. The building in its present form, however, probably dates from early in the twelfth century, when it was the principal residence of Count Henry, father of Afonso Henriques, first king of Portugal. Only ruins remain of the original residence (*alcacova*) within the enclosure.

The whole castle only escaped in 1836 by one vote in the municipal council from being used as a quarry for the construction of new houses in the town.

13 Street in Viana do Castelo

Vila nova da foz do Lima ('the new town at the mouth of the river Lima') was founded by Afonso III in 1258. He spoke of it as 'one of the towns of my kingdom which I much love'. It lies on the north bank of the river which was known in Roman times as the Limaea; the elder Pliny (*Natural History*, iv, 115) refers to marvellous fables current in his day about the Limaea as the River of Forgetfulness, perhaps a tribute to its beauty.

The Vianenses soon established themselves as shipbuilders, sea traders and navigators, prominent in the Portuguese age of discovery. In 1439 a colony of Jews from Catalonia settled there. Unlike Oporto, Viana made no strong opposition to *fidalgos* (nobles and persons entitled to bear coats of arms) residing in the town; consequently there are fine town houses *(casas brasonadas)* of noble and patrician families – Tavoras, Limas, Alpoins, Velhos, Reimões and a number of others. Each of these houses has its own private chapel, among which that of the Casa dos Malheiros Reimões (also known as the Casa da Praça) is outstanding architecturally. Its façade closes the street in the lower part of the photograph. Dedicated to São Francisco de Paula, this chapel is one of the masterpieces of the dramatic rococo style developed in the Minho around the mid-eighteenth century. It has close analogies to buildings dating from the third quarter of the eighteenth century at Braga (Falperra chapel, Casa do Raio) which are attributable to a local amateur architect, André Ribeiro Soares da Silva.

The Capela dos Malheiros resembles a piece of rococo furniture; but the material employed for the decoration is the ubiquitous grey granite of the Minho region. This intractable material influences the carving, but what is thereby lost in delicacy is more than gained in forcefulness and vitality. The *rocaille* 'ears' framing the window of the chapel add a fantastic touch to the decorative composition, which is startlingly projected by contrast with the plain white plaster of the surrounding wall.

Dominating Viana on the north side is the precipitous escarpment of Monte de Santa Luzia (nearly 800 ft. high), crowned by a huge Sanctuary church which was designed in the 1890s by a local architect in byzantine-romanesque style. A few hundred yards behind the Sanctuary is a *citânia* similar to that of Briteiros (*see* note 18).

14 MISERICÓRDIA, VIANA DO CASTELO

Viana, capital of the Alto Minho, is the chief town of the extreme north of Portugal. Founded seven hundred years ago, it had already become a flourishing centre of trade and shipping by the reign of Manuel I (1495–1521). The monuments dating from the sixteenth century in the principal square (formerly known as the Campo do Forno or Oven Place, and now the Praça da Republica) bear witness to this prosperity. In the middle of the Praça is a Renaissance fountain designed by João Lopes the elder; on the north side is the hospital (Misericórdia) with its three storeys of open loggias, built in 1589 by João Lopes the younger, son of the fountain designer; while on the east side stands the arcaded Town Hall, dating from the early sixteenth century.

The Misericórdia façade, seen here through one of the arches of the Town Hall, is unique in Portugal. The inspiration for its design evidently derives from Rhenish and Netherlandish 'Renaissance' compositions. The rusticated bands on either side (just visible bottom left), the perversely elaborate 'terms' supporting the entablatures of the two upper storeys, the unclassical corbels and frieze enrichments and the strapwork cartouche enclosing the sun in the pediment are closely related in spirit to the long series of engraved designs issued by Jan Vredeman de Vries during the second half of the sixteenth century and to the earlier grotesques of Cornelis Bos. The imaginary architecture drawn by de Vries, in his influential books of engravings, provides many examples of open arcades and loggias, including some in tiers above each other.

The northern derivation of the Misericórdia façade at Viana recalls to us that the merchants of the town carried on trade with northern Europe, venturing as far as Scandinavia and Russia.

15 BOM JESUS DO MONTE, NEAR BRAGA

The pilgrimage church of Bom Jesus, set high up on the wooded hillside of the Montanha de Espinho a few kilometres east of Braga, is approached from the foot of the hill through a park starting with winding paths between the trees. Half way up, the gradient becomes steeper and the ascent continues by a series of interwoven stone staircases. At intervals there are octagonal or square chapels containing realistic scenes of the Passion.

The infirm, or idle, visitor can make the ascent by a funicular railway concealed in the woods to the left. This railway was inaugurated in 1882 and still functions perfectly, never having had an accident.

However, for those who can manage it, an ascent by foot is rightly recommended by the guide books, for only thus will the culminating feature of the approach to the church, known as the Stairway of the Five Senses, be seen. This stairway incorporates a series of symbolic fountains and statues of biblical personages, starting in baroque idiom at the foot and progressively becoming more and more rococo in style at each level upwards.

The idea of laying out this splendid religious garden on the hillside was conceived in 1723 by the Archbishop of Braga, Dom Rodrigo de Moura Teles. Its precedents are Italian sixteenth-century secular gardens such as those at Caprarola (Villa Farnese), Bagnaia (Villa Lante) and Tivoli (Villa d'Este), and the religious park created on the slopes of the Sacro Monte near Varese, north-west of Milan, in the seventeenth century (first chapel commissioned 1604).

Originally the pagan elements in the symbolism of the statues and fountains was more pronounced; but in 1774 this was thought scandalous, and the statue of Midas was renamed Solomon, and so on. Nevertheless fountains of Diana, Mars, Mercury and Saturn have still survived next to the chapels in the lower park.

The church, built in 1784–1811 to designs by Carlos Luis Ferreira Amarante (a local architect who was the son of a Braga choirmaster), replaced an earlier circular or oval church completed in 1725, which in turn replaced a still earlier structure dating back to 1494.

The Bom Jesus *ensemble* is one of the great achievements of European baroque. A similar grand design was executed slightly later, but no less successfully, at Lamego on the other side of the River Douro; and later still, on a smaller scale, at Congonhas do Campo in Brazil (Minas Gerais).

16 THE CASTLE, VILA DA FEIRA

Vila da Feira lies between Oporto and Aveiro, a few miles inland from the coast. The town grew up in the Middle Ages as the urban focus of an extensive surrounding district known as the Terras de Santa Maria. The castle, on a hill south of the town, has an older history. Its site was already occupied in Roman times – to judge by the discovery, made during repairs to the castle carried out in 1912–17, of inscribed votive stones dedicated to a Lusitanian deity, Tueraeus. The hill was probably first fortified by the Suevi or Visigoths at some time between the sixth and eighth centuries AD. There was certainly a castle on the site early in the eleventh century. It was known as the Castelo de Santa Maria, and was of strategic importance in the early years of the kingdom of Portugal as the chief fortress of its region. João I (reigned 1385–1433), after establishing himself on the throne, granted the hereditary lordship of the Terras de Santa Maria to Álvaro Pereira, Marshal of the Realm. In 1488 Fernão Pereira, who had succeeded to the lordship of Santa Maria, was also made hereditary constable of the castle of Vila da Feira, which gave him, and his successors, virtually absolute authority throughout the region. His appointment as constable carried with it the obligation to restore the castle, which had fallen into decay. The present structure was thus largely built in the fifteenth century by Fernão and his son Rui Pereira (the latter being the *fidalgo* who was expelled from Oporto in 1474; *see* note 8). The earlier walls and towers must, however, have been incorporated in the new fortress.

The dominant feature of the castle is a huge, rectangular, vaulted keep, seen in this photograph from the bailey. It is constructed of granite with projecting square turrets at the four corners. These turrets are crowned by conical brick spires with granite finials – a striking feature which gives the castle its special character. In the south of Portugal, similar conical spires are quite usual – on the towers and turrets of churches at Évora, for example (*see* pl. 76); but their appearance at Vila de Feira is exotic in its northern environment.

Rui Pereira's heir, Diogo, was made Count of Santa Maria da Feira by Manuel I. The title became extinct in 1700 with the death of the eighth count, a notorious rake who left no legitimate offspring. The greater part of the property of the Counts of Feira then reverted to the Crown, and its revenues no doubt assisted towards the cost of building the pilgrimage church at the Cabo de Espichel (*see* note 52).

The last additions to the castle were made in the seventeenth and early eighteenth centuries. A curious hexagonal chapel (which survives) was built just outside and adjoining the entrance to the castle – behind the camera in the photograph. Also the medieval *alcáçova* (residence of the constable) was replaced by a fine arcaded house. This, however, was burnt out in 1872, and the stone structure, which remained substantially intact, was demolished in 1935 by the Directorate of National Monuments during works of 'renovation and reintegration'. Its forlorn site is here visible on the lower left-hand side.

17 Landscape in Trás-os-Montes

In Trás-os-Montes, a remote province of north-east Portugal, whole hillsides have been planted with eucalyptus and *Pinus pinaster* during the past forty years. This afforestation has completely changed the life of the inhabitants, most of whom were originally shepherds. The bushy tree in the foreground is a stone pine (*Pinus pinea*), the indigenous pine-tree, which is slower growing, less useful and more beautiful than *Pinus pinaster*.

18 Citânia de Briteiros

The hill-city, or 'Citânia', of Briteiros is the largest, most impressive of Celtic-Iberian remains in Portugal. It is situated in high country near Braga, and comprises flagged streets, the remains of a drainage system and a large number of habitations, some rectangular, other circular. Briteiros was first excavated in the 1870s by Dr Martins Sarmento, and the artifacts he found there are now in Guimarães, in the museum that was named after him.

Nearby, at a lower level, are the foundations of another town, that of Sabrosa, also excavated by Sarmento. But Sabrosa was deserted far earlier than Briteiros, which continued to be occupied during Roman times. The Romans reached Portugal around 217 BC, in pursuit of the Carthaginians. The Lusitanian hero Viriathus, the Portuguese counterpart of Vercingetorix or Boadicea, led a resistance movement which was active until 140 BC. By the end of the first century AD, the Roman occupation was complete. In some ways, Portugal is still the most Roman of European countries.

The construction of the round huts at Briteiros (some of which have been restored with thatched roofs to show their original appearance) is known as 'helicoidal': the irregularly shaped stones are laid in a spiral, in what is in effect one continuous course up to the roof.

The inhabitants of Briteiros were an agricultural people, who knew about the rotation of crops. The hill-city is strategically placed so that an enemy would be visible from a great distance.

19 LANDSCAPE IN THE BEIRA ALTA
Near the frontier between the Spanish city of Ciudad Rodrigo, and Guarda in Portugal, the plateau, or *meseta,* comes to an end and is replaced by rocky, infertile country, deeply divided by river valleys. Here, in a landscape of the Beira Alta (which means 'high boundary'), we see the sparse vegetation and unrewarding soil typical of this mountainous region.

20 AUTUMN PLOUGHING IN THE BEIRA ALTA
Autumn ploughing in the Beira Alta, between the valley of the Douro, which reaches the sea at Oporto, and the Mondego, which flows through Coimbra. The soil, dry after the long summer, floats away in dust clouds. The oxen, which are used for ploughing in northern Portugal, wear strange yokes padded with fringed leather. Farther north, yokes of elaborately carved wood are preferred.

21 CATTLE MARKET IN THE BEIRA ALTA
Country fairs, where cattle, sheep, horses, mules and pigs are bought and sold, are a prominent feature of country life in Portugal. One of the largest is at Vila Nogueira de Azeitão, near Lisbon. Barcelos, in the Minho, has a splendid market every Thursday,

where, in addition to animals, household objects and local pottery are sold. This photograph shows cattle on sale at a market in the Beira Alta.

22 LANDSCAPE NEAR VILAR FORMOSO

Another scene showing the type of cultivation found in the mountainous country near the frontier with Spain. The round haystacks, offering more resistance to violent winds, are typical of this part of the country.

23 SHRINE, BRAGA CATHEDRAL

This is a thirteenth-century shrine in the cloister of Braga Cathedral, close to a gate leading into the small courtyard which separates the Cathedral from the adjoining Misericórdia church. Under a trilobate arch stands the figure of St Nicholas, Bishop of Myra, revered in western Europe as protector of children and in the East as protector of sailors. (It has also been suggested that this mitred saint is not St Nicholas but a sixth-century bishop of Braga, Sao Martinho de Dume.)

Bracara Augusta, a city of fountains (more than sixty have been counted in the town), was one of the administrative capitals of Roman Spain, linked by Roman roads to the neighbouring capitals of Lugo and Astorga to the north-east and Santarém and Beja to the south. Christianity was certainly introduced into Spain during Roman times, but there is no sound evidence that this occurred very early. Nevertheless, Hispanic tradition has insisted that in the middle of the first century one of the twelve apostles, St James the Greater (Sant' Jago Maior or Santiago), brother of St John the Evangelist, brought the gospel to Spain and is buried at Santiago de Compostela in Galicia. Pious and patriotic Portuguese tradition relates that Santiago began his mission at Braga, and from his converts in that city chose nine disciples to preach the gospel throughout the Peninsula. The chief of these disciples was São Pedro de Rates, founder of the see of Braga, whose remains are the most revered of the holy relics in the Cathedral. (Extraordinary stories were told of this most ancient saint: for example, that he was originally a Jew named Malachi, or Samuel, who at the time of Nebuchadnezzar's dispersal of the Israelites fled to Spain, where he died and was buried near Granada, but was restored to life after six hundred years by Santiago, who converted him, baptized him Peter, and sent him to Braga to preach the gospel. This marvellous history was still given official currency in the Braga Breviary printed in the eighteenth century.)

Belief in the tradition of São Pedro de Rates enabled the citizens of Braga to claim that their city was the primitive centre of Hispanic Christianity and first Peninsular see, giving their archbishops primacy over all others in Spain and Portugal. Since the early fourth century the bishops of the whole of the north-west of the Peninsula were apparently suffragans of Braga, and this persisted at least until the end of the twelfth century.

Architecturally, however, Braga Cathedral never lived up to the grandeur and pretensions of its archbishops. The present structure, no doubt the successor to earlier churches on the site, was begun in the late eleventh or early twelfth century. It was built on a Cluniac model under the auspices of Henry of Burgundy and his wife Dona Teresa, Countess of Portugal (daughter of Alfonso VI of Castile and Leon). But only the general plan of the building and two doorways survive of the romanesque edifice. During subsequent centuries all the resources and architectural enterprises of the archbishops was devoted to modifying and rebuilding, rather than enlarging, the romanesque structure. Some of this later work was of high quality, particularly the chancel and porch, for which an energetic and forceful archbishop of the early sixteenth century, Dom Diogo de Sousa, was responsible. Like a Roman prelate of his time, Dom Diogo planted a *vigna* outside the city walls as a summer retreat, reformed the urban street system and instituted a school of classical studies; but the style employed by the architect of this princely Renaissance humanist in his additions to the Cathedral was Gothic.

24 The Tomb of Pedro I, Alcobaça

The great monastic church at Alcobaça contains a number of royal tombs of the thirteenth and fourteenth centuries, among which two are outstanding works of art, namely those of Pedro I, illustrated here, and of his mistress-wife, Dona Iñez de Castro; they were evidently designed and executed as a pair.

The Royal Abbey of St Mary of Alcobaça was founded as a Cistercian monastery by the first king of Portugal, Afonso Henriques, probably in thanksgiving for military successes against the Infidel. Begun *c.* 1153, the building took seventy years to complete. The church closely follows the plan of those of the Cistercian parent-house of Clairvaux and of Pontigny-in-the-Meadows in north Burgundy (begun 1114). All three are characterized by their immense length: Alcobaça is 365 feet long.

In 1834 Alcobaça, along with all other monasteries in Portugal, was dissolved; but a vivid picture has come down to us of life there in the last years of its existence as a monastic house, thanks to a visit paid by William Beckford at the end of the eighteenth century. He was the guest of the monks for several weeks, and describes in his fascinating *Recollections of an Excursion to the Monasteries of Alcobaça and Batalha* how he was entertained by them with sumptuous feasts, and even with plays and operas performed by some of the younger members of the community. Everywhere at Alcobaça he found 'an original mixture of simplicity and magnificence'.

Pedro I, eighth king of Portugal, had the famous pair of tombs at Alcobaça made for himself and Dona Iñez soon after his accession to the throne in 1357: that of Dona Iñez had certainly been completed by 1361, when her embalmed body was transferred from Santa Clara Coimbra to its new resting place. Dona Iñez had been beheaded on

7 January 1355. Three counsellors of Afonso IV, father of Pedro, were directly responsible for her execution, apparently acting under orders from the King. The reasons for this atrocity remain obscure – an obscurity perceptibly thickened by the romantic imagination of nineteenth-century writers quite ignorant of fourteenth-century historical circumstances. It is certain that Dom Afonso wanted his heir, Pedro, to remarry after the death in 1345 of the latter's wife, in order to secure the succession. But Pedro refused to remarry, out of what seems to have been a quite genuine devotion to his mistress Dona Iñez. She was certainly the favourite among his several mistresses. Later he said that he had married her secretly in the year before her death. This may well be true; but, so far as Afonso was concerned, his son was endangering the succession by refusing to produce legitimate offspring, for which his many bastards were no substitute. Indeed, contemporary Spanish history demonstrated only too clearly the dangers of bastards as incitements to civil war. The execution of Dona Iñez can thus be explained, though not excused, as an 'act of state'.

The tombs, carved in white limestone, form a pair. In each of them a richly decorated sarcophagus is supported by six heraldic beasts (Dona Iñez' tomb by sphinxes, Dom Pedro's by lions, two of which are visible at the bottom of the photograph). On top of the sarcophagus lies the life-size figure of the deceased, with open eyes as if awakened from the dead. Six angels, gazing towards heaven, support the upper part of the body with outstretched arms. Three of the angels kneel on each side, apparently lifting the body at the head, shoulders and waist. The angel on the right of the photograph and the one opposite also hold incense censers. These angels are the most charming and poignant features of both tombs. The recumbent figures of the King and Dona Iñez are impressive state effigies, not realistic portraits. He holds the hilt of his sword in his right hand and the scabbard with his left. She lightly grasps a pair of folded gloves with both hands.

The sides of the tombs are carved with great elaboration. The principal decorative feature is a series of niches containing religious scenes in high relief under triangular gables filled with varied tracery (four of these niches are visible in the photograph). Behind the tops of the gables and of the pinnacles between them is another series of arched niches containing very small delicately carved figures only a few inches high. Round the top is an exquisitely delicate arcade interrupted at regular intervals by panels displaying the royal arms of Portugal. The quality of the carving is superlative throughout, making these tombs major masterpieces of European Gothic sculpture. But they pose problems which will probably never be resolved: in particular who designed them, who executed them and what the significance is of the decorative themes—especially of the miniature rose window, full of figures, at the head of Pedro's sarcophagus with its inscription in inverted Gothic letters, which seems to read: ATÉ A FIM DO MUNDO ('Until the end of the world').

Both tombs were severely damaged in 1810, when French troops carried out a systematic campaign of looting and destruction at Alcobaça. It was after this, it seems, in order that the damage should be less obvious, that the two tombs were moved from the crossing where they had originally stood to a chamber leading off the south transept. There they were placed with their feet towards each other, from which rearrangement there grew up the charming but wholly fictitious story that Dom Pedro had ordered the tombs to be placed end to end, so that at the Resurrection he and Dona Iñez would rise and meet each other face to face. Recent restorations, however, have ruthlessly separated the lovers to opposite sides of the nave.

25 Village Church, Sangalhos

Most of the great buildings of eighteenth-century Portugal were the work of foreign architects. Their baroque influence filtered down to the simple churches of country villages, the great majority of which have a baroque façade, often in front of a more ancient building, as in this church at Sangalhos between Aveiro and Coimbra.

The quite elaborate, but not very well proportioned tower is a separate architectural element, revealing a rustic desire to imitate the grandeur of a great baroque church. This tower has been added on to a façade of the simplest kind. The charm of the latter can be appreciated by blocking out the tower with one's hand, which also enables one to recognize the close kinship of this Sangalhos façade with those of the small chapels in the extreme south of Portugal illustrated in plate 95.

26 The Old Cathedral, Coimbra

The small romanesque Cathedral of Coimbra stands on the western slope of the hill on which the town is built. At the top of the hill is the University – its clock tower (1728–33) can just be seen behind the long roof of one of the wings of the main university quadrangle on the right-hand side of the photograph.

The Old Cathedral was begun in 1162, on the site of an earlier church, and was consecrated in 1184. Its architect was, it seems, a certain Master Robert, a Frenchman from Basse-Auvergne who was called from Lisbon to Coimbra. He had evidently formed his stylistic notions from acquaintance with the churches on the famous pilgrimage route, the so-called *camino francés*, down to Santiago de Compostela.

In 1772, after the suppression of the Society of Jesus in the Portuguese dominions, the enormous church of their Coimbra College (built 1598–1698), which lies a few hundred yards away up the road to the left in the photograph, became the New Cathedral (Sé Nova) of Coimbra. The Sé Velha, or Old Cathedral, which we see here is now simply the church of the town parish of São Cristóvão.

In many respects the Sé Velha follows, on a reduced scale, the design of Santiago (largely completed by 1128), except for its rectangular compactness, in which it follows the example of smaller pilgrimage churches on the route to Santiago, such as San Martín de Frómista (dating from *c.* 1066) between Burgos and Leon. Particularly striking is the fortified appearance of the Sé Velha (Santiago, too, was fortified in the twelfth century): one notices the battlements, the turret-like treatment of the buttresses and central bay of the façade, the big nave window designed like a door with a machicolated sill to defend the real doorway below and the slit windows (lighting the aisles) on either side.

On the north side, just visible at the extreme left of the photograph, is a projecting portal surmounted by a loggia, above which an attic storey is carried to the full height of the building and crowned by a lantern. This addition was made in the second quarter of the sixteenth century in French Renaissance style. It is known as the Porta Especiosa, or Fair Doorway, and is enriched with sculptured decoration in niches and medallions.

Inside the Cathedral there are two fine reredoses. One behind the high altar in the central apse is a splendid Gothic example dating from 1498–1588, elaborately carved and gilded: it is the work of two northern craftsmen – Oliver of Ghent and John of Ypres. The second one is in the small apse to the left of the high altar, the Chapel of St Peter. It is beautifully designed and executed in early French Renaissance style dating from *c.* 1530. Both reredoses, differing so profoundly in style, were nevertheless presented to the Cathedral by the same bishop, Dom Jorge de Almeida (a contemporary of Dom Diogo de Sousa, Archbishop of Braga: *see* note 23). His own tomb lies in the Chapel of St Peter.

27 Conimbriga

Conimbriga lies in the country a few miles south of Coimbra. It is situated on a rocky promontory perforated with caves, between two glens. Originally a Lusitanian-Celtic town, already mentioned as an *oppidum* in the first century AD by Pliny (*Natural History*, iv, 113), it was thoroughly Romanized during the imperial era and grew rich – to judge by the splendour of the buildings so far excavated, among which is the palatial house seen here. Ample water was provided for Roman Conimbriga by an aqueduct from the copious nearby spring of Alcabideque, where there may still be seen traces of the Roman cistern, while the associated Roman water tower still survives. The road from Conimbriga to Aeminium (Coimbra) was of sufficient importance to justify constructing a substantial viaduct to carry it over the adjacent valley.

The tip of the Conimbriga promontory is defended by a formidable circuit of walls, up to four metres thick and eight metres high. These walls enclose a roughly triangular space measuring approximately 400 metres along each side from the apex and 200 metres across the spine of the ridge. In the section of wall across the ridge there are two gates, the more important of these comprising a carefully constructed covered passage between salient towers (visible in silhouette at the top left-hand side of the photograph). The wall across the ridge cuts through the town, leaving important buildings outside it. Presumably, therefore, it was constructed at a late date, perhaps in the fourth century, when barbarian invasions were becoming a serious threat. In such circumstances it would have been necessary to make best use of the terrain for defensive purposes irrespective of residential convenience. Evidence of hasty construction of the walls at Conimbriga, if not some measure of desperation on the part of its inhabitants, is provided by the quantity of votive tablets, tombstones and even statues which were incorporated in the defensive fabric.

Sacked by the Suevi in 468, Conimbriga was reconstituted by the Visigoths and became the short-lived seat of a bishopric. Habitation had, however, ceased by the time the region was reconquered by the Christians from the Moors, and prior to the excavations in recent times the site of Conimbriga was planted as an orchard of olive trees.

28 UNDERFLOOR HEATING, CONIMBRIGA
In the 'hypocaust' system of heating developed by the Romans, warm air from a 'hypocausis', or stokehole, was spread through a building by one of three methods: hollow tiles covering the walls could be used to conduct the heat into chimneys; traps in the floor could be used to admit it directly into the room; or (the method apparently used at Conimbriga), by means of narrow passages such as shown in this photograph, the warm air could be circulated under the entire floor, which, being made of thick concrete, was a good conductor of heat.

29 DETAIL OF MOSAIC, CONIMBRIGA
In this detail from one of the mosaic floors, two birds, apparently moorhens, carry a garland in their beaks.

30 DRAIN COVER, CONIMBRIGA
A drain cover at Conimbriga repeats the flower-like decoration found in the mosaic shown plate 29.

31 MOSAIC, CONIMBRIGA
Many of the mosaic floors at Conimbriga are in good repair. This one shows Perseus carrying the head of the Medusa, whose gaze will turn the sea monster to stone. Andromeda, threatened by the monster, is not represented.

32 TOMB OF A DAUGHTER OF SANCHO I, LORVÃO
The Convent of Lorvão lies in a narrow, wooded valley about ten miles north-east of Coimbra. The local industry of the small adjoining town is the manufacture of *palitos*, the hygienic wooden toothpicks – eulogized by Sir Richard Burton – which are

universally used by the Portuguese. The first religious establishment at Lorvão was a monastery, probably founded in the ninth century. This was converted into a nunnery in the year 1200 by the Infanta Dona Teresa, who had returned from Spain in 1196 after being separated from her husband, the king of Leon; the evicted monks were transferred to Pedroso, near Oporto. The present imposing range of buildings dates almost entirely from between 1630 and 1765.

In the chancel of the church on either side of the high altar are preserved the remains of two daughters of Sancho I, Dona Teresa and her younger unmarried sister Dona Sancha (died 1229). The latter had founded the Bernardine nunnery of Gelas, close to Coimbra, in 1217. They were soon deemed saints, miracles were recorded and both sisters were canonized by a Bull of Pope Clement XI dated 23 December 1705. In 1713 the abbess of Lorvão commissioned new reliquary coffins from an Oporto silversmith, Manuel Carneiro da Silva, to which the bones of the two saints were transferred on 17 October 1715 at a splendid ceremony attended by the Count-Bishop of Coimbra, the Abbot of Alcobaça and the principal persons of the whole region. The inner caskets of these baroque reliquaries are covered with crimson velvet, visible through outer casings of open-work silver, wrought in a pattern of acanthus sprays.

33 CHOIR-STALLS, LORVÃO

Between the fifteenth and the end of the eighteenth century, throughout Spain and Portugal, there was an increasing demand for decorative wood-carving (*talha*), especially wood-carved reredoses, to enrich the interiors of churches. With so much patronage, the skill and prestige of the specialized craftsmen employed for such work reached a very high level. Most Portuguese *talha* was executed in chestnut wood, which, after priming with gesso, was gilded and coloured. But good quality utilitarian furniture was also required, for which gilding and painting would be less suitable – for example, the seats of choir-stalls and, of course, chairs and tables. For these purposes there was a preference for exotic woods, especially *jacaranda* (Brazilian rosewood) left in their natural state and thus revealing their rich colour, fine texture and attractive veining.

Early in the eighteenth century at the nunnery of Arouca, between Oporto and Viseu, 108 stalls were provided for the *côro baixo*, the part of the church reserved for the nuns. The stalls themselves are of rosewood, but the high ornamental backs and the elaborate cresting at the top are of chestnut wood, richly gilded and framing panel pictures of pious themes. The 116 stalls in the *côro baixo* at Lorvão are later than those at Arouca, belonging to the second half of the eighteenth century though still baroque in style. Unlike the choir-stalls at Arouca, those at Lorvão are made entirely of rosewood, including their high backs, on the lower part of which are saints carved in relief, instead of paintings as at Arouca.

The natural wood emphasizes the high quality of the workmanship; only one carved panel in the series of saints, which represents a female martyr, is gilded and coloured.

It is quite likely that the nuns of Lorvão felt a need to emulate those of Arouca in thus embellishing their *côro baixo*. The two convents were curiously linked by an ancient royal connexion, since both owed their prestige to the patronage of saintly daughters of Sancho I: Arouca to the Infanta Dona Malfalda or Matilda (died 1256, canonized 1792), and Lorvão to her elder sister the Infanta Dona Teresa (died 1250, canonized 1705). Both these ladies were married to Spanish kings – Dona Mafalda to Henry I of Sastile and Dona Teresa to Alfonso IX of Leon – and both had their marriages annulled on grounds of consanguinity. On return to Portugal, each of these former Spanish queens adopted a religious life and respectively reformed the ancient convents of Arouca and Lorvão as Bernardine nunneries under strict Cistercian rule. One is reminded, irreverently, of an old rhyme:

> *King David and King Solomon*
> *Led merry, merry lives:*
> *They had many, many concubines*
> *And many, many wives.*
> *But when old age caught up on them*
> *They had many, many qualms;*
> *So King Solomon wrote the Proverbs*
> *And King David wrote the Psalms.*

34 THE UNIVERSITY LIBRARY, COIMBRA

The Royal Library of the University of Coimbra was built and decorated during the second and third decades of the eighteenth century. It is one of the finest baroque libraries in Europe, comparable to the best of those in the monasteries of Austria, Bavaria and Switzerland, for example that of St Gallen. The patterned marble flooring and the charming *trompe l'œil* ceiling paintings (which give extra height to the rooms with their illusion of architectural recession) are characteristic of such baroque designs. Other features are peculiar to this library, in particular the green, red and gold japanning of the bookcases and the pairs of pillars supporting the galleries by which the upper shelves are reached. These Ionic pillars or *estípites* (a Spanish and Portuguese word derived from the Latin *stipes*, a stock) are of classical heredity, but they gaily and elegantly break every possible classical rule for the Ionic order. The idea of the shaft tapering downwards probably derives from the herm steles of classical antiquity, revived for use as structural members by Renaissance architects (often called 'terms': see, for example, plate 14). Michelangelo seems to have invented the idea of applying the downward tapering shaft to a classical column or pilaster, employing it at the library of San Lorenzo, Florence.

The architect is unknown, but the wood-carving shows the influence of Claude de Laprade (1682–1738), a French sculptor who spent his working life in Portugal. The overall impression is classical, but a closer inspection reveals that the shelves, and the ingenious step-ladders which fold away into them, are exquisitely ornamented with *chinoiserie* decorations in green, red and gold. The University Library represents, therefore, not only a masterpiece of the baroque but also an important example of the 'Dream of Cathay' which fascinated Europe in the seventeenth and eighteenth centuries. Portugal, with its ancient colony of Macão, was especially open to such oriental influences.

Part Two LISBON AND ITS SURROUNDINGS

35

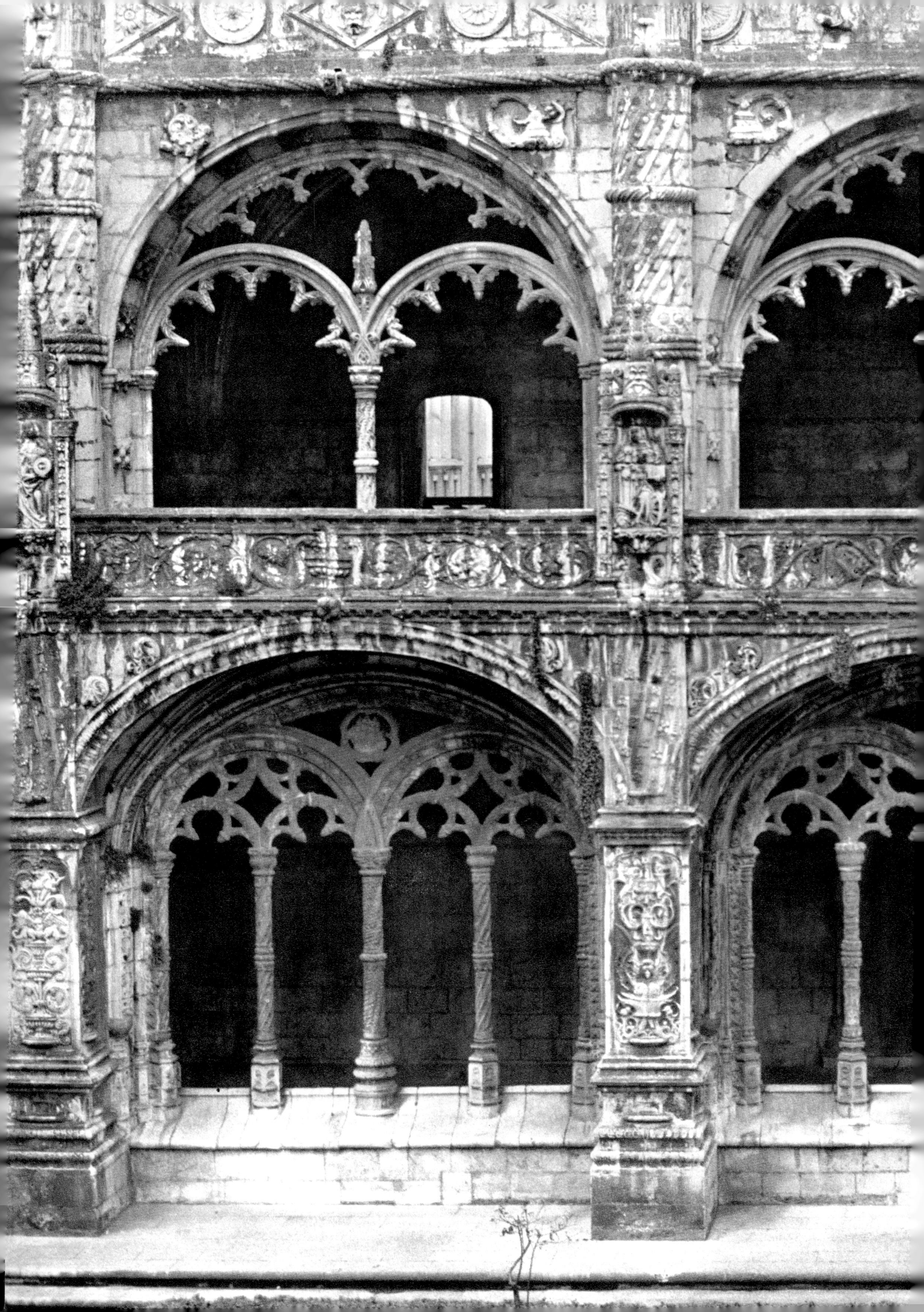

36

37

38

40

41

42

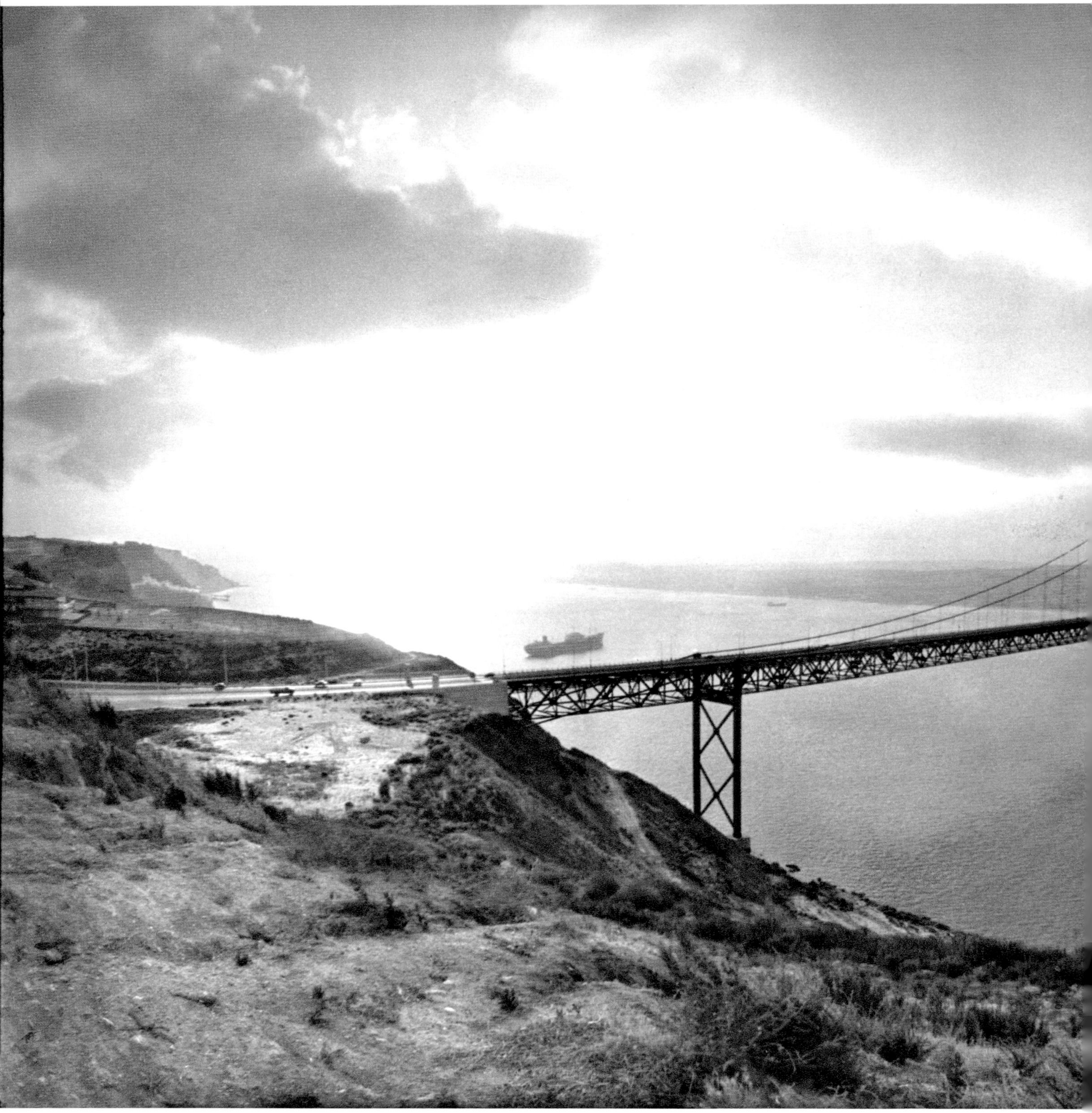

44

45

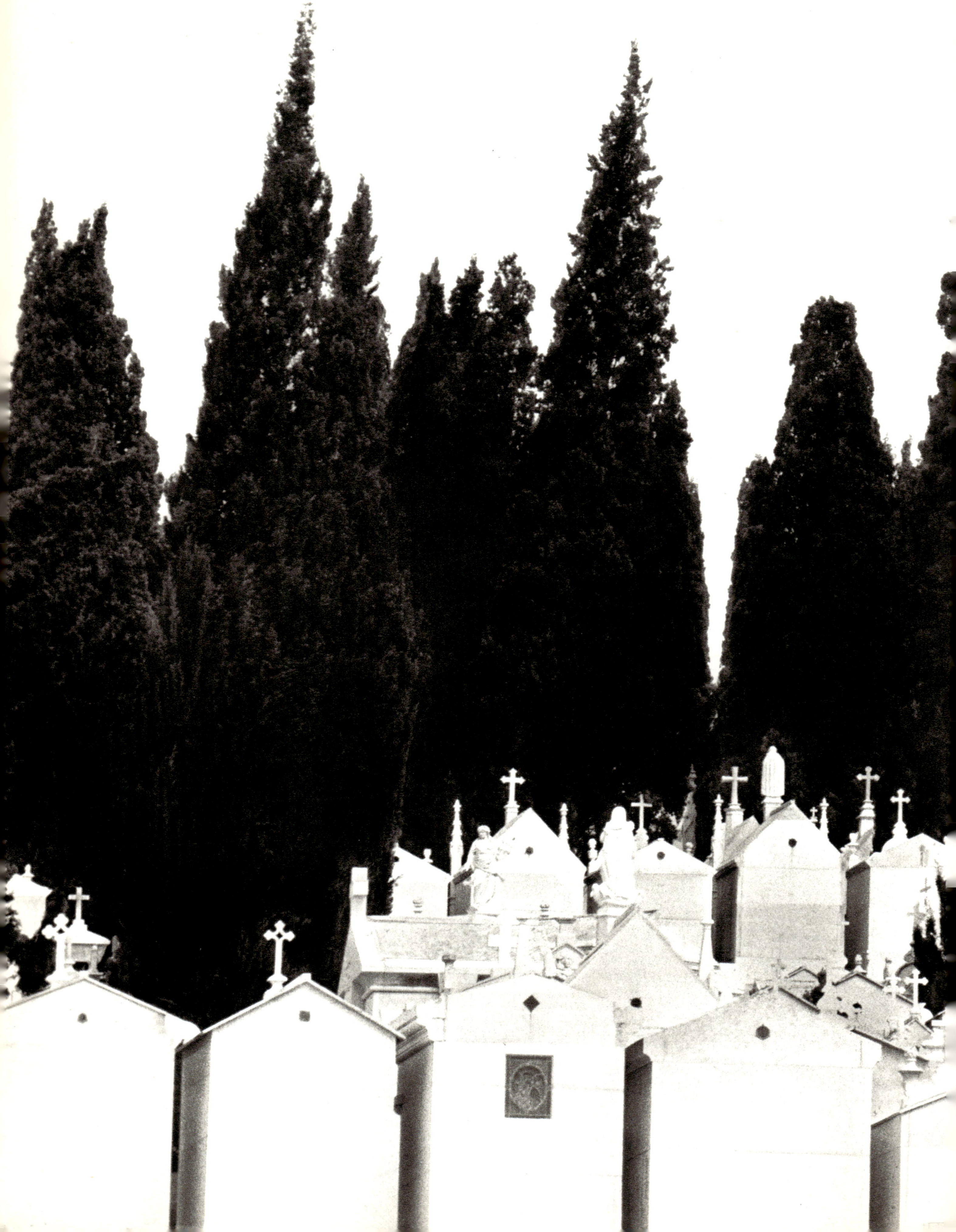

46

47

48

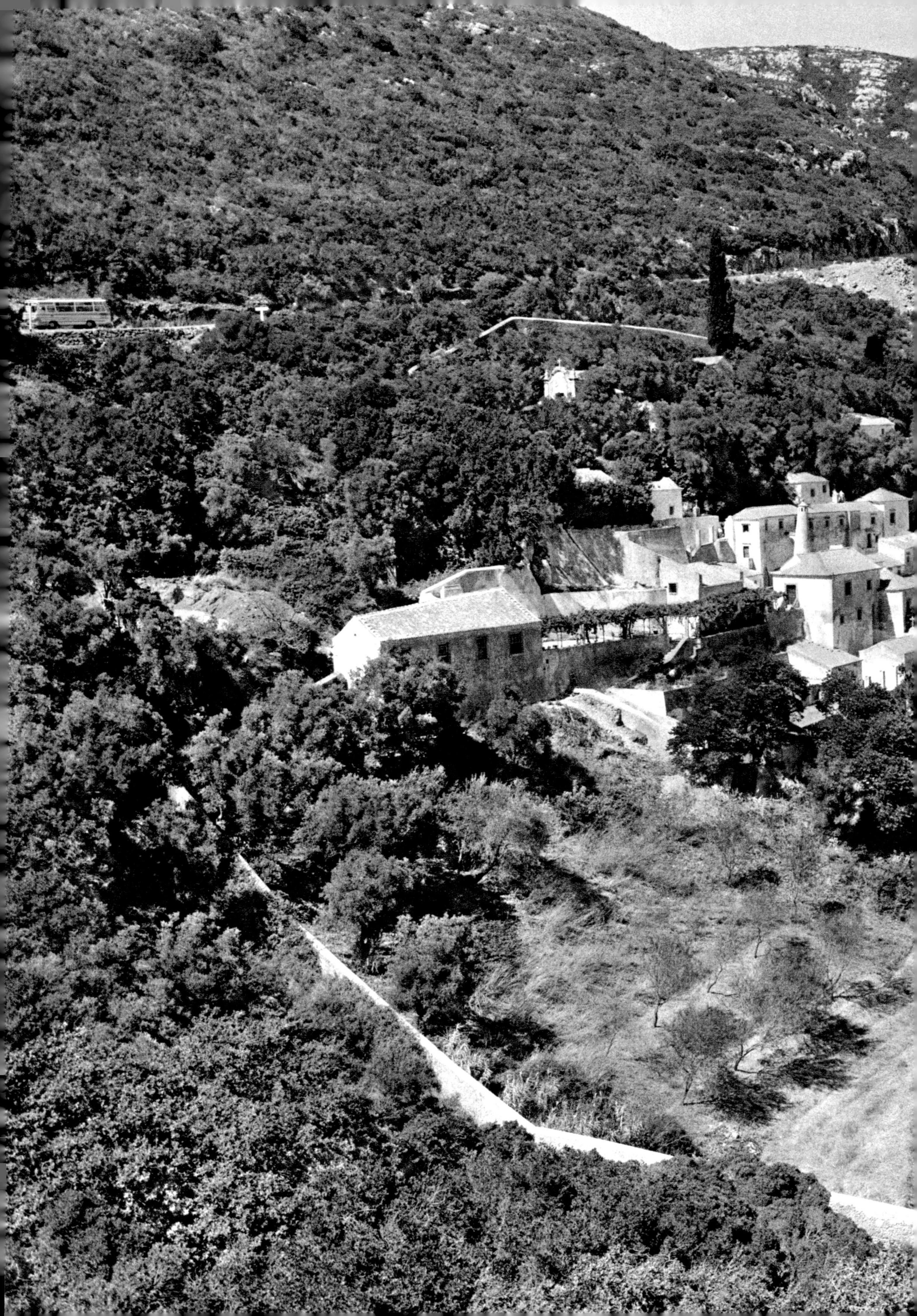

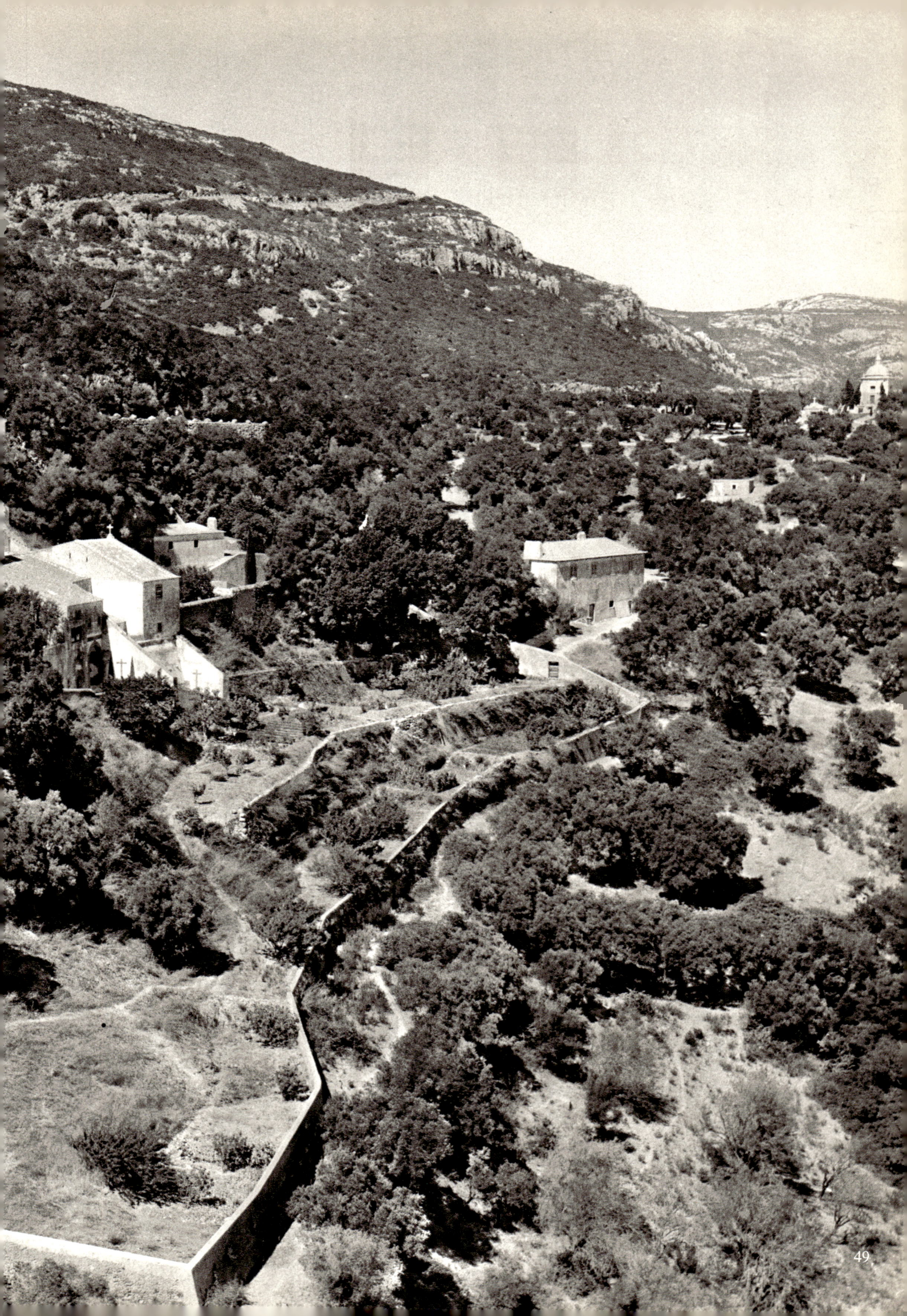

50

51

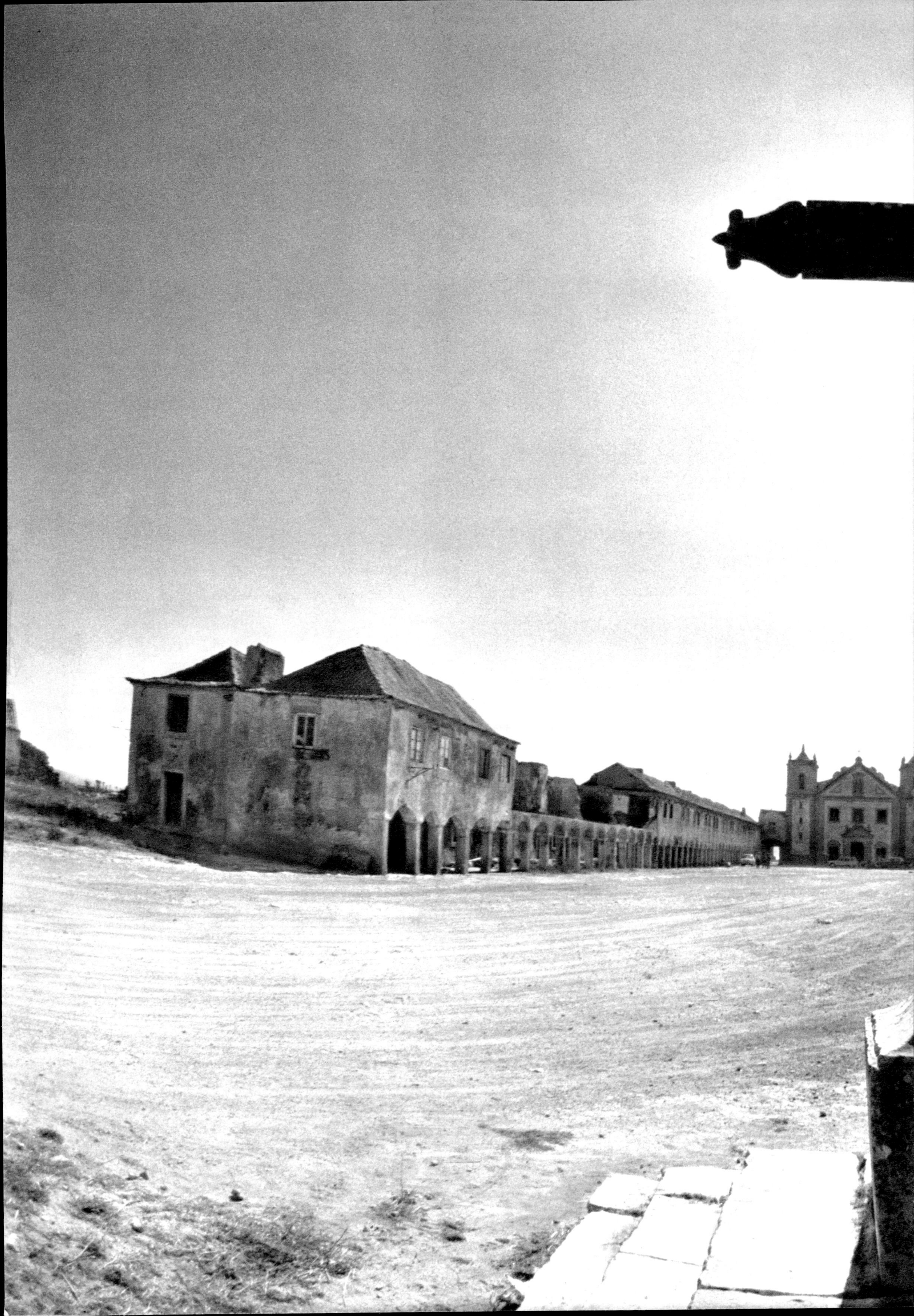

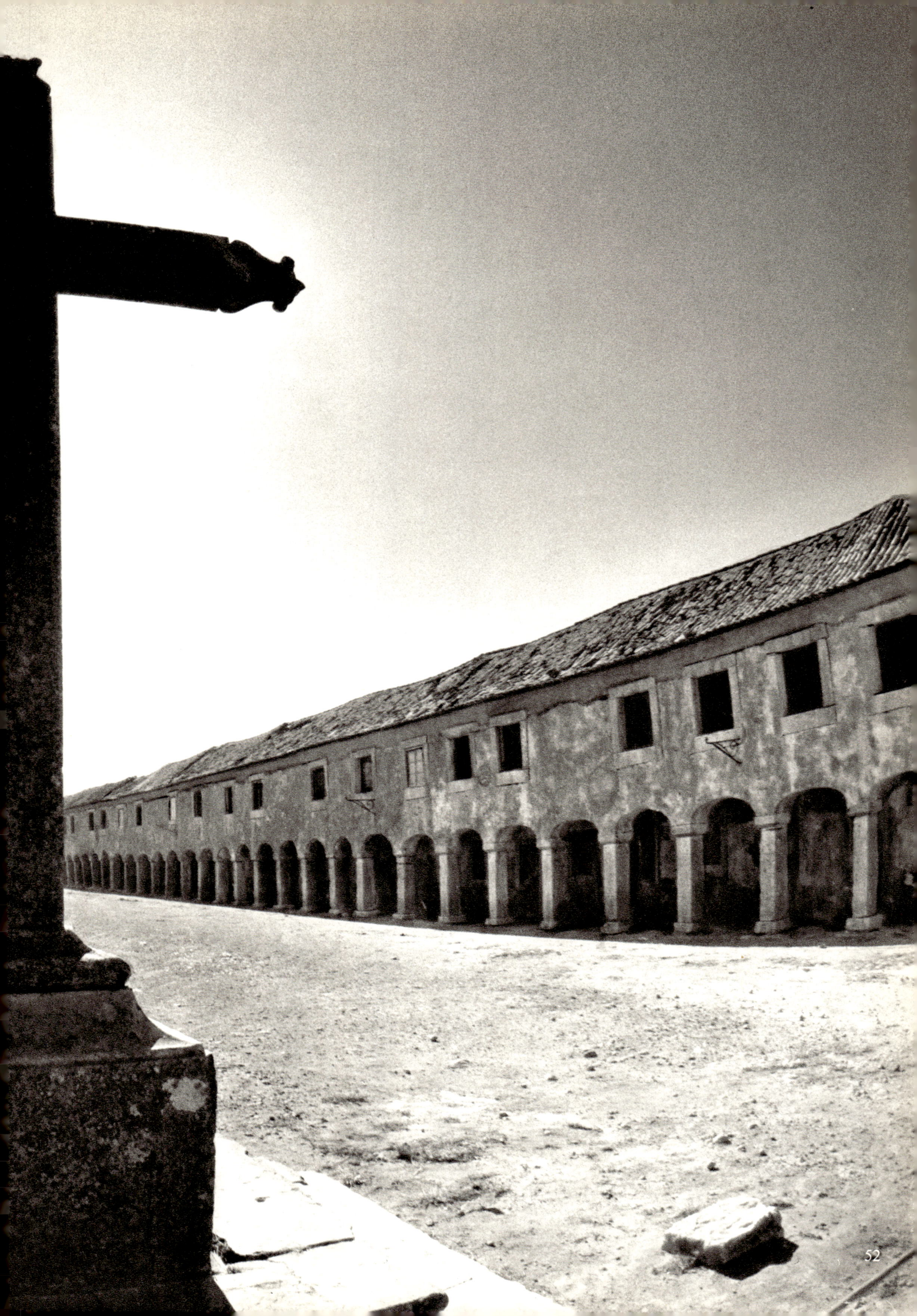

53

54

DIVAE
MAR
VIRGI

56

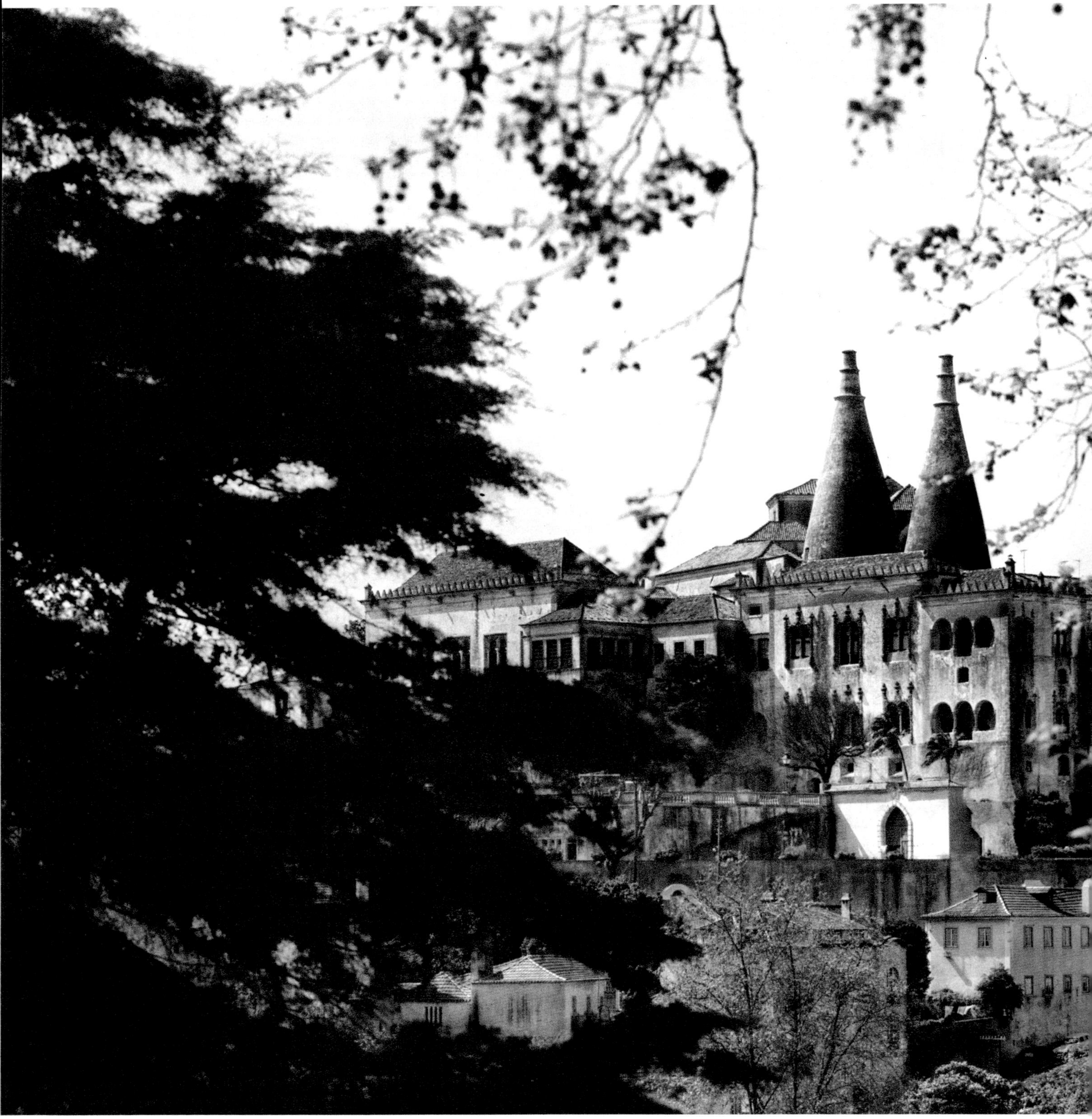

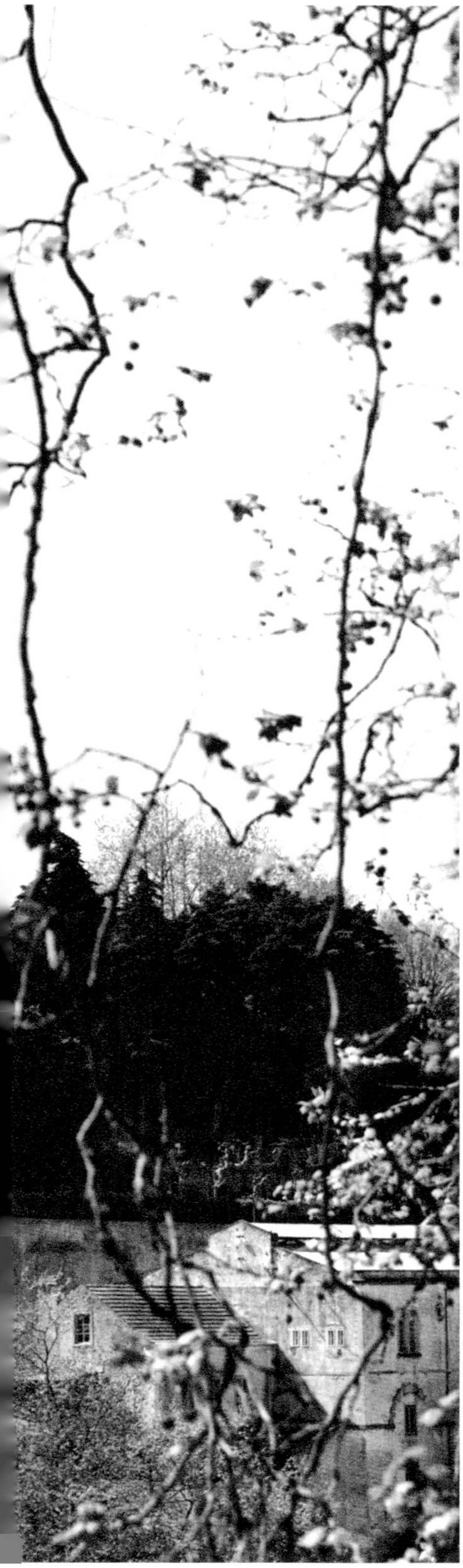

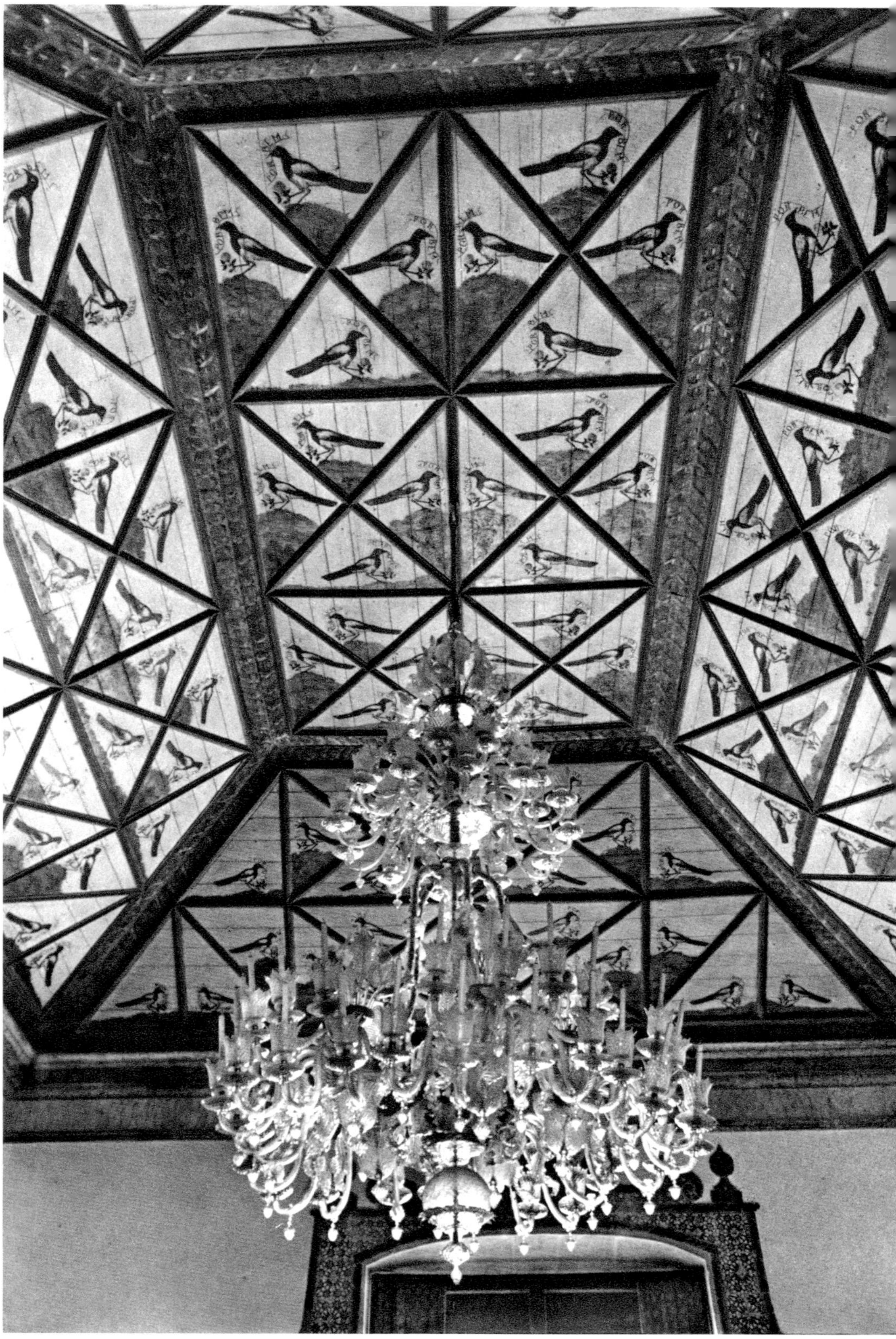

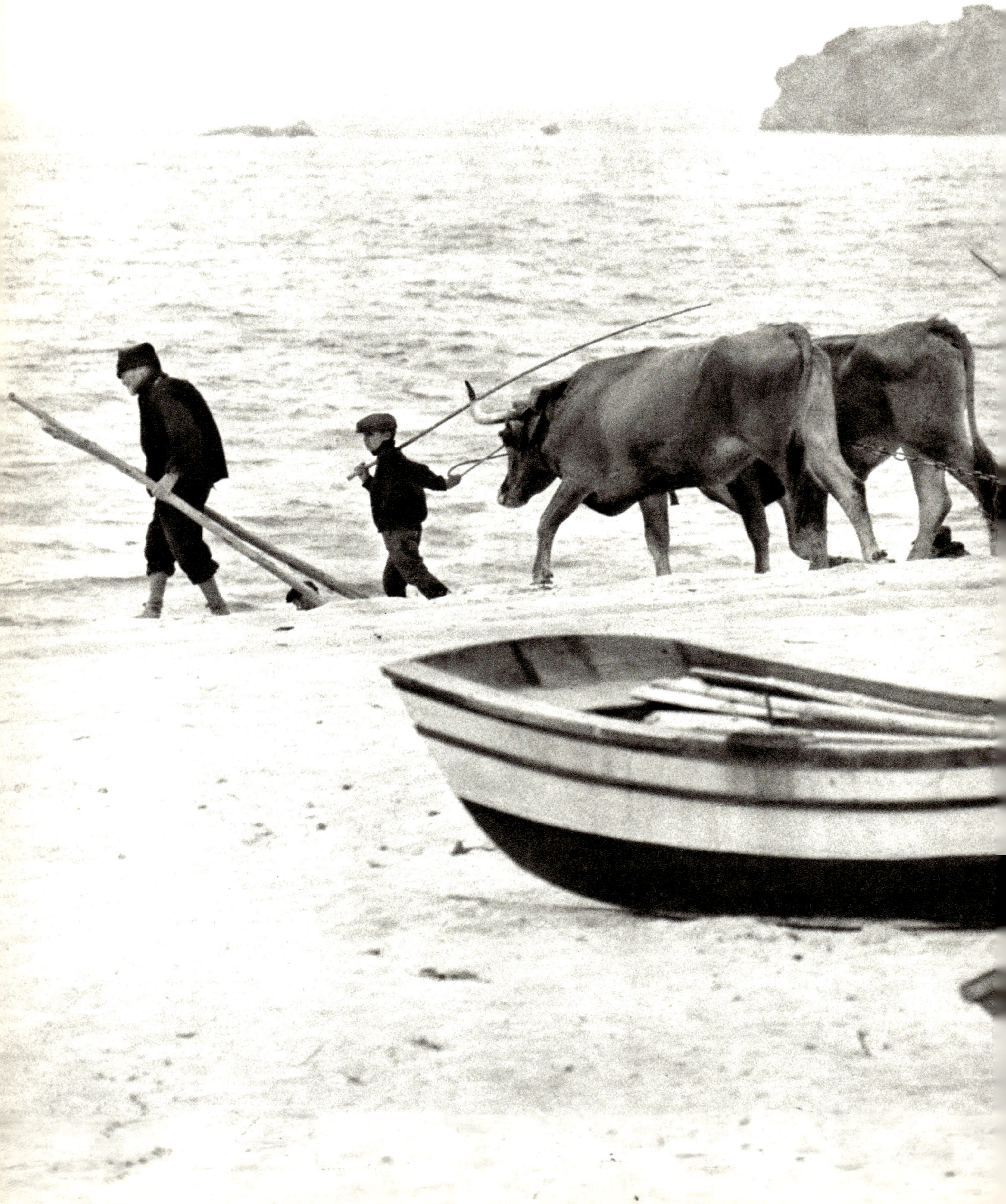

60

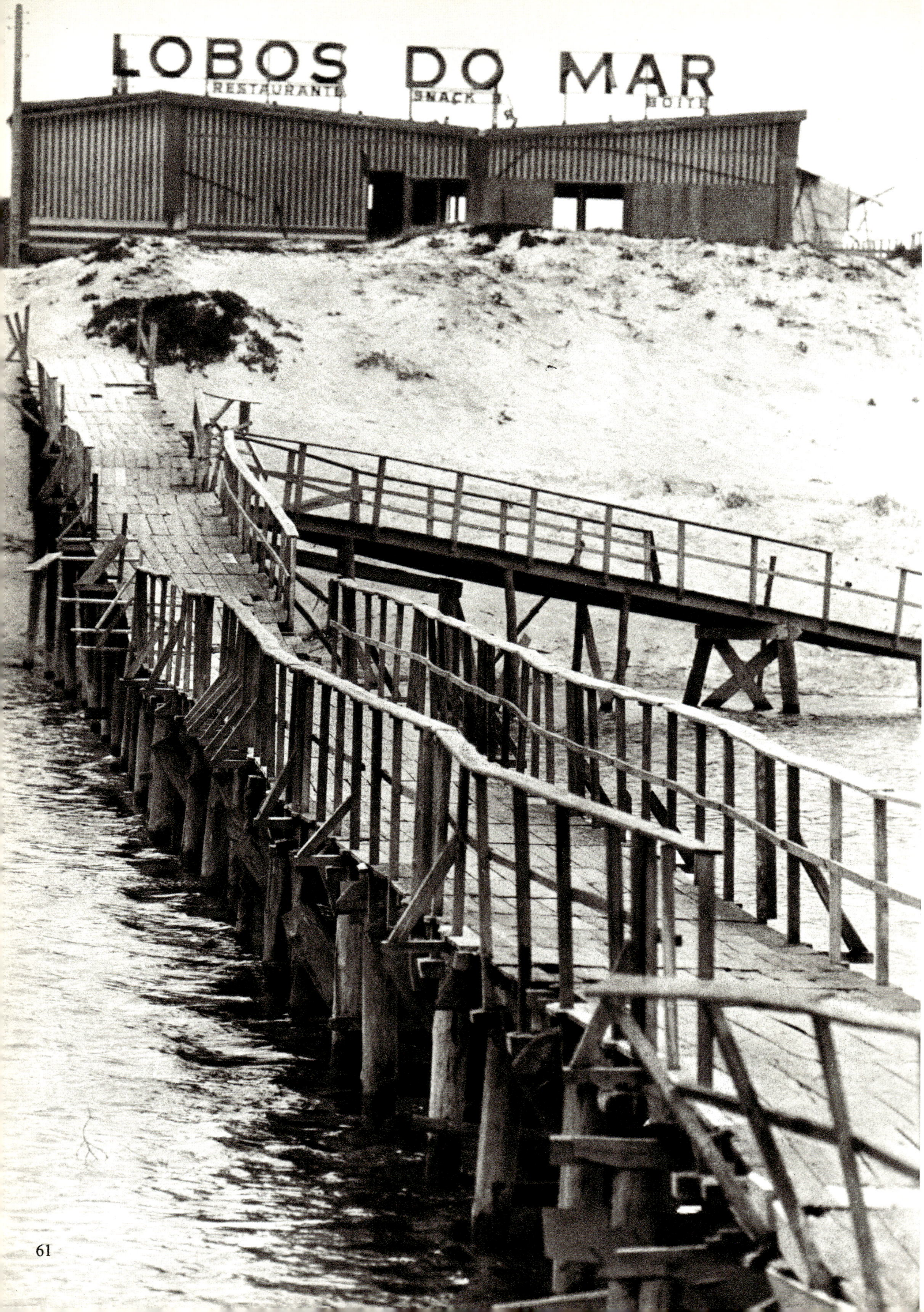
LOBOS DO MAR
RESTAURANTE
SNACK
BOITE

62

63

64

65

66

68

69

70

71

72

73

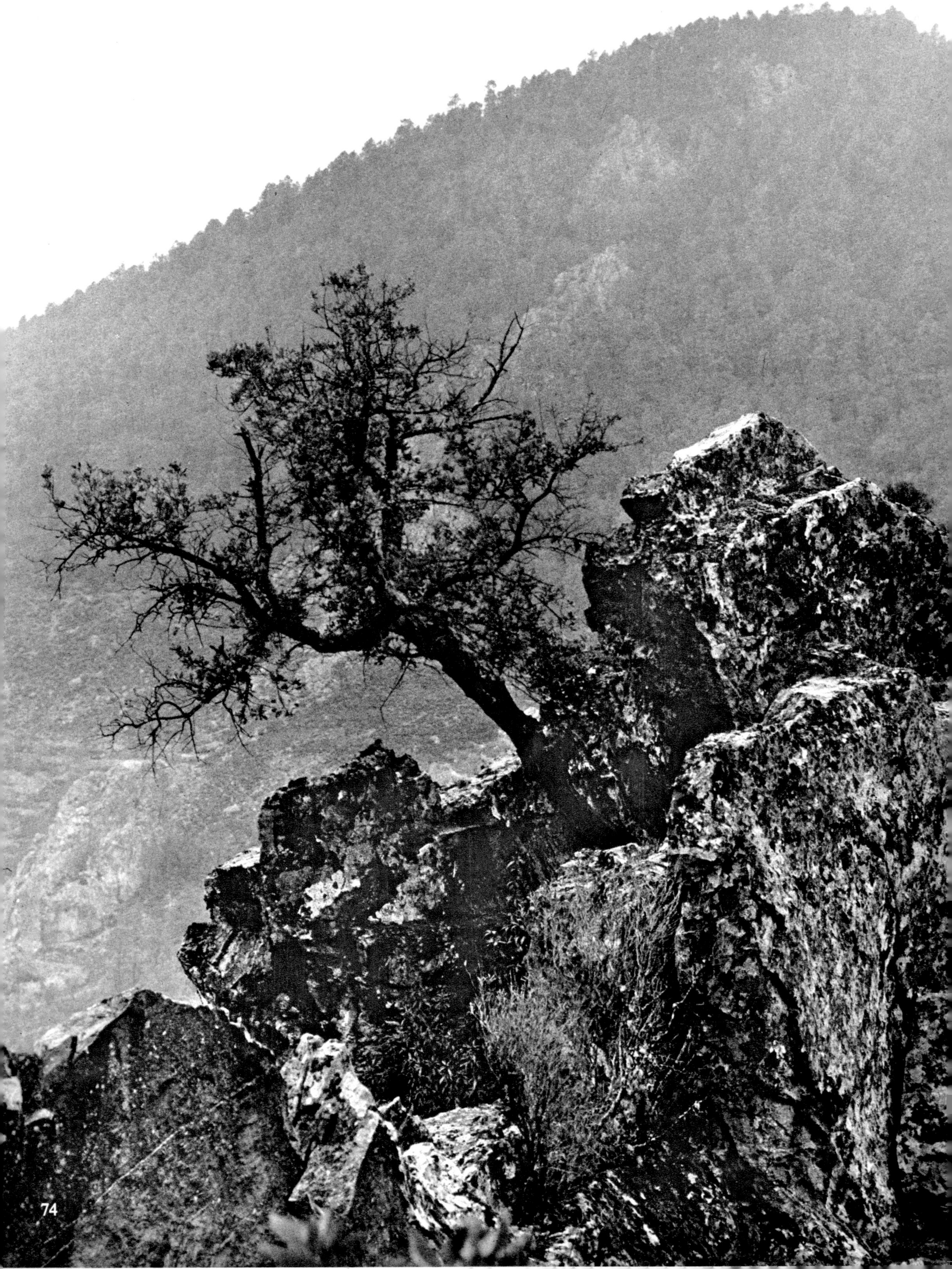

75

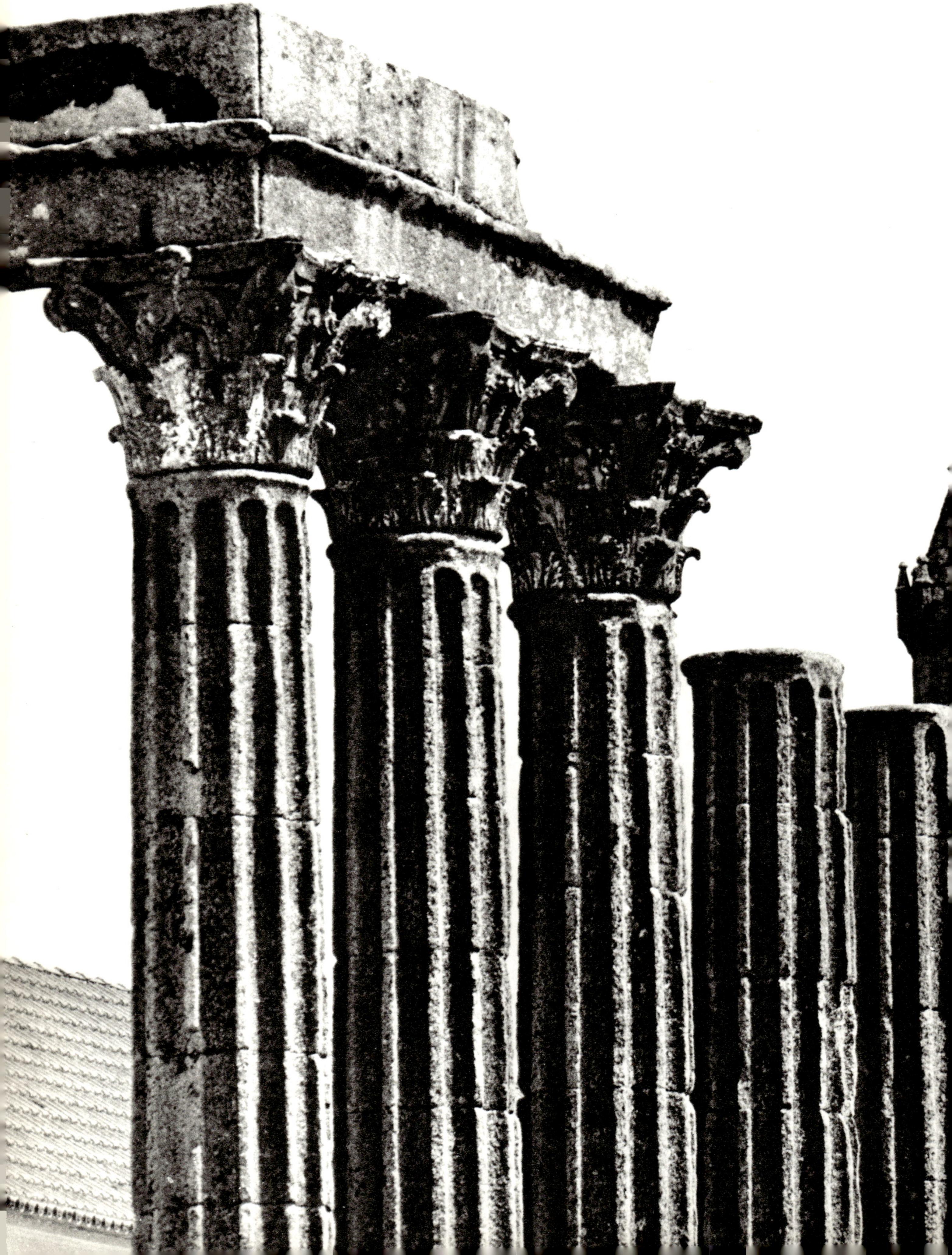

76

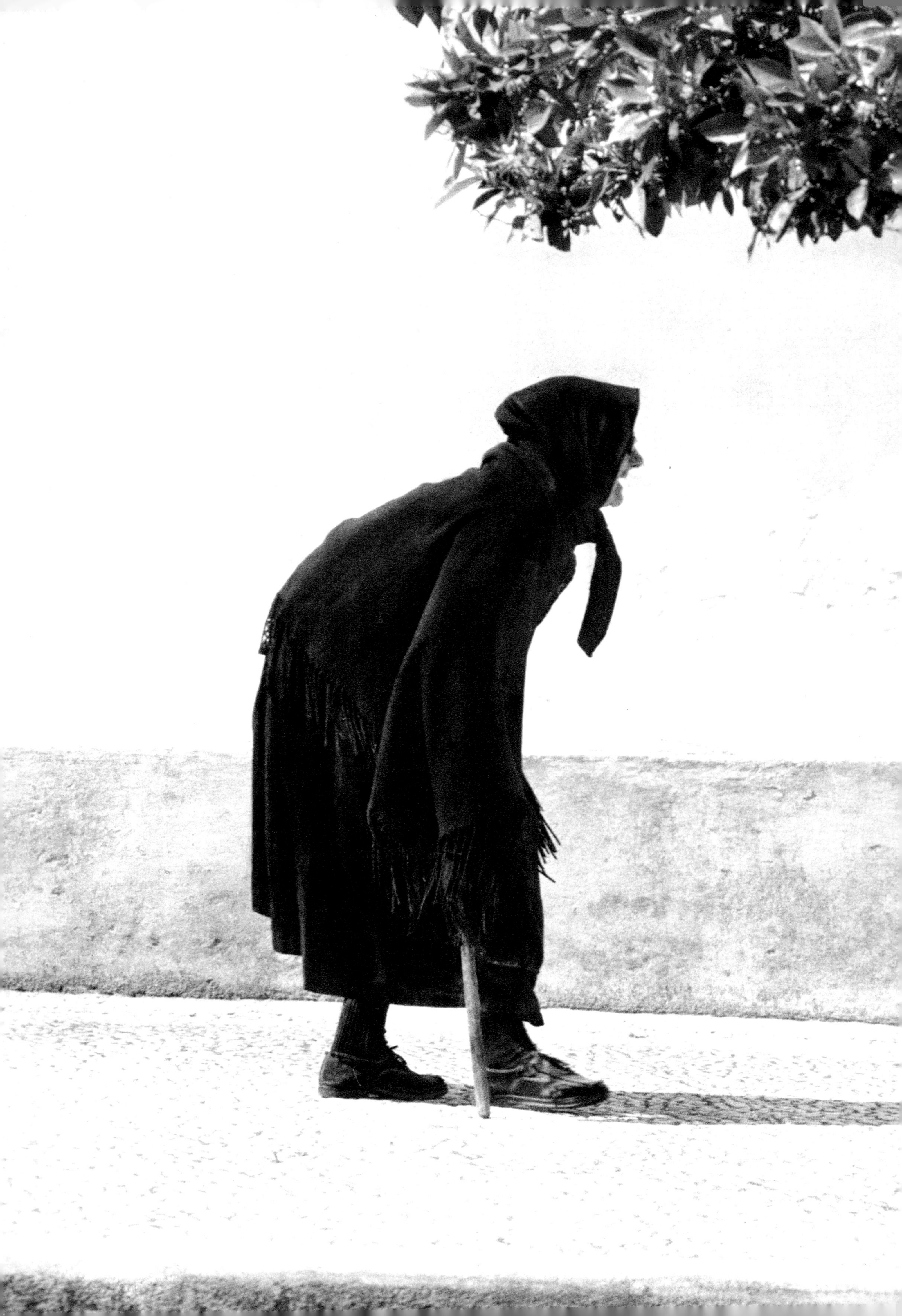

78

79

80

NOTES ON PLATES 35–80

35 DETAIL OF COLUMN, JERÓNIMOS CLOISTERS, LISBON

The Mosteiro dos Jerónimos (monastery of the Hieronymites) at Belém (Bethlehem), near Lisbon, was founded by Manuel I in 1496, one year before Vasco da Gama's pioneering sea-voyage to the Indies. Thus, contrary to popular belief, it does not commemorate this tremendous achievement. The monastery church and cloisters are, nevertheless, the supreme example of an architectural style which reflects, not only the fantastic material wealth, but also the national self-confidence and expansion of imaginative perception, brought about by the great voyages of discovery. The stone-carving on this single pier indicates clearly that the Manueline style, as it is known, represents an elaborate evolution of Late Gothic.

36 THE JERÓNIMOS CLOISTERS

The cloisters of the Hieronymite monastery (like the church itself) are a composite work, built over a period of something like thirty years, between the second and the fifth decades of the sixteenth century, under the supervision of three successive architects. It is not therefore surprising that the result is stylistically hybrid. What is surprising is that the outcome of successive phases of building and decoration in different styles should convey a real sense of unified design. The splendid appearance of the structure is certainly enhanced by the building material employed, namely the local white limestone known as *pedra* (or *marmore*) *lioz*, which weathers to various shades of golden yellow and brown.

Not all critics have considered the cloisters equally successful as a work of art. Haupt (*Die Baukunst der Renaissance in Portugal*, 1890) considered them 'perhaps the most beautiful cloisters in the world'. Watson (*Portuguese Architecture*, 1908) found the ornament excessive and criticized the proportions, especially the depressed shape of the lower arches, as ungraceful; for him therefore the total effect was 'splendid but not really pleasing'. The *Guia de Portugal* (1924) describes the Belém cloisters as 'robust, exuberant, turgid'.

The lower cloister is a vaulted Gothic structure which can safely be attributed to the first architect of the monastery, Diogo Boitac (died before 1528) and dated within the reign of Manuel I (d. 1521). The exterior of this cloister was overlaid by a series of projecting piers supporting elliptical arches decorated with Renaissance ornament in the elaborate style known as 'plateresque' from its use on the silverware (*platería*) of the period. This second campaign is reasonably attributed to the second architect of the monastery, João de Castilho (died *c*. 1552), who was also responsible for beginning the upper cloister, which seems to have been concluded in the 1540s by a third architect, Diogo de Torralva (1500–66), judging by the style of some of the vaults and the dates 1542 and 1544 on keystones.

Manuel I, the Fortunate, was an imaginative initiator of building programmes (and other expensive ventures), but he left their completion to his successors, in particular to his pious son João III, who dutifully carried out his father's grand schemes as best he could at a time when Portugal had already become a good deal poorer. In 1542, João III's minister of finance, the Count of Castanheira, observed that the greater part of the cost of the Belém monastery had been incurred during João III's reign, 'at least the cost of the better and more sumptuous work'. (*Annaes de El Rei D. João Terceiro por Fr. Luiz de Sousa*, ed. Herculano, Lisbon 1844, p. 404).

37 Town Houses, Lisbon

The majority of the town houses of Lisbon are in the classical or 'Pombaline' style, called after the Marquis of Pombal, who took charge of the reconstruction of the city after the great earthquake of 1755. Here there is a variation in the usual rectilinear pattern, with Gothic windows in a regular façade.

Portugal has suffered from many earthquakes. Most of these have been mere tremors, like that of 28 February 1969. The effects of others have been relatively localized, like that of 27 December 1722 which was felt with great severity only in the Algarve, and that of 11 November 1858 which was particularly destructive at Setúbal. Over the past thousand years several earthquakes have been so severe and widespread in their effects that they have earned the appellation 'great', in particular those of 24 August 1356, 26 January 1531 and 1 November 1755. There is no reason to suppose that the last was more severe than the other two, but the consequential effects at Lisbon were exceptionally destructive to life and property. Like the other great earthquakes, that of 1755 was felt over a very wide area; Salamanca, for example, some 250 miles away, was so severely shaken that the cupola over the crossing of the new cathedral fell. All three were felt throughout Europe.

Knowledge of this long history of seismic violence, and recollection of the 1755 earthquake in particular, has influenced the architecture of Lisbon; building regulations have been imposed by the city authorities, particularly of course on height. So deep is the memory of the 1755 earthquake (preceded by two other great earthquakes at intervals of approximately two hundred years) that many people in Lisbon were convinced that there would be another great earthquake in 1955.

38 FOUNTAIN AND VIEW OF THE CITY, LISBON

Lisbon, like Rome (and also Oporto), is traditionally held to be built on seven hills. This fountain provides a decorative focus for a small *alameda*, or tree-shaded walk, along the side of the Praça de São Pedro de Alcántara. It is also a *miradouro* (belvedere) because it is situated on the brow of one of Lisbon's steepest hills, ascended from the valley below by a funicular. Behind us is a quarter (*bairro*) of the city called the Bairro Alto; in front, if we walked round to the other side of the fountain, we should enjoy a splendid view over the eastern quarters of the town including the Monte do Castelo.

The marble pool in which the fountain stands once adorned the park of the Bemposta Palace, built for Catherine of Braganza when she returned from England to Portugal after the death of her husband Charles II. Since 1851 the Paço da Bemposta has been the Portuguese Military Staff College. It lies about three quarters of a mile north-east, that is half-left, from the spot where this photograph was taken.

39 PRAÇA DE SÃO PAULO, LISBON

Black-and-white pavements are a speciality of the streets of Lisbon, and recall Lisbon to mind when one sees them in Portuguese-speaking cities overseas. Wave patterns, executed in similar mosaics, pave the promenade of Copacabana, a famous seaside suburb of Rio de Janeiro. This example is in the Praça de São Paulo, in the south of Lisbon, west of the Praça do Comércio and a few hundred yards from the Tagus.

40 TRAFFIC POLICEMAN IN THE PRAÇA DO COMÉRCIO, LISBON

In the middle of the magnificent waterfront along the Tagus, the Praça do Comércio is today a whirling mass of motor traffic. It is kept under control by the rhythmical, elegant gestures of policemen like this one. Standing under a striped sunshade, he wears a solar topee, a favourite headgear among imperial nations.

41 Praça do Comércio with the Equestrian Statue of José I, Lisbon

The original Terreiro do Paço, with the royal palace built by Manuel I, was engulfed during the earthquake and tidal wave of 1755. The new square and the lower part of the city were planned and rebuilt as a complete unity, which has been called 'the greatest uniform architectural undertaking of the Age of the Enlightenment'. The principal architect was Eugénio dos Santos (1711–60), but the idea of the equestrian statue probably came from the Marquis of Pombal. In the best-known portrait of Pombal, a maquette of this statue, the work of Machado de Castro (1731–1822) is placed on the table beside him. Pombal was skilled at flattering his easy-going king, who appears in an untypically martial pose, with floating plumes on his helmet, riding a charger which is trampling on serpents, and accompanied by two groups of statues flanking the pedestal: 'Triumph leading a rearing Horse' and (not visible in the photograph) 'Fame conducting an Elephant', in reference to Portuguese rule in the East. Pombal himself is not omitted from the memorial. His portrait in profile can be seen on the bas-relief medallion on the pedestal. In the reign of Maria I, during the violent reaction to Pombal's policies, this was removed, but the artist who had made it managed to preserve it. After the Liberal Restoration of 1834, the artist's nephew told Marshal Saldanha, Pombal's grandson, of the existence of the medallion, and it was restored to its original position.

42 Street Scene, Lisbon

The paved streets of the capital curve and undulate, following the contours of the seven hills. Here it is a tough climb for a domestic servant who hurries back from market with her daily purchases, and an easy downward slope for a member of the middle classes on his way to a government office; but the visitor from the country, with his buttoned-up woollen shirt and unfurled umbrella, stands in mild bewilderment in the very middle of the road.

43 Ponte Salazar, Lisbon

The new suspension bridge over the Tagus is the final realization of a series of projects which have been talked about for nearly a hundred years. By opening up the southern part of Portugal, it has already produced tremendous development and economic change in the Outra Banda, the peninsula which lies opposite Lisbon, and has brought the Algarve nearer to the capital.

The bridge stands 230 feet above the river, tall enough to allow the largest ships to pass into the great natural harbour of the Tagus. The caissons on which the 623-foot towers are supported extend down through 98 feet of mud and 65 feet of sand and rock to a basalt bed-rock, and are the deepest in the whole world. The bridge stretches 7,546 feet over the river and connects with 14 miles of motorway.

44 GROUP OF FISHING BOATS, ALCOCHETE
The small port of Alcochete, near Lisbon, is renowned for its colourful fishing boats. For a closer view of their gay decoration, see plate VIII.

45 THE WATERFRONT, LISBON
On the edge of the Tagus, a group of the massive, shawled fish-sellers known as *varinas* haggle for the morning's catch. This will be sold in one of the many markets of Lisbon; or else the women themselves, carrying the fish in broad, open baskets on their heads, will tramp from street to street and door to door through the city, crying their wares.

46 CEMETERY AT LISBON
Under a row of black, funereal cypresses, which were introduced into Portugal from Italy, lines of family sepulchres. In Portugal, the coffins are laid on shelves in these tombs, which are often adorned with photographic plaques and gaudy bunches of artificial flowers.

47 THE TAGUS AT LISBON
A sailing barge goes upstream, crossing the path of one of the many ferryboats that bring commuters from Cacilhas to Lisbon. In the muddy foreshore, a man searches for the little clams (*ameijoas*) which are a favourite dish in Lisbon.

48 THE ALFAMA, LISBON
The Alfama, a tortuous labyrinth of narrow streets and flights of steps (*'escadinhas'*), is the oldest of the hilltop districts to survive the great earthquake of 1755. It dates from Visigothic times and later became the Moorish and Jewish quarter. Today most of the houses huddled round the Romanesque cathedral and the Castelo de São Jorge date from the sixteenth and seventeenth centuries.

49 CONVENTO NOVO, SERRA DA ARRÁBIDA
The Serra da Arrábida (frontier or boundary range) rises sharply from the sea coast west of Setúbal. From its summit one looks eastward over the estuary of the Sado river, southwards over the Atlantic Ocean and northwards over the peninsula which the Portuguese call the Outra Banda on to the Tagus estuary with Lisbon beyond.

The order of Arrábida was founded by a Franciscan friar, Martinho de Santa Maria (died 1547), who came from Cartagena in Spain. He was a scion of the family of

Benevides, Counts of San Estéban del Puerto. While on pilgrimage to the famous sanctuary of Our Lady of Guadalupe in Estremadura, Martinho, then an old man, met a cousin of his, the Portuguese grandee João de Lencastre (1501-71) Duke of Aveiro, who proposed to the venerable friar that he should found a monastery of penitents in the Serra da Arrábida. The proposal was accepted and the monastery, known as the Convento Novo, was founded by Fr. Martinho in 1542, with the assistance of the great Franciscan reformer St Peter of Alcántara (1499-1562).

The discipline of the Franciscan friars of Arrábida was strict and their life solitary. Consequently their reputation for sanctity soon increased and spread. Their patrons, the powerful family of de Lencastre, acquainted the court with their virtues. The Cardinal-King Henrique, João IV and Pedro II all took a close personal interest in them. New Arrábidan houses were founded and there were twenty-one in Portugal by the end of the seventeenth century. Pedro II's sister Catherine, wife of Charles II of England, even founded an Arrábidan house in London. Meanwhile the parent house continued to grow, and the slopes of the Serra adjacent to the monastery were gradually sprinkled with small subsidiary buildings – cells, hermitages, and chapels dedicated to Franciscan saints. At night angels were heard to sing in the Serra; and when Cosimo III, Grand Duke of Tuscany, visited Portugal in 1673 he is said to have taken a greater interest in the Convento Novo de Nossa Senhora da Arrábida than in anything else he saw in the kingdom. The devotion of the anchorite brothers to their wild but extremely beautiful mountain retreat is charmingly expressed in the verses of the contemplative poet, Agostinho da Cruz:

> *Oh serra das Estrellas tão vizinha*
> *Que nunca de ti, Serra, me apartara!*
> *Ou quando se partisse esta Alma minha*
> *Da terra, nesta serra me enterrara!*

('O thou mountain range, so close a neighbour of the stars, I pray that I shall never be separated from thee. Or when this soul of mind has departed from the earth, I pray that in this mountain range I shall be interred'.)

Under João V, the prestige and influence of the friars of Arrábida was almost equal to that of the Jesuits, and it was the prophecy of a particularly holy Arrábidan friar, António de São José, famous for the severity of his self-mortifications, that constrained João to build the enormous monastery-palace of Mafra (40 km. north-west of Lisbon) as an Arrábidan house.

50 Church of Jesus, Setúbal

This is the earliest important building in the Manueline style and was in fact begun in the reign preceding that of Manuel I. The architect, Diogo Boitac (fl. 1490-1525), who was probably of French origin, went on to design the great church of the Jerónimos at Belém.

In the church of the former Franciscan nunnery of Jesus, six piers made of the dark marble from nearby Arrábida support the roof of the nave. Their rope-like forms, corkscrewing alternately from left to right and from right to left, give the church a strange, restless impression. More ropes of stone decorate the apse and the surrounds of the windows. The green-and-white tiles in the apse are in the simple Moorish style favoured by King Manuel himself and found in his palace at Sintra; if they date from the seventeenth century, as seems possible, they represent a subsequent reversion to that style. The pictorial *azulejos* (coloured tiles of Moorish origin) which form a dado along the walls of the aisles betray their eighteenth-century date by their rococo frames. Until quite recently the church was full of baroque *talha dorada* (gilded woodwork: *see* note 33), and a fine series of sixteenth-century paintings. The chancel window was once filled with early sixteenth-century stained glass.

As this church is always cited as the earliest example of the Manueline style of architecture or perhaps more correctly architectural decoration, it is worth briefly considering precisely what the Manueline style is. Quite a number of examples of it are illustrated in this book – not only the great monuments at Belém (plates 35 and 36), Sintra (plate 58), Tomar (plates 65, 66 and 67) and Batalha (plates 69, 72 and 73), but also minor examples such as the portal of the chapel at Sines (plate 102).

It can be argued quite convincingly that there are insufficient common characteristics to justify classifying these varied works as members of one general style; the reader can form his own opinion by studying the illustrations. It is true, however, that there was tremendous building activity in Portugal at a period roughly coinciding with the reign of Manuel I, the Fortunate (1495–1521), and it has been found convenient to apply a general term to this remarkable series of structures.

Insofar as Manueline can be defined as a particular style, it is (like rococo) a style of architectural decoration, as opposed to any peculiarity in its spatial planning or constructional principles. The latter remained basically Gothic. Contributory sources discernible in Manueline decoration are North European 'flamboyant' Gothic, Castilian 'plateresque' Gothic, Iberian *mudéjar* (the work of Moorish craftsmen working in Moorish idiom for Christian masters), French Renaissance and Castilian 'plateresque' Renaissance. The degree to which these various sources were utilized and combined with each other varied with date, region, material employed and the artists and craftsmen responsible: in other words there are virtually as many styles as monuments.

A few characteristics emerge which are peculiar to Manueline architecture within the overall European context of the end of the Gothic era. These are: first, the pervasive influence of the *mudéjar* inheritance, often recessive but still perceptible; secondly, the frequency of vegetable themes in the decoration, treated in a most realistic way; thirdly, the prominence of twisted and spiral forms, used on every possible occasion, particularly for structural members, including even buttresses. The effects achieved curiously combine the massivity of Romanesque, the drama and chiaroscuro of baroque and the disquieting contradictions of mannerism.

51 Street in Setúbal

In spite of a large increase in modern building since the construction of the bridge over the Tagus, Setúbal remains an attractive town, with wide, cobbled streets and square-built houses, usually overhung with washing. A minor disadvantage is the often overpowering smell of sardines from the large canning factories near the docks.

52 Pilgrimage Church, Cabo de Espichel

The church of Nossa Senhora Santa Maria da Pedra de Mua (commonly known as the Senhora do Cabo) was built between 1701 and 1707 at Cabo de Espichel, the south-western extremity of the Outra Banda, the peninsula which juts out into the Atlantic on the south side of the Tagus estuary.

Since the middle ages a small image of Our Lady, who had miraculously appeared on the Mua rock at the tip of the cape, had been preserved in a small chapel on the brink of the cliff. This precious image was transferred to the new sanctuary church which was the first of a series of important pilgrimage churches built in Portugal during the eighteenth century.

The church of Nossa Senhora de Mua was evidently regarded in its time as a major architectural undertaking. It was sponsored by João V's brother Dom Francisco (1691–1747), who had at his disposal an immense income, including the revenues of extinct noble families, such as the Counts of Vila da Feira, which had reverted to the crown when the line died out in 1700 (*see* note 16). Nevertheless, the only features which give the ensemble any sense of monumentality are the long arcaded ranges of pilgrim lodgings (the *arraial*, or encampment) dating from later in the eighteenth century.

The church, which is built of plastered brick with stone trim, was described at the time as *uma magestosa igreja*. But its majesty is only that of a moderate size (35 by 20 m.). Otherwise it has 'all the characteristics of peasant architecture' and strikingly reveals the low ebb to which the arts had declined in Portugal as a result of the country's poverty and political difficulties during the seventeenth century. This neglect was not confined to architecture. The Portuguese painter Felix da Costa, whose *Antiguidade da Arte da Pintura* was written in the 1680s (though not published until 1967), prefaced his book with an epistle addressed to an influential politician in which 'his lordship's patronage is sought in order that the art of painting may remain alive in this kingdom, where it is so forsaken as to be almost extinguished'.

The contrast between Nossa Senhora de Mua and Bom Jesus do Monte (plate 15) demonstrates the tremendous advance made by the Portuguese in architectural skill and imagination during the eighteenth century, thanks to the stimulus of renewed patronage.

53 CASA DAS ÁGUAS, QUINTA DA BACALHOA

The oddly-named 'Quinta da Bacalhoa' – the 'Farm of the Lady Codfish' – lies beside the road running south from Lisbon to Setúbal. It derives its name from one of its owners, Maria de Medonça, whose husband, the Commander of Goa, was nick-named 'O Bacalhau', the codfish. The house and gardens, which originated in the early sixteenth century, are unique, not only as the only Portuguese country estate surviving from this period, but also from the point of view of architectural development. Although the Quinta dates from the reign of Manuel I, it has nothing of the fantastica-tion of the Manueline style. The influences are Moorish and Florentine: the Casa das Águas, the garden pavilion, was decorated with pictorial *azulejos* and plaques, some of which came from the Florentine workshops of the Della Robbias. Most of these have disappeared during later periods of neglect, but two surviving examples are shown in plates III and IV. This 'House of Waters' overlooks a large tank, oriental in aspect and strongly reminiscent of the oasis gardens of Morocco, such as the Menara near Marrakesh.

In 1903 the Quinta was bought as a country retreat by the pleasure-loving King Carlos I and gained a somewhat dubious reputation. Because of this, one is told, Queen Amélia allowed it to fall into disrepair after her husband's assassination in 1908. After changing hands yet again, the Quinta da Bacalhoa was bought in 1937 by an American lady, the late Mrs Scoville, who restored much of its former beauty.

54 THE GARDEN FRONT, PALACE OF QUELUZ

The original Palace of Queluz, pictured here, was built in 1747–52 for Dom Pedro, brother of José I, who married his niece, Maria I, and acted as regent during her frequent periods of insanity. Queluz was badly damaged by fire in 1934, and a part of the gardens was destroyed in the disastrous floods of 1967. It remains, however, one of the most beautiful of Portuguese houses. The little palace, its gardens and surrounding buildings, just off the road from Lisbon to Sintra, are like the setting for a Mozart opera.

The chief architect of Queluz was the Portuguese Mateus Vicente (1706–86), who also designed the church of the Estrêla in Lisbon. The upper gardens, known as the Neptune Garden, were designed by the French sculptor and architect Jean-Baptiste

Robillon, a disciple of Le Nôtre. Among the statues are charming sphinxes with Elizabethan ruffs round their necks, one of which is seen in the foreground of the photograph.

55 REREDOS, MONASTERY CHAPEL, PENA

The monastery chapel and cloister are all that remain of the original Convento da Pena (or Penha, meaning 'crag'), which, after the dissolution of the Portuguese monasteries in 1834, became part of the castle built by Ferdinand of Coburg. The reredos, in alabaster and black marble, is by the French sculptor Nicolas Chanterène, who was active in Portugal from 1517 to 1550. According to some authorities, it was Chanterène who introduced the style of the Renaissance to Portugal. His work, however, was limited to sculpture, and some of it appears in an architectural framework that is still Manueline in style. The Pena reredos is dated 1532, and shows a triumphant statue of the Virgin and Child, beneath which is a relief of the dead Christ in the arms of angels.

The carving of the two principal sculptural groups and five subsidiary ones is very fine and delicate, but the figures in the various niches are quite different from each other in scale. The details of the surrounding architecture are likewise beautifully executed, but the columns and niches are of different sizes, the entablature broken uncomfortably far forward over the columns and the side bays severed from each other by the central bay with which they have no proper connection. The result is a rich, tumultuous composition, creating a strong sense of disquiet because it altogether lacks unity. A capricious use of black marble adds to the chaotic effect. Chanterène was happily ignorant of the rules of classical architecture, as can be seen from such enormous solecisms as the superimposition of a Doric frieze upon Ionic columns.

Parts of a long Latin inscription carved in Roman capital letters can be seen on the frieze of the lower entablatures and to the left of the altar. This records that the altar, with its reredos, was completed and dedicated by João III in 1532 to the Virgin Mary (the words DIVAE MARIAE VIRGINI are partly visible at the bottom left-hand side of the photograph). The occasion was the happy birth of a prince, Dom Manuel, to João's 'incomparable wife' Dona Catharina, a sister of the Emperor Charles V. This prince, who was born on 1 November 1531, died on 14 April 1537.

56 THE CASTLE OF PENA

The Castle of Pena was built by the King-Consort, Ferdinand of Coburg, husband of Maria II (1834–53) and cousin of Prince Albert. This massive construction is super-imposed, like an enormous lid, on the small monastery built by Manuel I and used by him, it is said, as a look-out for the returning fleet of Vasco da Gama, the discoverer of India (1499). 'On the suppression of the monasteries, the Pena was bought by a private gentleman, from whom it was shortly afterwards purchased by the king Dom Fernando. By him it has been restored with much taste' (*Murray's Guide,* 3rd edn., 1876). In fact, the castle, designed by a German, Baron Eschwege, between 1840 and 1850, is Portugal's version of Balmoral. After the Queen's death in 1853, the king-consort continued to live here with his mistress, an opera singer. The building is surrounded by magnificent wild gardens, from most parts of which it is fortunately invisible.

57 Serra de Sintra

The Serra de Sintra lies west of Lisbon close to the Atlantic coast. One of its sharp granite peaks is crowned by the Pena monastery and palace (plate 56). Two neighbouring peaks (on the right in this photograph – the second being concealed by the nearer one) were fortified by the Moors with a large castle, the battlements of which are visible on the skyline.

Among the few monumental remains of the Moorish occupation which have survived in Portugal, their castles at Mértola, Silves (*see* note 106) and Sintra are the most considerable, and of these Sintra is the most impressive. It has five massive square towers connected by curtain walls strung out along huge outcrops of granite. Despite fourteenth-century reconstructions and various repairs executed to make good earthquake damage, the Moorish design has not been substantially altered, and the pyramidal termination of the merlons, which is such a characteristic feature of Moorish military architecture, has survived the restorations.

The camera is pointing west, towards the Atlantic, and the Royal Palace (plate 58) is in the valley to the right.

The beauties of the Serra de Sintra have been celebrated by Portuguese poets since Gil Vicente, the 'Portuguese Plautus', and the epic poet Luiz de Camões, both of whom wrote in the sixteenth century. Vicente described it as a terrestrial paradise, a sentiment independently echoed by many foreign visitors including Robert Southey, Byron (in *Childe Harold*) and George Borrow. A Spanish proverb asserts that 'to see the whole world and to leave out Sintra is truly to travel blindfold'.

58 The Royal Palace, Sintra

The Royal Palace of Sintra, Moorish in origin, was largely rebuilt by João I, the first king of the House of Aviz, at the beginning of the fifteenth century, and again by Manuel I a hundred years later. On the outer walls, windows of Moorish, Gothic, Manueline and classical styles appear side by side, and the whole building is dominated by the two peculiar conical kitchen chimneys. Beckford wrote in 1787: 'The Alhambra itself cannot well be more *morisco* in point of architecture than this confused pile which crowns the summit of a rocky eminence and is broken into a variety of picturesque recesses and projections ... From the windows, which are all of an oriental fantastic shape, crinkled and crankled, and supported by twisted pillars of smooth marble, various striking views of the cliffs of Sintra are commanded.'

Sintra was to be increasingly celebrated by travellers in search of the picturesque. Robert Southey, a few years later, described it as 'the most blessed corner of all the habitable globe.'

59 SALA DAS PEGAS (MAGPIE ROOM), ROYAL PALACE, SINTRA
'The ceiling is painted all over with magpies; each bird holds in its claw a rose branch, and in its beak a label with the motto *Por bem*—"For good". It is said that Dom João I was detected by his queen, our Philippa of Lancaster, in the act of saluting one of her maids of honour on the cheek, while presenting her with a rose, and that he replied (on the principle of "Honi soit qui mal y pense") to the Queen's look of indignation, "É por bem, minha senhora." But in order to satirize and silence the gossip of the court on the subject, he ordered that the room should be closed for a time, and in the interval the ceiling was painted with magpies' *(Murray's Guide, 1875)*.

Whatever the truth in this story, 'Por bem' was simply the motto of the monarch and is inscribed on his sarcophagus at Batalha. The ceiling, in its present state, was painted during the seventeenth century.

60 FISHERMEN ON THE SHORE, NAZARÉ
Nazaré is a fishing village which has become a famous tourist attraction. Since the Middle Ages, a great many harbours have silted up with sand; fishermen are obliged to put out from the open shore. In other parts of Portugal nowadays, the boats are dragged to and from the sea by tractors; in Nazaré oxen are still used. Here, too, people still wear a form of traditional costume: the men, shirts and trousers of tartan patterns, and long, tasselled stocking-caps; the younger women, short skirts with a large number of petticoats under them, which cause them to stand out like a ballet-dancer's tutu.

There is a much-quoted theory that the seafaring people of Nazaré, like the *varinas* or fishwives of Lisbon, are descended from early Phoenician settlers, but there seems to be no evidence to support this.

61 BEACH RESTAURANT, NAZARÉ
At Nazaré, before the tourist season begins: a rickety jetty leads up to a deserted restaurant called 'Sea Wolves'.

62 A STORK'S NEST AT MONFORTE
Storks are still commonly seen near the villages and towns of Portugal. When these huge migratory birds begin to circle overhead in the bright sky, people know that

spring has come. Here a stork and a weathercock combine to ornament the roof of a chapel near the Spanish frontier.

63 FOR SALE

A house, with a medieval window, is up for sale in the medieval town of Óbidos. The form of this window may derive from the *ajimez*, an aperture with twin arched lights separated by a column, which was used in Moorish architecture and inherited by the Christians in Spain and Portugal who adapted it stylistically – in particular changing the shape of the arches from the horseshoe form preferred by Moslem architects to ogival (as here) or round (as in Manuel's additions to the palace of Sintra, plate 58). On the other hand the Manueline predeliction for twin arched lights may also have been influenced by Christian Romanesque precedents; the triforium windows of the Old Cathedral at Coimbra exemplify the latter tradition (plate 26).

64 STREET IN ÓBIDOS

Once you have passed through the medieval gates of Óbidos, you enter a world cut off from the present day. The streets are roughly paved and impassable to cars. The houses dazzle with white wash, and wrought iron and flowering plants decorate odd corners. Although it has become something of a mecca for tourists, Óbidos remains one of the most enchanting of small Portuguese towns.

Just north of Óbidos, on the road to the spa of Caldas da Rainha, there stands the Royal Sanctuary Church of Nosso Senhor de Pedra Fria, Our Lord of the Cold Stone. It was one of a series of major pilgrimage churches built in Portugal during the eighteenth century (plates 15 and 52 illustrate two others). Sponsored personally by João V, the church of the Senhor de Pedra was designed by Captain Rodrigo Franco, architect of the Palacio da Mitra – the palace of the Patriarch of Lisbon. It was built between 1740 and 1747 on a hexagonal plan with a pyramidal roof, no doubt inspired by the *Architettura* of Sebastiano Serlio (*see* note 86).

The antiquity of the cult of the Lord of the Stone is witnessed by the revered image which gives its name to the Sanctuary. It is a tiny, extremely primitive figure in a most curious, almost dancing attitude, carved in low relief on a stone cross which looks as if it might originally have been a menhir. This extraordinary icon may, it is thought, date from the eighth century AD; but it could well be much earlier.

65 WEST WINDOW, CHURCH OF THE CONVENT OF CHRIST, TOMAR

After the papal suppression of the Order of Knights Templar in 1314, the Portuguese King Diniz founded his own organization, called the Knights of Christ. To them he transferred the property of the Templars at Tomar. The Knights of Christ were to assist in Portugal's first imperial ambitions, the Moroccan campaigns of the early fifteenth century, and their emblem, the Cross, was stitched on to the sails of the caravels that later circled the earth. In 1523, the Order was changed from one of chivalry to one of monasticism, but royal generosity to the monastery and church of the Order at Tomar continued throughout the reign of João III (1521–57).

The nave of the monastery church is the work of Diogo de Arruda (fl. 1500–31), the brother of the architect of the Tower of Belém (*see* plate 44). At Tomar, the Manueline tendency to naturalism and the use of exotic forms of decoration reaches an extravagant climax, and the window set in the west wall is perhaps the most celebrated, or notorious, example of the style. At its base an old man upholds a gnarled tree-root – perhaps a representation of Jesse in the Trees of Jesse, symbolizing the human ancestry of Christ. Above, a miscellany of decorative elements, including knotted ropes, branched coral, and stylized plant forms resembling seaweed and globe artichokes, culminates in two finials with the armillary spheres which were the personal emblem of King Manuel, the royal coat of arms, and, high above all, the Cross of the Military Order itself.

66 DETAIL OF WEST WINDOW, CONVENT OF CHRIST, TOMAR
The Manueline nave at Tomar, built between 1510 and 1514, is one of the last great architectural works in Portugal to be entirely free from Renaissance influence. Two or three years later, Renaissance forms were to appear at the Mosteiro dos Jerónimos at Belém (*see* pl. 36) in the work of João Castilho, and elsewhere in the work of Nicolas Chanterène (*see* pl. 55). But at Tomar, Diogo de Arruda kept to the style indigenous to Portugal. Yet here, too, in the thistle-heads and twisted ropes, there is a suggestion of the grotesque of the Mannerist period, the rioting forms of baroque, and perhaps even of the fantasies of Gaudì at Barcelona in the early years of this century.

67 THE ORDER OF THE GARTER, CHURCH OF THE TEMPLARS, TOMAR
Among the details on a pilaster of the nave at Tomar is this stylized representation of the Order of the Garter (omitting the motto 'Honi soit qui mal y pense'), which commemorates the connection between the English and Portuguese royal families, and in particular the presentation of the Order to Dom Manuel by Henry VII.

68 SANCTUARY, CHURCH OF THE TEMPLARS, TOMAR
The oldest part of the monastery church at Tomar, to which the Manueline nave was added later, dates from the twelfth century and, like other churches of the suppressed order, was built on the pattern of the Mosque of Omar, Jerusalem. The outside wall has sixteen sides, and the central sanctuary is octagonal. At the time when the nave was added (thus turning the Templars' church into the apse of the whole building), the

sanctuary and the sixteen walls of the ambulatory were extensively decorated, and the roof vaults ornamented with the emblems of the Order of Christ, the royal family and Dom Manuel himself. The paintings on the sanctuary are possibly the work of the royal painter, Jorge Afonso, who died in 1540.

69 THE UNFINISHED CHAPELS, BATALHA

The Dominican monastery of St Mary of Victory, usually known as Batalha ('the Battle'), was built by João I in fulfilment of a vow made on the nearby battlefield of Aljubarotta (see Introduction, p. 21). It is possible that his wife, Philippa of Lancaster, who retained a British attitude of gentle superiority to things Portuguese, suggested the name, in reference to Battle Abbey, near Hastings in England. The construction of the church and its cloisters continued through the fifteenth century, the last major addition being 'os Capelas imperfeitas', the unfinished chapels, intended as a pantheon for the royal house of Aviz.

These chapels have an extremely intricate ground plan, with seven minor chapels leading out of the central octagon, the eighth side being filled by the door into the cathedral (at the bottom in the photograph). Between these seven side chapels were to be six others, even smaller. But the central octagon was left roofless. The whole structure breaks off in mid-air: the completion of the original dream can take place only in the imagination of the spectator.

Why were the chapels left unfinished? Mateus Fernandes, the most Gothic of Manueline architects, died in 1515, and Diogo Boitac, who succeeded him and built the seven piers, had a stronger, more assertive style. The king changed his mind and decided he would be buried at Belém. And the Renaissance came to Portugal. Above the door can be seen the loggia designed by João de Castilho and dated 1533. It is classical in style, for by this date the Gothic style, a splendid survival in peripheral countries like England and Portugal, had become hopelessly out of fashion.

70 THE FOUNDER'S CHAPEL, BATALHA

There has been much debate about outside influences on the architecture of Batalha, since there was a strong English element at the court of Queen Philippa. The original plan was certainly by a Portuguese architect, Afonso Domingues; but his work was continued by Ouguete or Huguete, who was probably of English origin and perhaps a disciple of Henry Yevell, the architect of Westminster Abbey. Huguete built the mortuary chapel of the founder and his family, which was part of the original plan of the church. The eight piers support an octagonal lantern tower, with vaulting in the form of an eight-pointed star with carved bosses. The chapel contains the sarcophagus of João, who died in 1433, and Philippa, who had died in 1416, at the time of the expedition to Ceuta in Morocco, the beginning of Portuguese imperialism. Around the walls are the tombs of Fernão, the 'constant prince', who died at Fez after years of captivity; João, Grand Master of the Order of Santiago; Henrique, famous as Henry the Navigator; and Pedro, Duke of Coimbra, killed in a civil war resulting from a family quarrel.

71 THE ROYAL CLOISTER, BATALHA

The Royal Cloister at the Church of St Mary of Victory is the work of the original architect, Afonso Domingues. The stone traceries within the arches are believed to be by Diogo Boitac. These screens of stylized foliage, which break the sunlight into strange patterns, show the style at its exotic best, a sophisticated continuation of the strong structure of the original Gothic. Apart from their obvious Moorish influence, the cloisters call to mind certain Indian architectural sculpture; there is, however, no evidence of any direct imitation, although the Portuguese had just established colonies in India.

72 DOORWAY OF THE UNFINISHED CHAPELS, BATALHA

The great doorway of the 'Capelas imperfeitas', which is dated 1509, is the work of Mateus Fernandes, the closest of contemporary architects to the Gothic of northern Europe. The photograph shows the inside of the doorway as seen from the roofless octagon of the chapels. Its series of interlacing arches has often been compared with the north portal of St Mary Redcliffe in Bristol, England, of which Professor Nikolaus Pevsner has written: 'The foliage of the capitals turns away from nature, and the resulting forms are vaguely reminiscent of seaweed (though definitely not imitations of it); bossy, nobbly – and again undulating in their surfaces.' This masterpiece of Mateus Fernandes, however, is less seaweed-like than other work of the same period. But the fact that St Mary Redcliffe was built nearly 200 years earlier (c. 1330) reinforces the idea that the Manueline was a provincial development of Gothic, a development that in England was to some extent interrupted by the comparative austerity of the Perpendicular style.

73 DETAIL OF THE UNFINISHED CHAPELS, BATALHA

The monastery at Batalha is built of a hard limestone, almost the colour of ivory. The magnificent use to which Mateus Fernandes put this material is shown in this detail of the great doorway, in which hard-edged, polygonal blocks, supporting pilasters decorated as though with plaited ribbon, are contrasted with the undulating lines of stems, leaves and seed-pods.

74 IN THE VALLEY OF THE TAGUS

A view across the Zêzere river, a tributary of the Tagus, in the direction of the Serra da Estrêla, the highest mountain range in central Portugal.

75 AQUEDUTO DE PRATA, ÉVORA

Évora is situated at the point where the watersheds of the rivers Tagus, Sado and Guadiana intersect. The 'aqueduct of [the water of] silver', otherwise known as the aqueduct of Sertorius, starts its course in a hill eleven kilometres northwest of Évora where it receives the waters of two springs, the original *fontes de agua da Prata*. Winding in undulating country, through which it passes mostly below ground, it collects the contribution of twenty-eight springs and is then carried on arches (four of which are here visible), attaining a height of thirty metres, for the last two kilometres of its course to Évora. In the sixteenth century it was believed that an aqueduct following the same route had been built by Quintus Sertorius (died 72 BC), enemy of Sulla and self-styled *dux Lusitanorum*, to supply Roman Évora (Ebora Liberalitas Julia) with water. The modern aqueduct, begun soon after 1531, was therefore regarded as a restoration of Sertorius' lost structure. The putative architect was Francisco de Arruda who held the post of *mestre das obras da comarca do Alemtejo* from 1531 to 1547, and was therefore probably also architect of the Elvas aqueduct (plate 78). Both in its design and in its course, the Évora aqueduct is more regular than that of Elvas, a fact which lends support to stories that the piers of the Aqueduto da Prata were built upon Roman foundations unearthed by the sixteenth-century classical scholar André de Resende, who reputedly supervised the design.

The inauguration of the aqueduct by João III took place in the presence of the whole court in the afternoon of 28 March 1537, when water first flowed from a fountain in the main square of the town, the Praça do Geraldo. The event was celebrated by bullfights.

The original fountain in the Praça do Geraldo consisted of four marble lions' heads inserted into a Roman triumphal arch. This arch was destroyed in 1570 by order of the Cardinal Infante Dom Henrique, and the existing fountain, one of the most charming features of the town, installed late in 1571.

Camões celebrated the aqueduto da Prata in his *Lusiads* (Canto iii):

> *Onde ora as aguas nítidas de argento*
> *Vem sustenar de longo a terra, e a gente;*
> *Pelos arcos reais que cento e cento*
> *Nos ares se alevantam nobremente.*

('Where now the sparkling waters of silver come from afar to sustain the land and the people, carried upon regal arches which hundred upon hundred rise nobly in the air.')

76 Temple of Diana and Cathedral Lantern, Évora

We are on the central hill, formerly the acropolis, of Évora, looking south-east. In the foreground are five of the surviving fourteen columns of a Roman temple probably dating from about AD 200. Behind is the *zimbório* or lantern-tower over the crossing of the cathedral: the battlements visible below the *zimbório* from left to right respectively crown the west wall of the north transept and the north wall of the nave.

The Roman temple was built on a high podium, 15 by 25 metres, with the main entrance facing south; and it seems to have been entirely constructed of granite except for the finely carved capitals and bases of the columns which were executed in Estremoz marble. The twenty-foot granite shafts of the columns have only twelve instead of the proper twenty-four flutes, which gives them a decidedly rustic appearance. In the late seventeenth century a learned Jesuit antiquary, Padre Manuel Fialho, propounded the theory that the temple was dedicated to Diana. This is, however, most unlikely. A dedication to Endovélico, the Jupiter Liberalis of the Celtic Lusitani, has recently been proposed. This attribution is supported by the north–south orientation of the temple, by the Roman name of the town (Ebora Liberalitas) and by the discovery close to the temple in 1862 of a marble thumb apparently belonging to a masculine figure more than twice life size.

The partial destruction of the temple may date back to the early Christian era, perhaps around AD 400. Subsequently its remains were incorporated into a Visigothic fort. From at least 1403 until 1836 it was used as a public slaughterhouse. The structural accretions of twelve or fourteen hundred years were finally removed in 1870.

The cathedral of Santa Maria of Évora, like the adjacent Roman temple, is almost entirely built of local granite, which has darkened with exposure. The battlements, however, are of brick; and the chancel, begun in 1718 to a design given by J. F. Ludovice, architect of Mafra, is of Estremoz marble. Évora cathedral is one of the best preserved and largest of Portuguese medieval churches. The existing structure occupies the site of a late twelfth-century church, perhaps a converted mosque. It was probably begun during the episcopate of Dom Durando Paes (1267–83) counsellor of Afonso III, and largely completed during the reign of Afonso IV (1325–57), with later additions. The three-aisle, Latin cross plan follows that of the twelfth-century cathedral of Lisbon, and apart from pointed arches, which have been used throughout, it is completely Romanesque in style.

The design of the late thirteenth-century *zimbório* derives from twelfth-century Périgourdin and Poitevin prototypes. Similar lanterns were built by French architects at Jerusalem (the church of the Holy Sepulchre) in the mid twelfth century, and subsequently in Spain at Zamora, Salamanca, Toro and Plasencia during the late twelfth and early thirteenth centuries. The Évora lantern especially recalls that of the Old Cathedral at Salamanca, known as the Torre del Gallo and dating from about 1180, a whole century earlier. Both have conical spires (that of Évora on an octagonal base) covered with typically Poitevin 'fish-scales' carved in relief on the stone.

77 OLD WOMAN AND ORANGE TREE, VILA VIÇOSA

The historic town of Vila Viçosa is not far from the Spanish frontier. In addition to an old castle, it contains the enormous seventeenth-century palace of the Dukes of Braganza, who, at the accession of João IV in 1640, became the ruling family. The straight streets are lined with whitewashed houses, and planted with orange and lemon trees, under which this old lady is taking an afternoon walk.

78 THE AMOREIRA AQUEDUCT, ELVAS

The Amoreira aqueduct, over four miles in length, brings water to the walled fortress city of Elvas, which faces Badajoz across the frontier formed by the Guadiana river. The aqueduct, which is remarkable for its four tiers of rounded arches, was designed by Franscisco de Arruda, the architect of the Tower of Belém (*see* pl. VII).

Over most of the distance the water flows at ground level or through subterranean conduits; but for more than a mile, across the São Francisco and Rossio valleys, the channel is raised as much as 31 metres above the ground. In all there are 843 arches, some dozens of which can be seen in the photograph. The irregular, un-Roman, trajectory of the structure is also clearly visible – contrasting with the regularity of the contemporary Évora aqueduct (*see* plate 75).

79 THE FORMER COLLEGE OF THE JESUITS, ÉVORA

In response to pressure from his brothers Dom Luis, Constable of Portugal, and Dom Henrique, Cardinal Archbishop of Lisbon, Dom João III authorized the institution of a Jesuit College at Évora in 1550. Dedicated to the Holy Ghost, it was officially inaugurated in 1553. Six years later, on the initiative of Dom Henrique, it was raised to the status of a University by Papal Bull, with all faculties except Civil Law and Medicine. It was closed when the Society of Jesus was suppressed in Portugal in 1759; and from 1841 to the present day most of the building has been occupied by a state secondary school (*liceu nacional*). During the last ten years other parts of the building have been utilized for various religious and educational purposes and for administrative offices and storage of archives.

The photograph is taken from the south-west arcade of the former Terreiro dos Estudantes, a large quadrangle, 43 by 39 metres, surrounded by two storeys of arcades with 144 Tuscan columns: 52 of the lower order belong to the first building phase of 1559–80, the rest being of late seventeenth-century construction (from 1687). The three-bay façade visible through the nearer arch is the principal ornamental feature of the courtyard, situated in the middle of the north-west side, facing the entrance. It was originally built as the collegiate chapel, but converted to become the Sala dos Actos or Hall of Disputation in 1574 when the enormous Igreja Nova (adjoining the south-west arcade, behind the point where we are standing) was opened for worship in 1574.

The façade of the Sala dos Actos, executed in white and black Estremoz marble, was completed in its present form during the years 1715-25. The Tuscan, Ionic and Corinthian orders are properly employed in ascending sequence, the last two being treated with unrestrained baroque licence. The lozenge-shaped panels between and above the three first-floor windows are examples of the *almofada* (cushion) decoration which was favoured by Portuguese architects particularly during the seventeenth century. In the panel above the middle window there is an inscription in honour of the founder of the University, who at the end of his life was King as well as Cardinal.

The façade is terminated in fully baroque fashion, presenting a series of emblems. The central panel encloses a shield, supported by half-length canephorae, which displays the arms of Portugal (*as quinas portuguezas*) surmounted by a cardinal's hat and royal crown. This panel is flanked by Corinthian pilasters, the shafts of which project in a series of enriched scrolls. These pilasters sustain the volutes of a broken curvilinear pediment, high above which two cherubim adore the crowning feature of the composition – a medallion in which is inscribed the cipher IHXS (*In Hac Cruce Salus*). Upon the lateral acroteria sit large, dignified figures of personified Virtues, who respectively hold, from left to right, a sceptre and the sun, the moon and a crozier – symbols of the royal and pontifical offices which the founder of the university occupied. In this photograph only the sun is visible.

80 CHURCH OF S. FRANCISCO, ÉVORA

The charnel-house or bone-chapel was the macabre form of decorative art favoured in Capuchin, or Franciscan, churches of the sixteenth and seventeenth century. At Évora there is this inscription:

Nós ossos que aqui estamos
Pelos vossos esperamos

('We, the bones who are already here, are waiting for yours.') In fact, the Portuguese people seem to lack the morbid obsession with the physical aspects of death common among the Spaniards and the Mexicans.

The monastery of São Francisco at Évora, was founded in the thirteenth century. Leading out from the south transept of the church is a long wing, built in the sixteenth century, containing the chapter house, a chapel dedicated to the Senhor dos Passos and finally the bone-chapel (Capela dos Ossos). The latter is an extensive rectangular room divided longitudinally into three naves and transversely into four bays. Originally it may have been a dormitory. The pillars supporting the vaults have granite capitals coarsely carved in characteristic Manueline style, with gross interwoven ropes or thick vegetable stems; they are attributable to Diogo or Francisco de Arruda, who were successively architects of the monastery over the years 1524–47. The turgid style of these capitals certainly conforms with that of the decoration of the west front of the church of Christ at Tomar and the Tower of Belém – respectively associated with these same two Arruda brothers. The naive frescoes on the vaults were painted in the early nineteenth century.

Part Three THE ALGARVE AND THE SOUTH

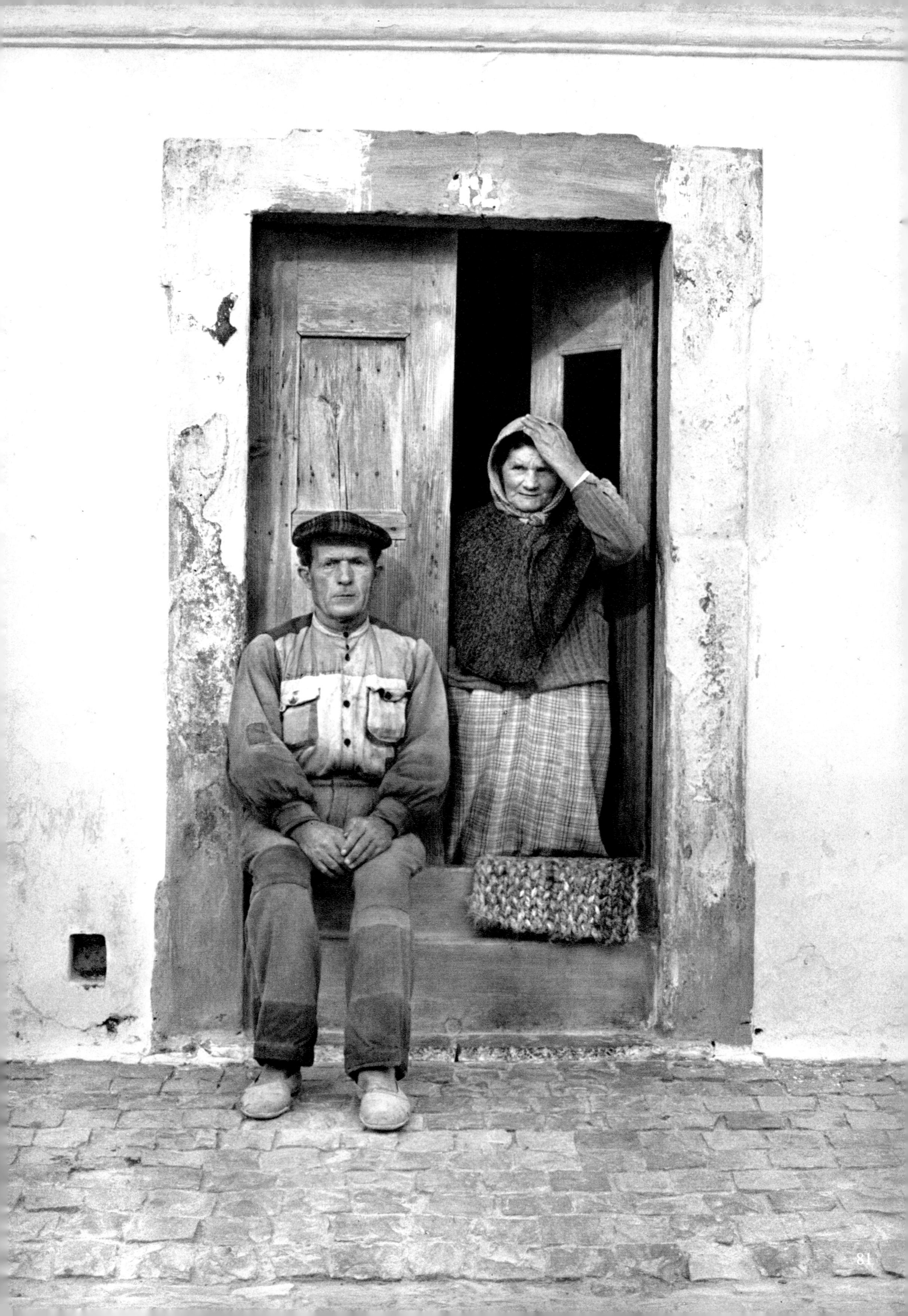

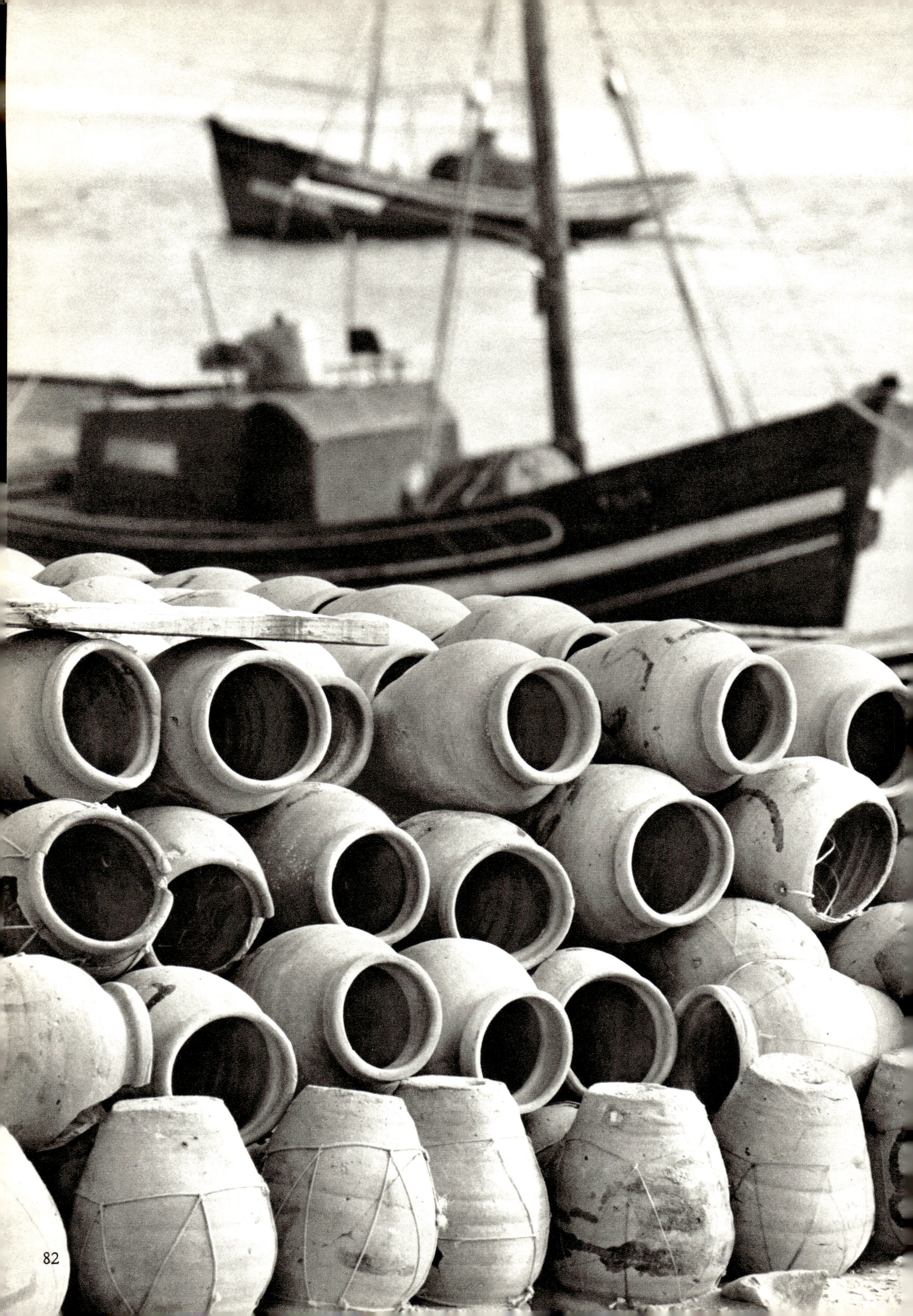

83

84

85

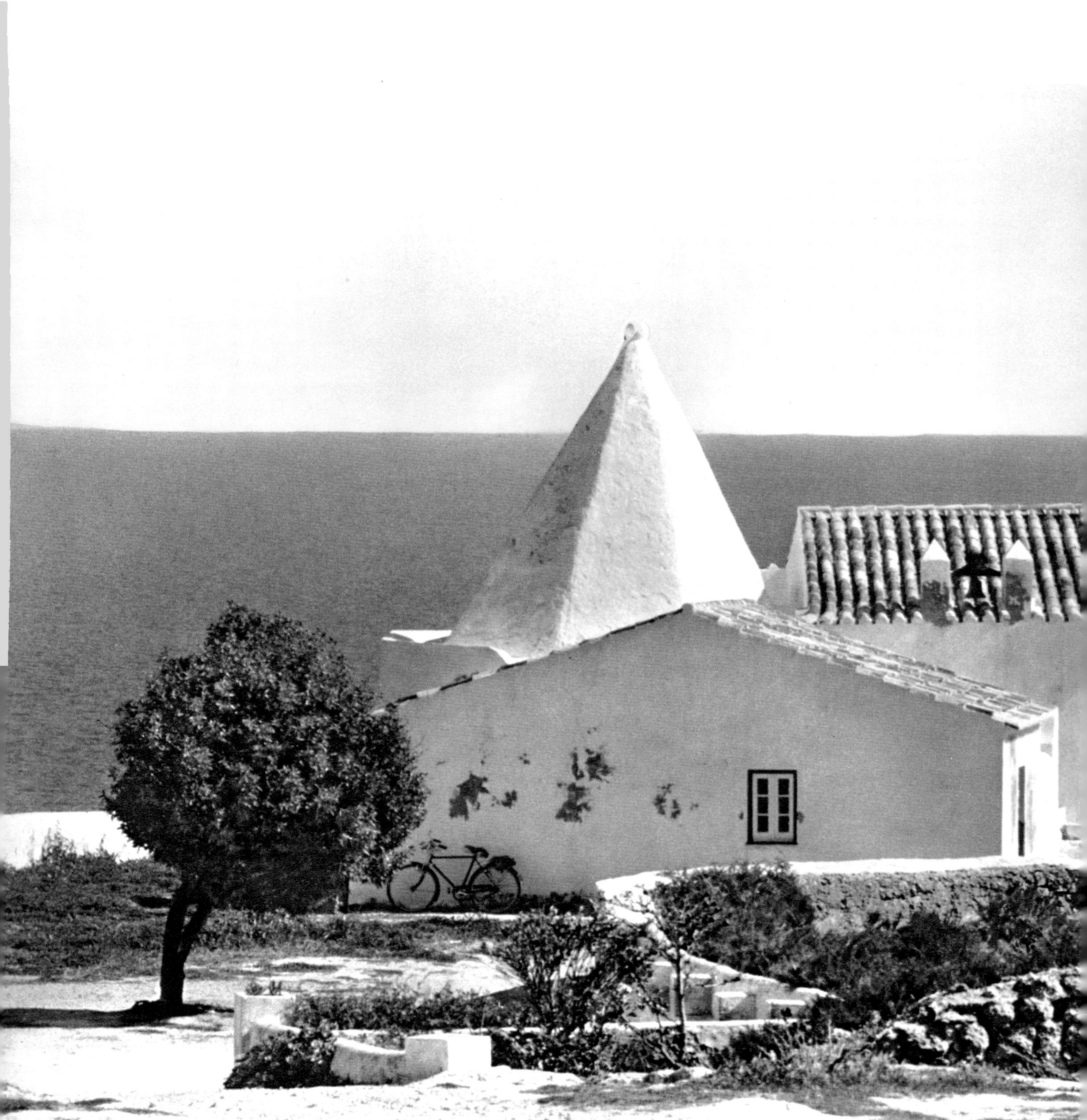

87

88

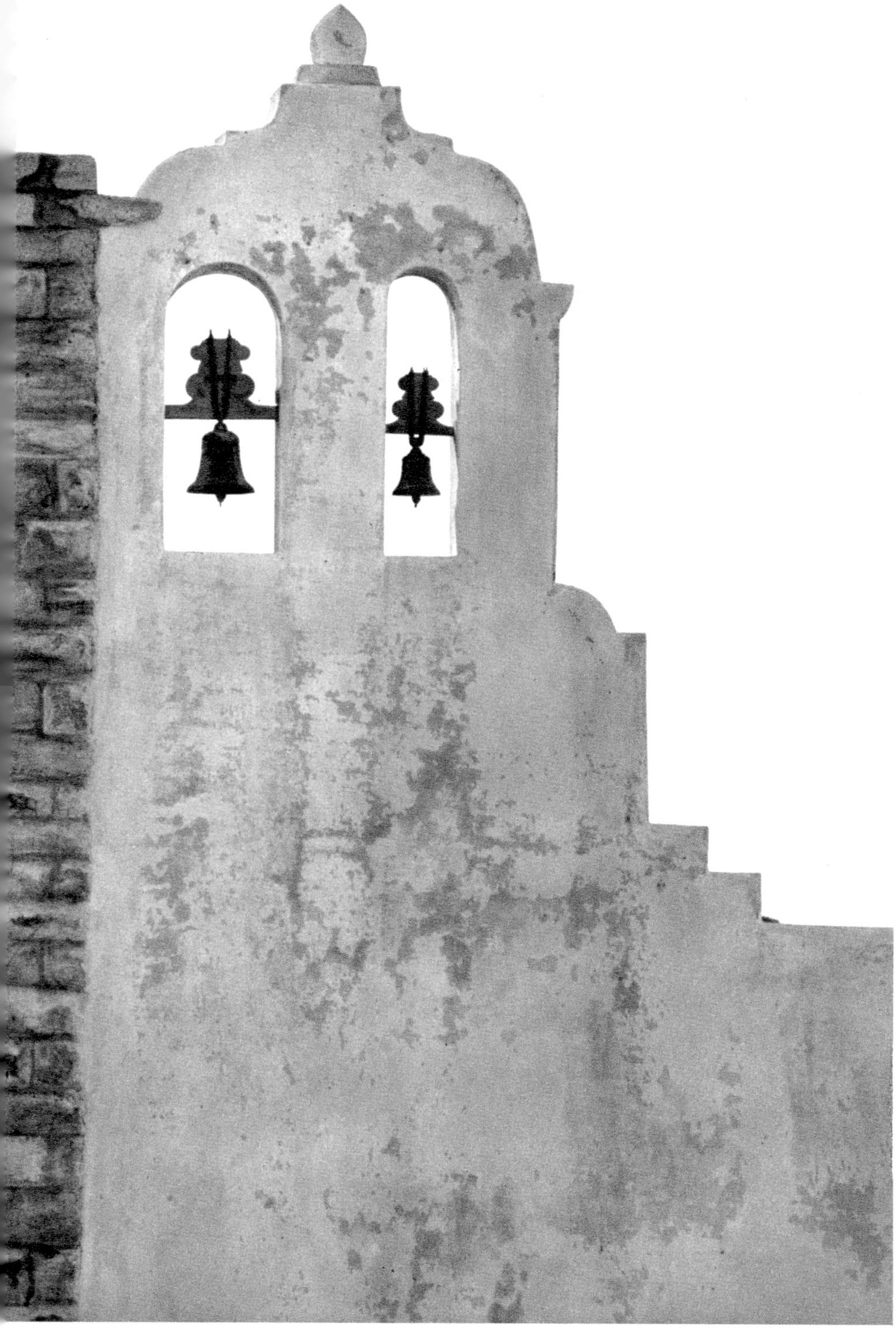

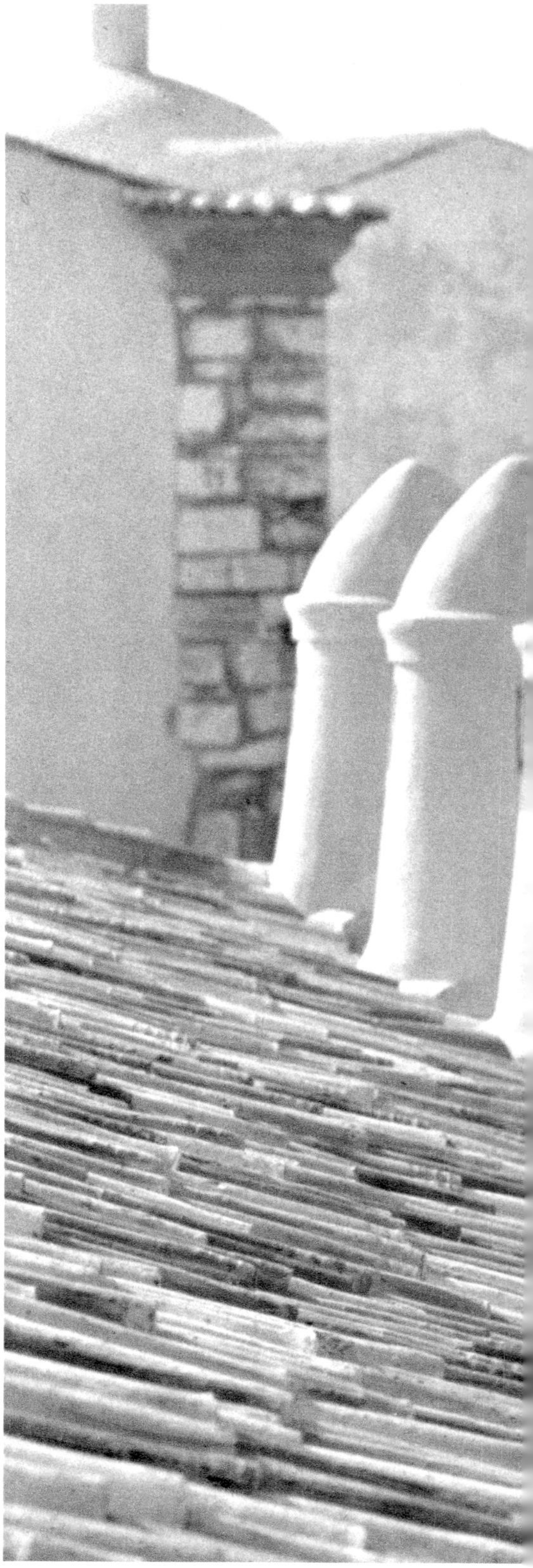

90

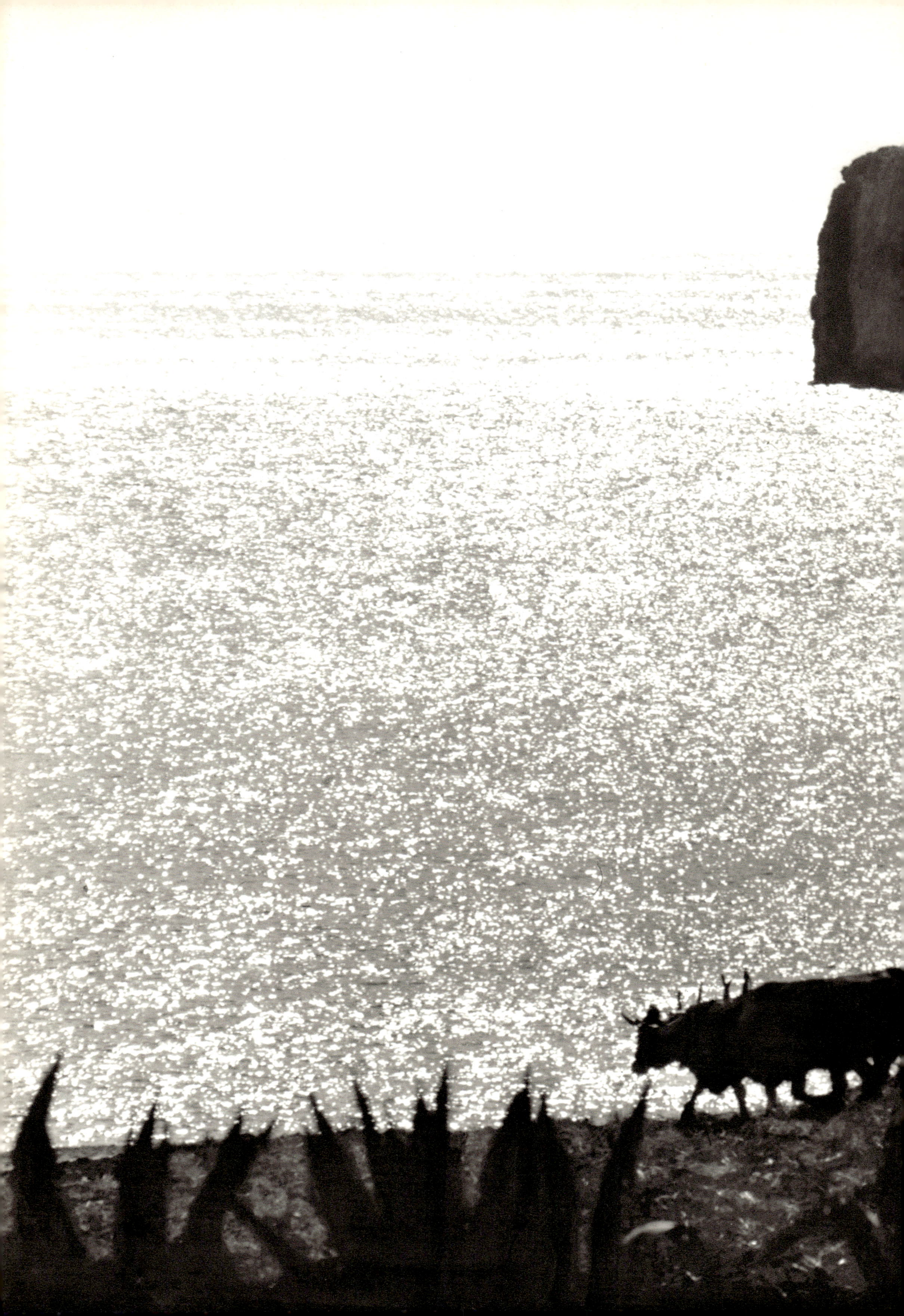

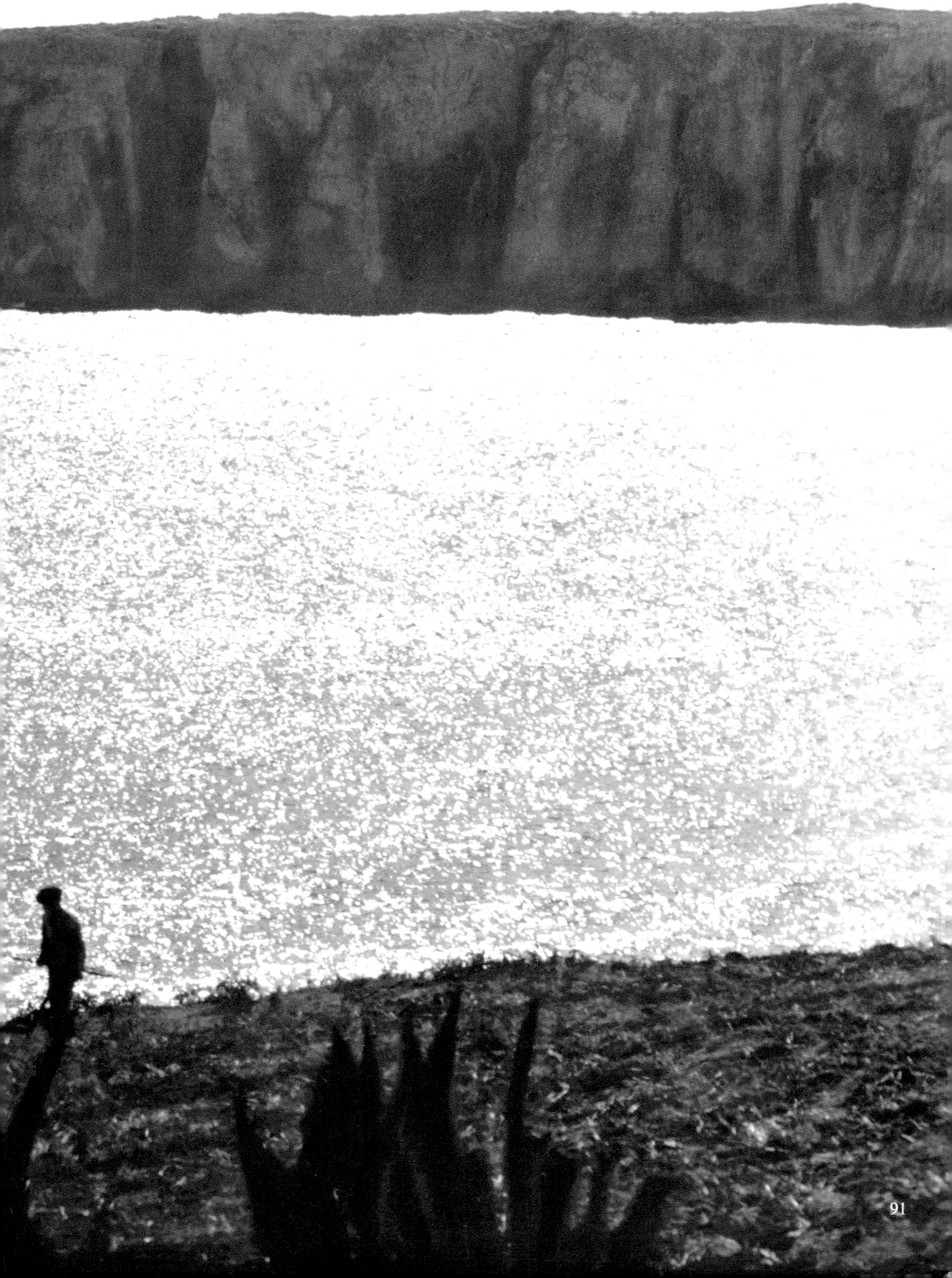

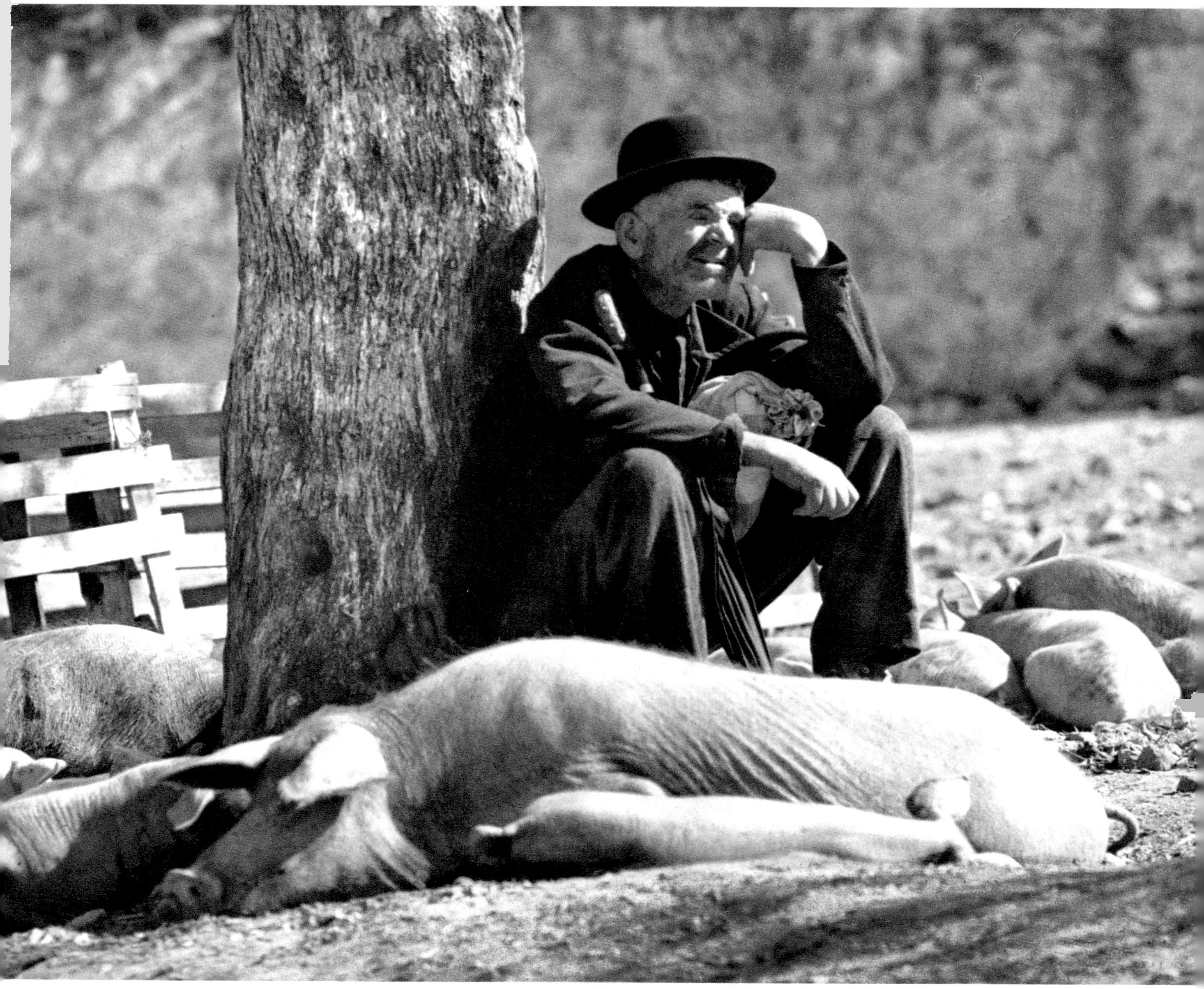

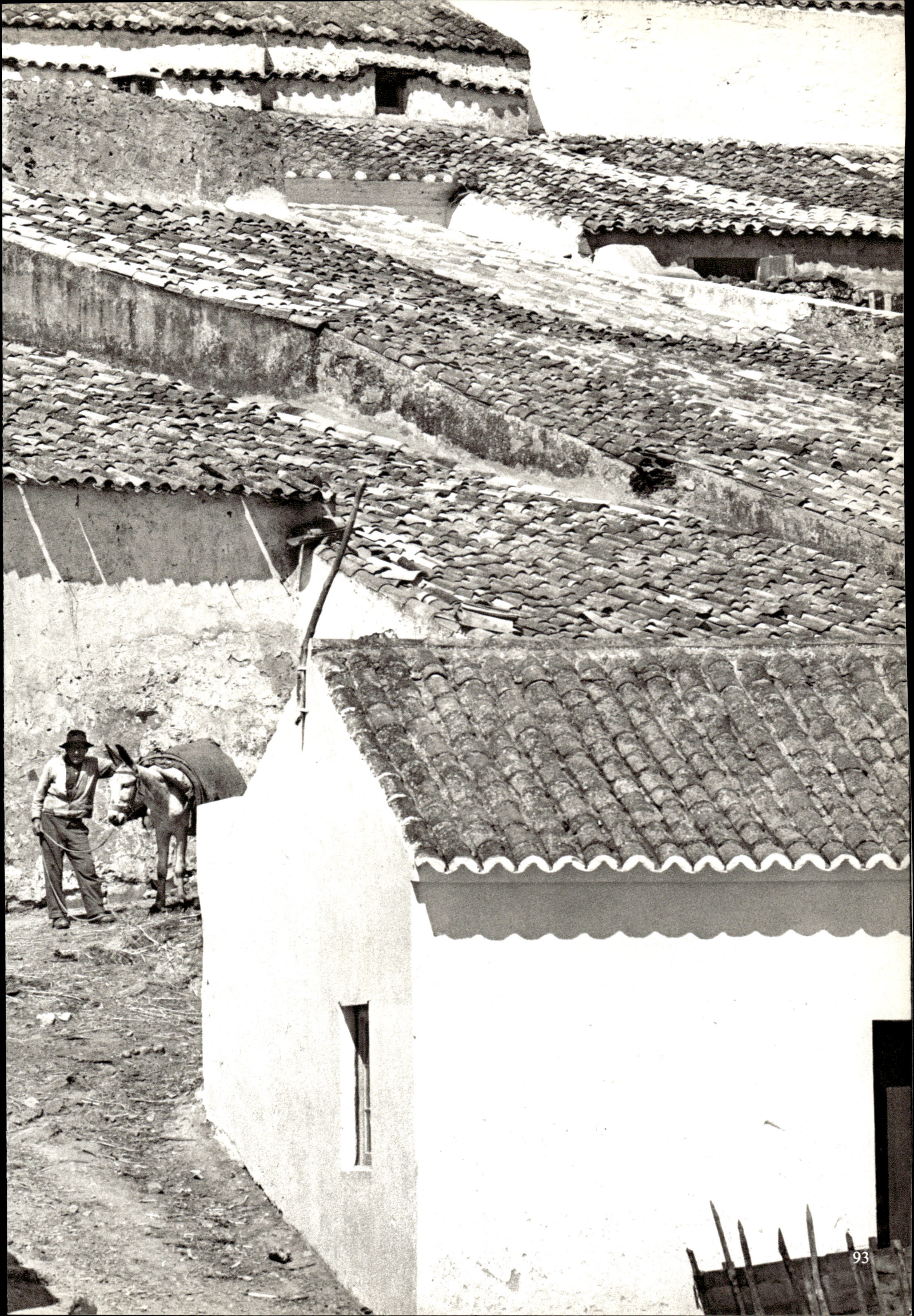

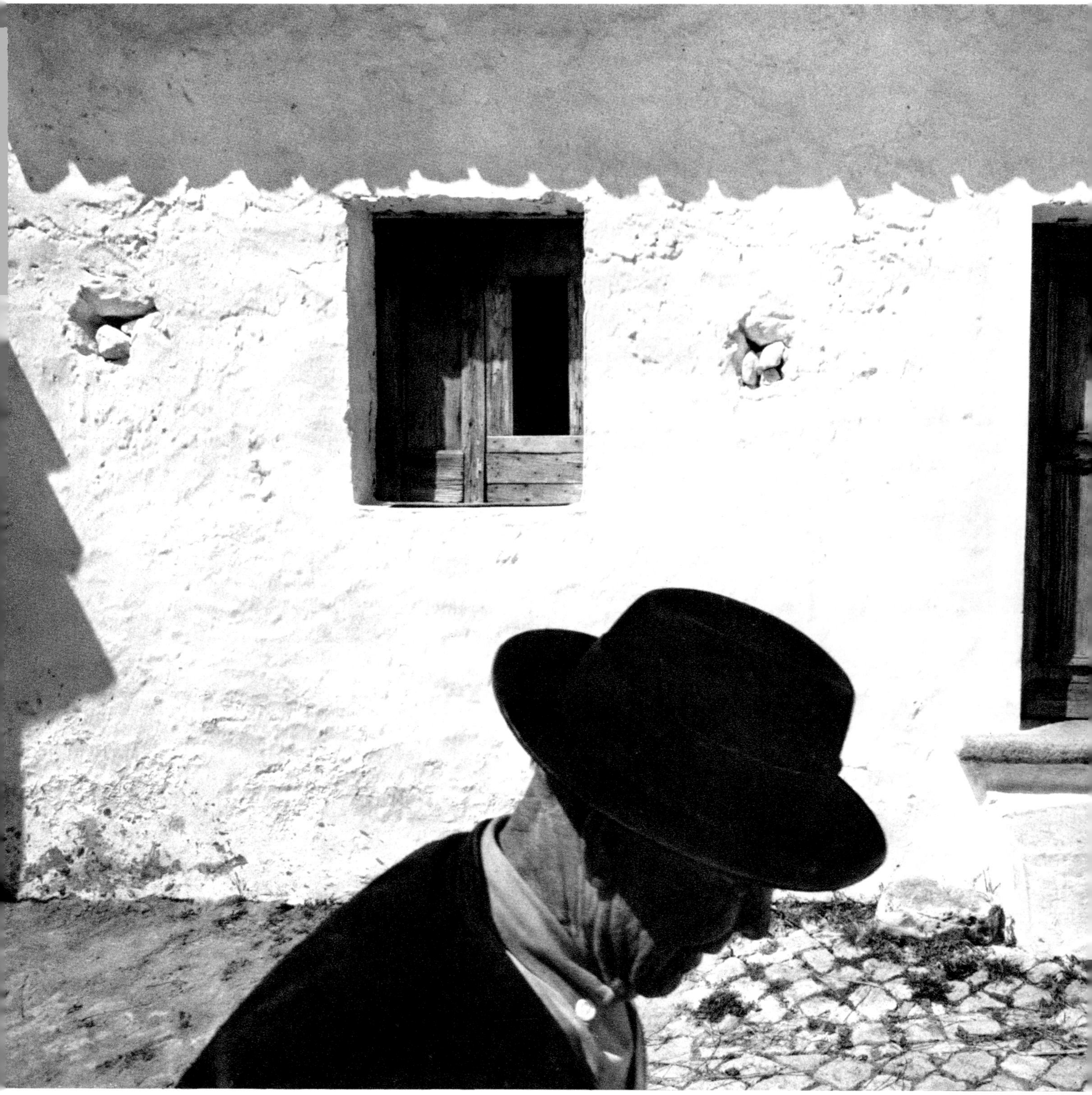

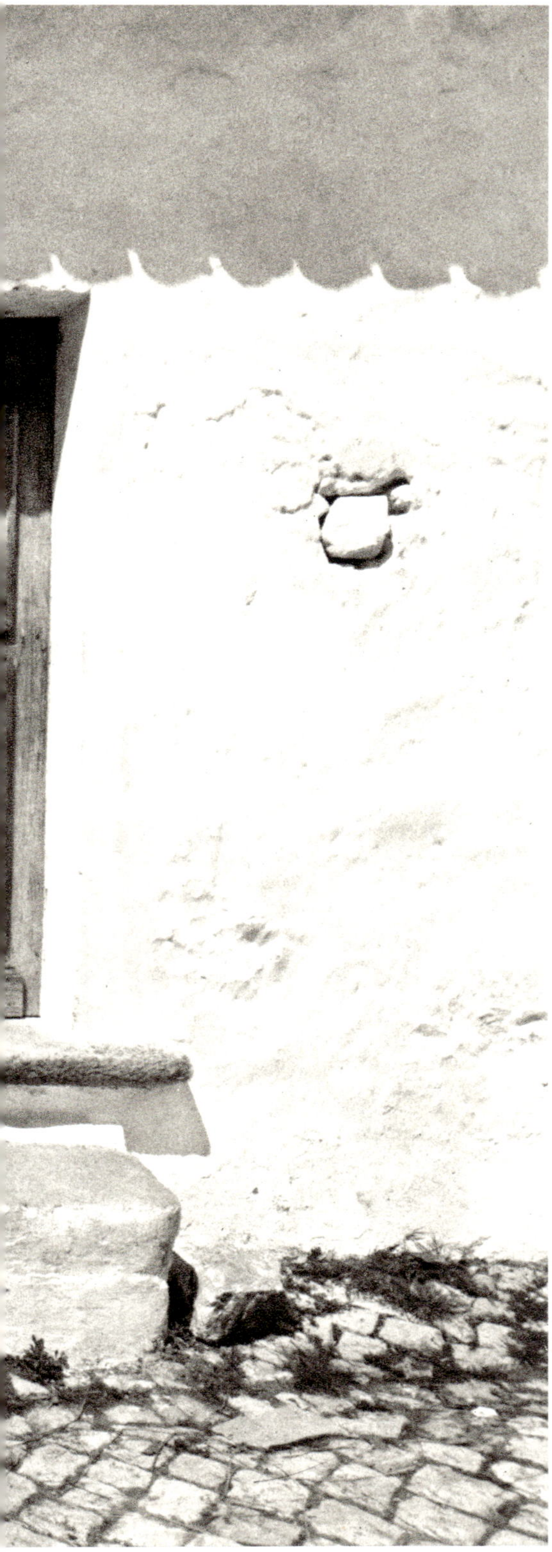
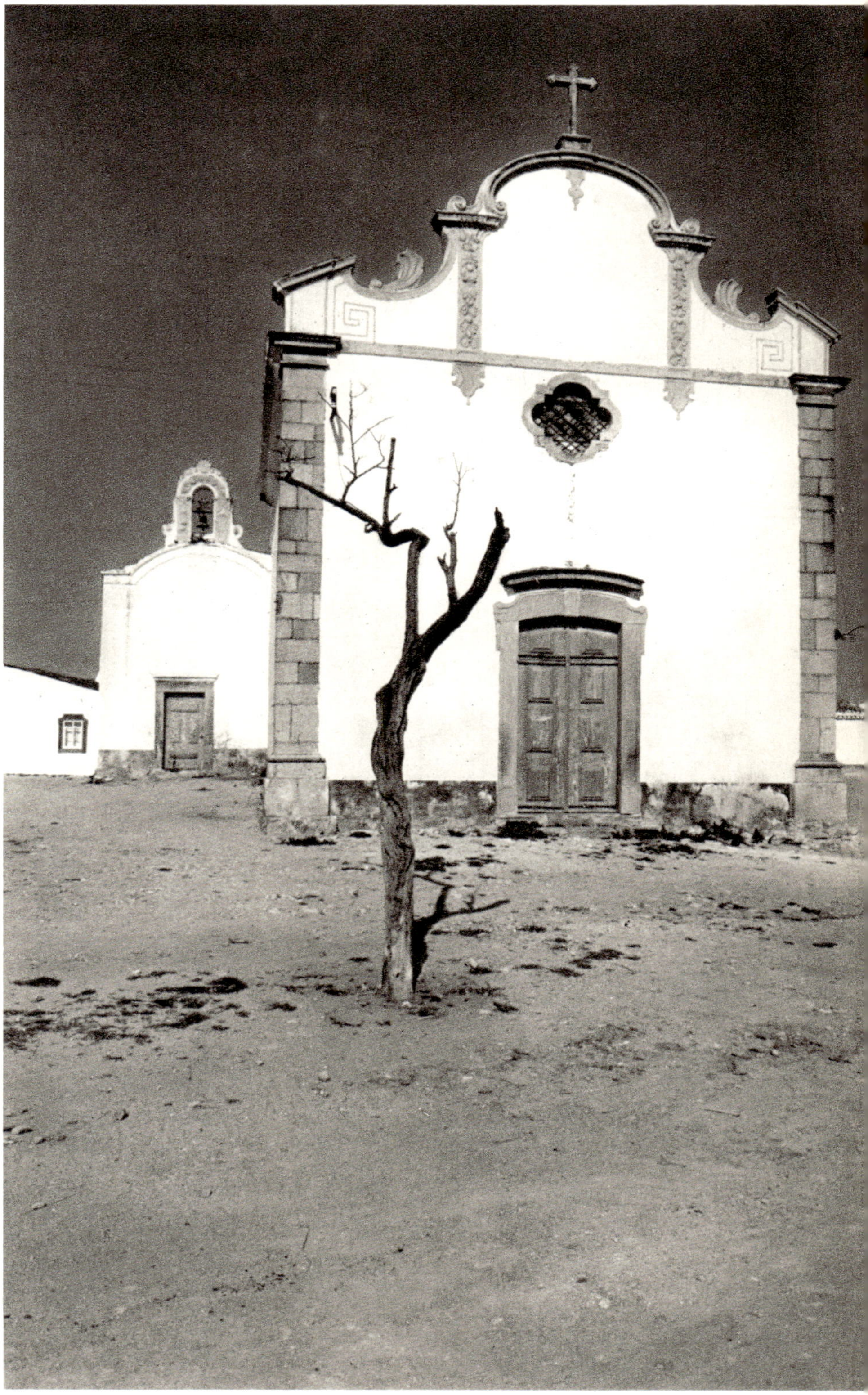

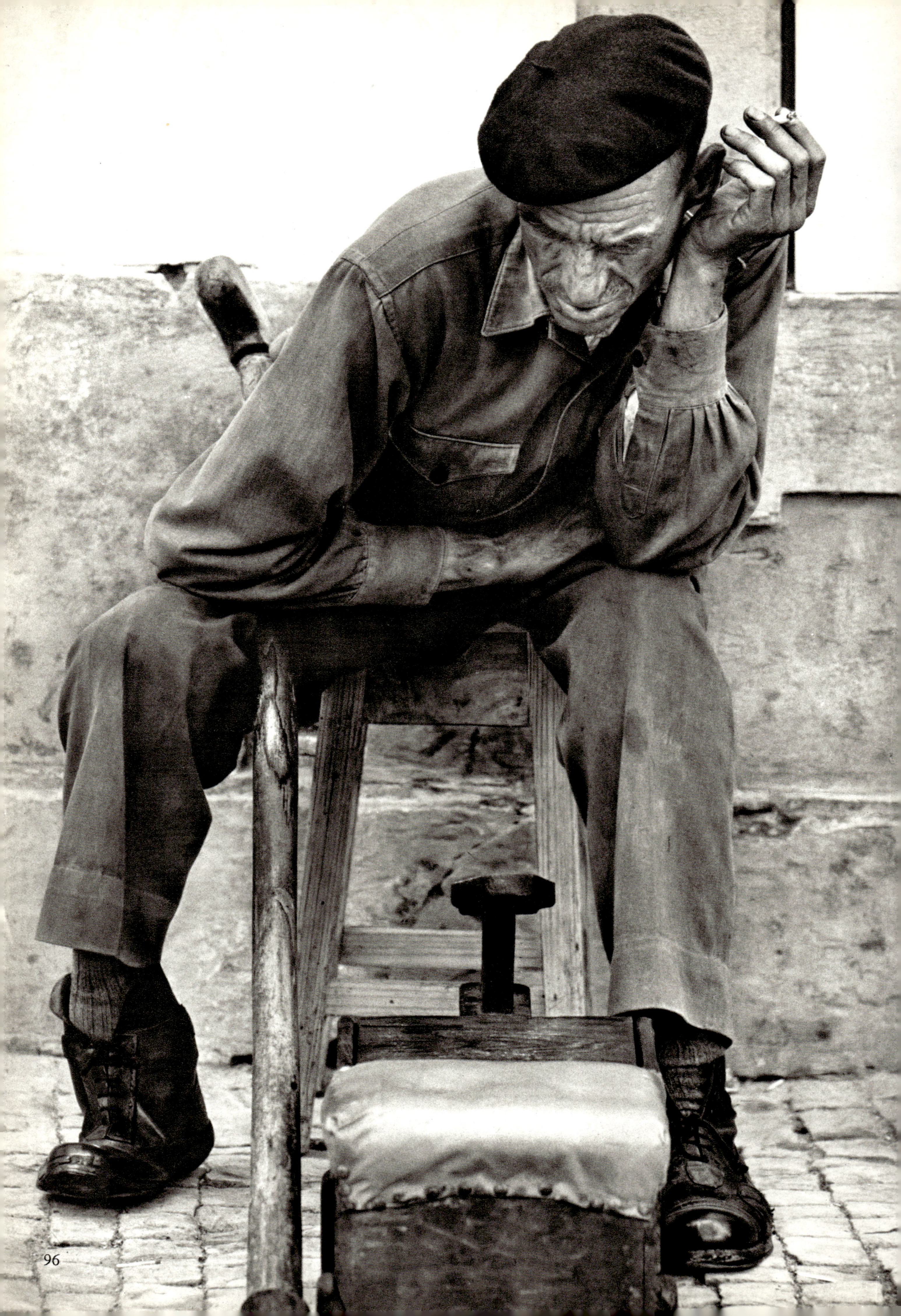

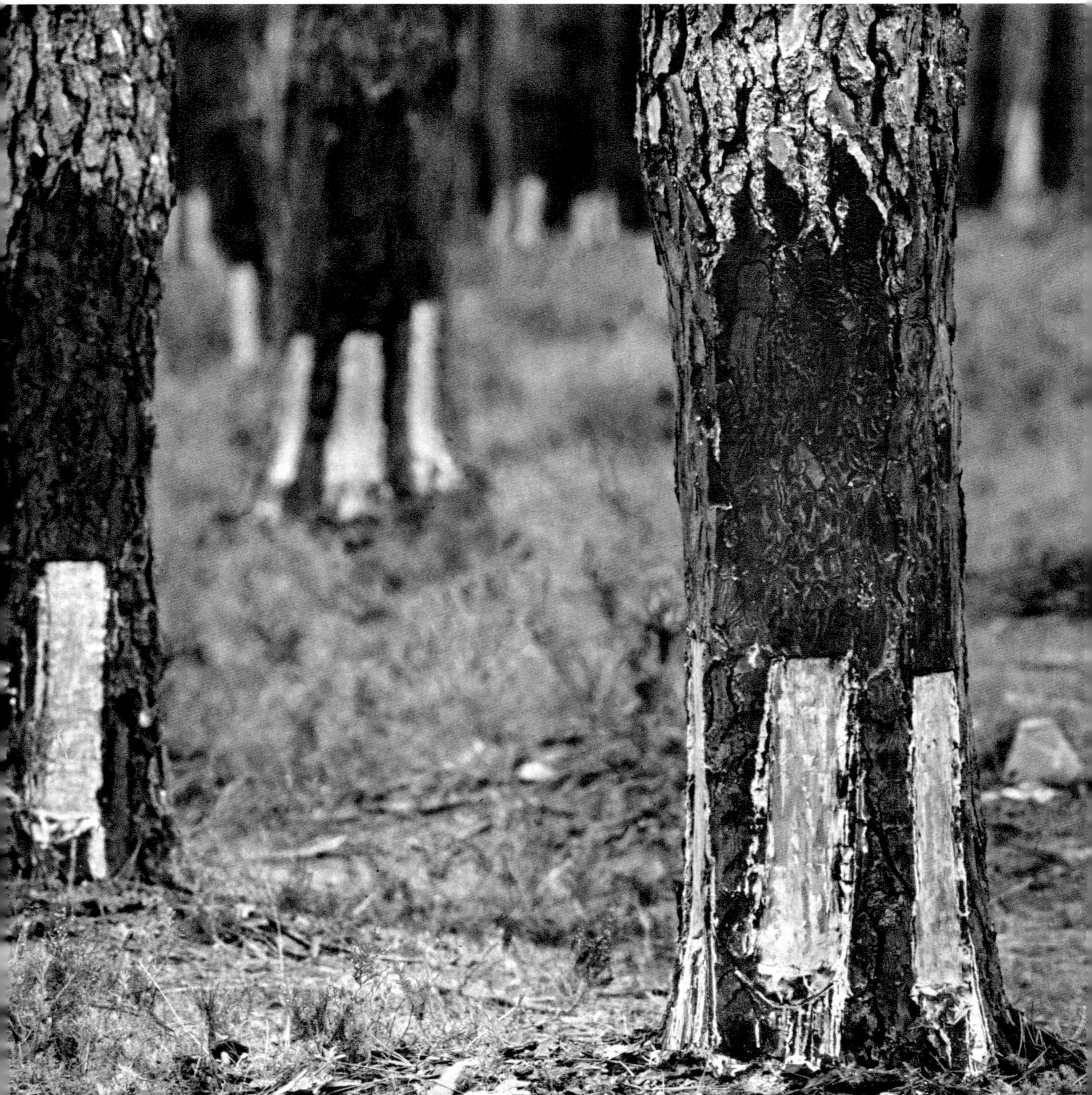

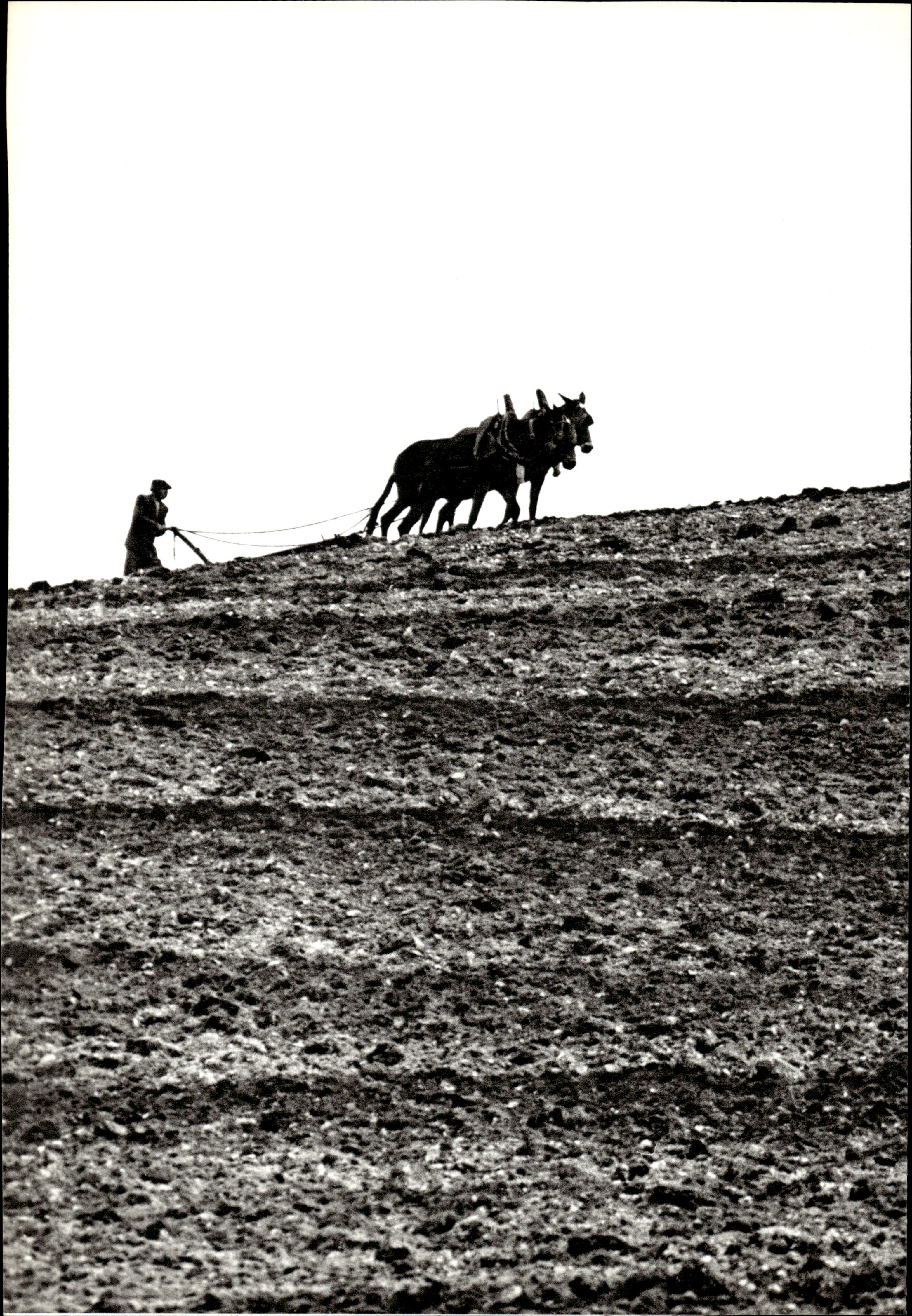

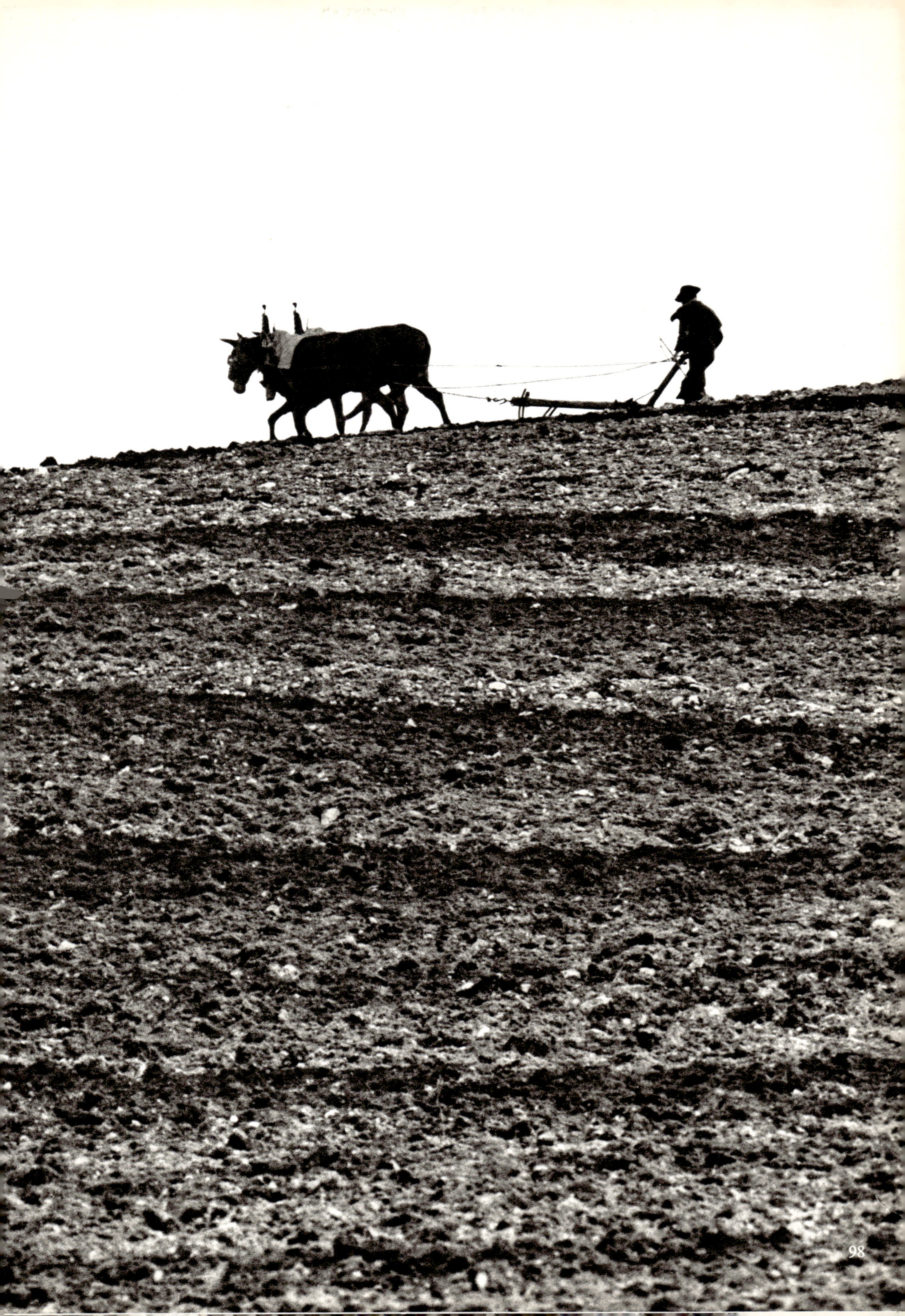

99

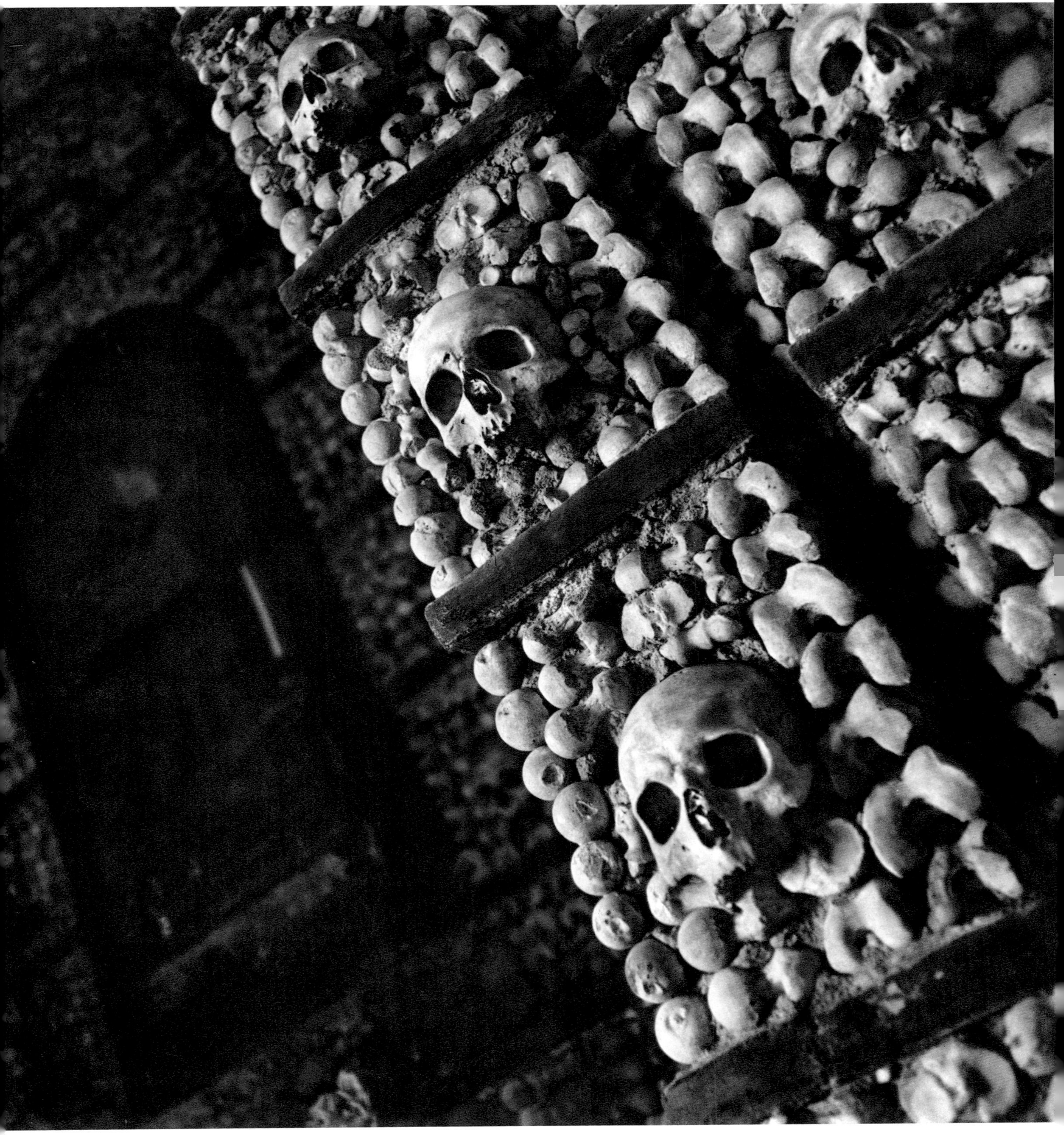

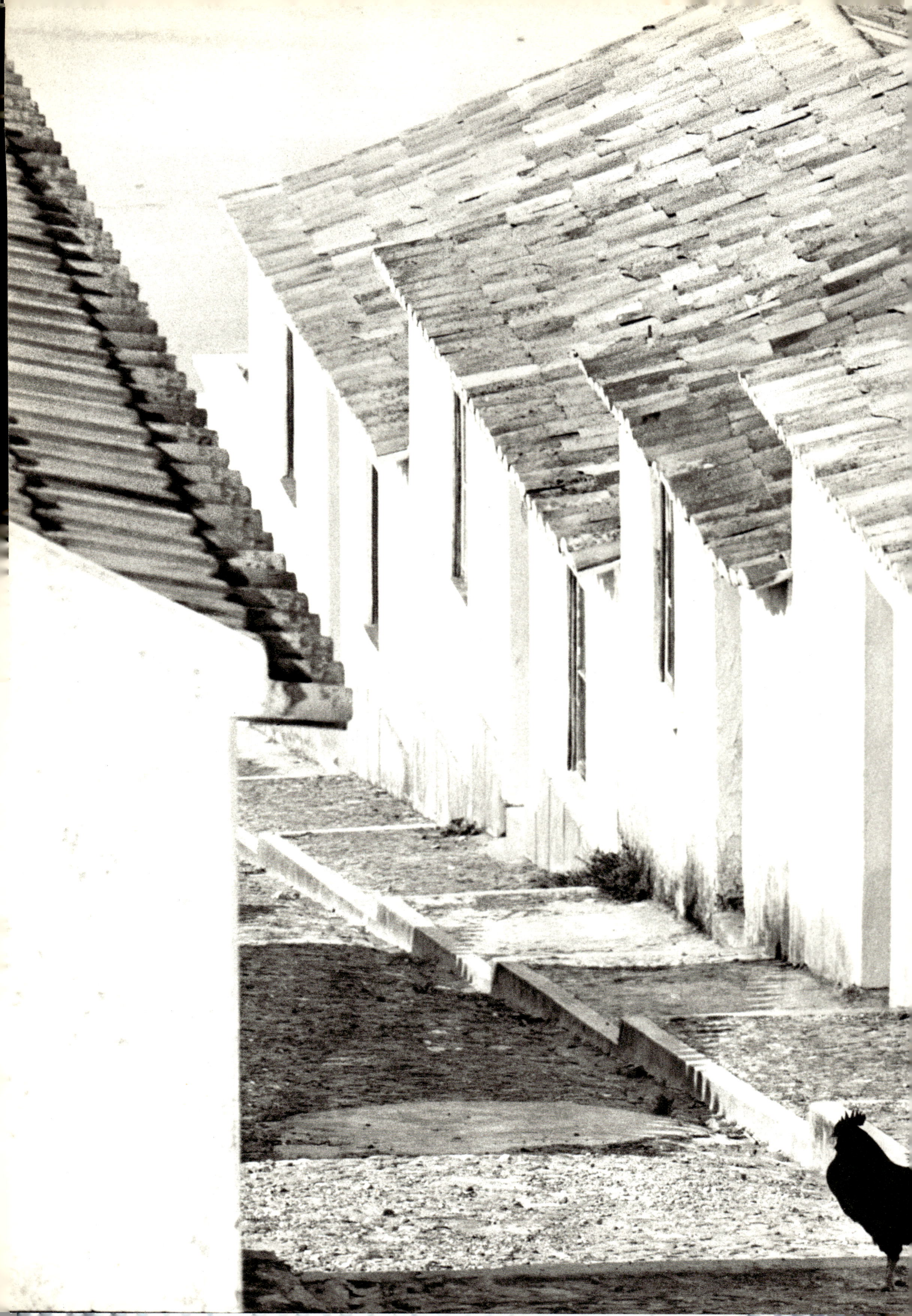

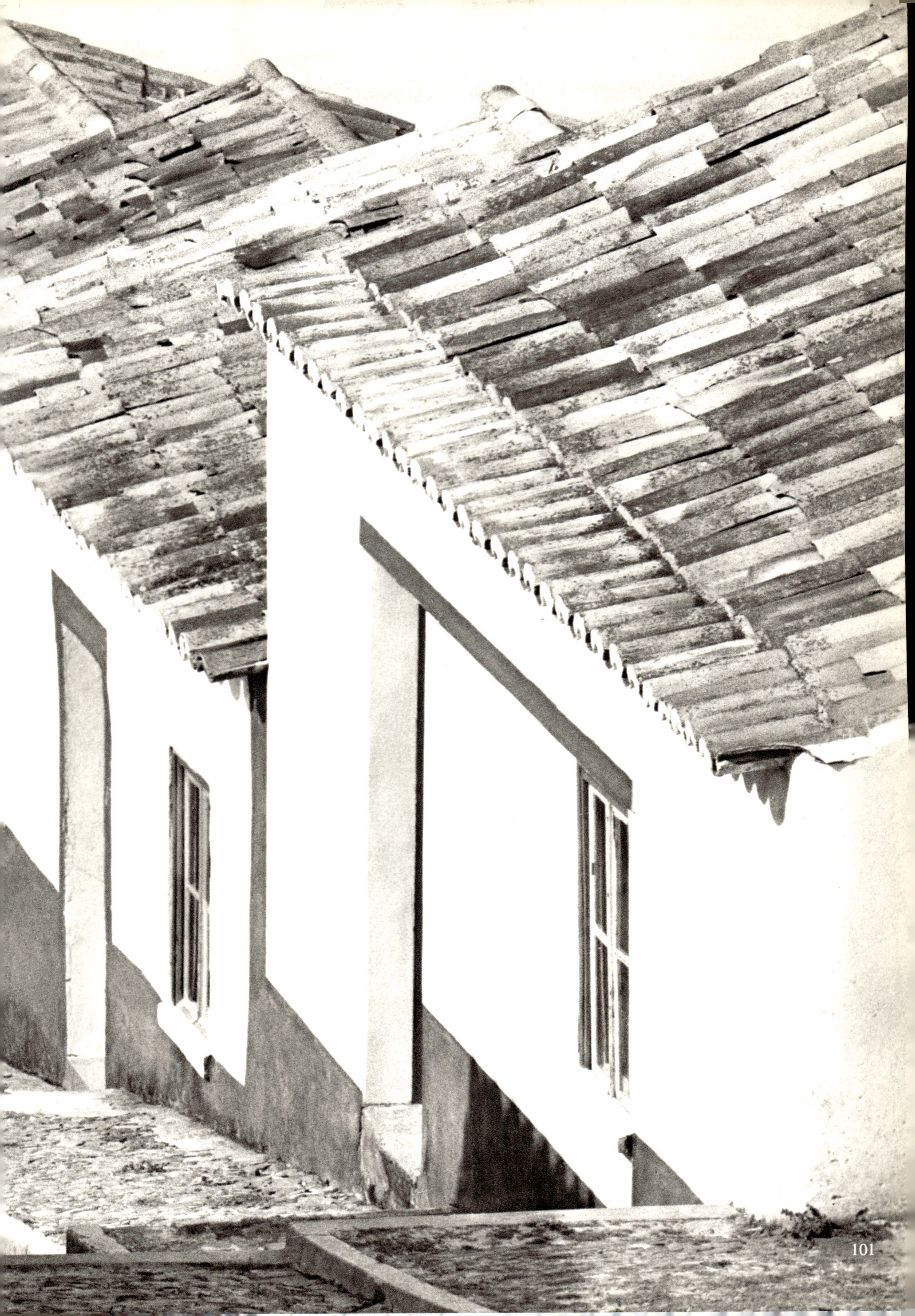

102

103

104

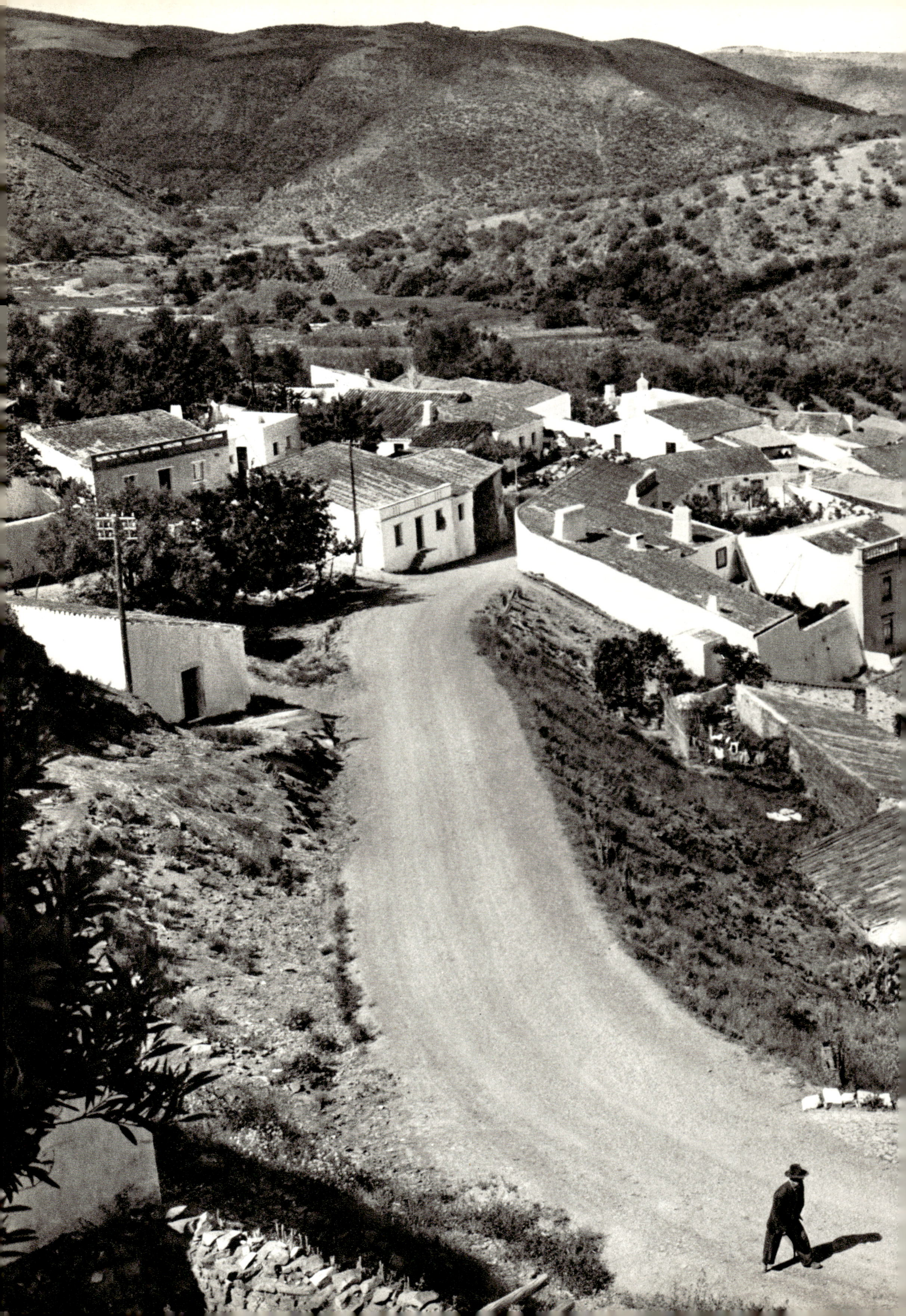

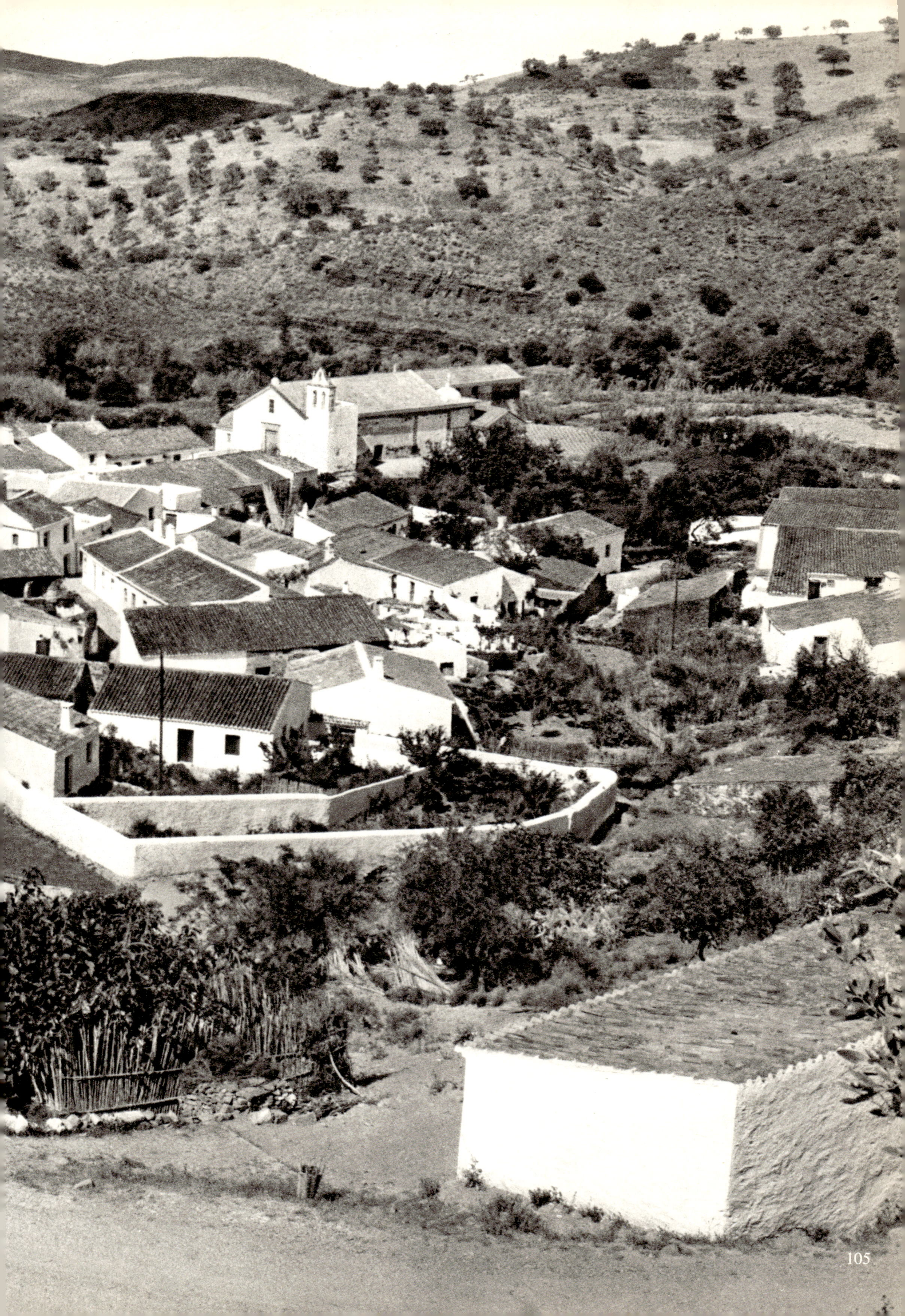

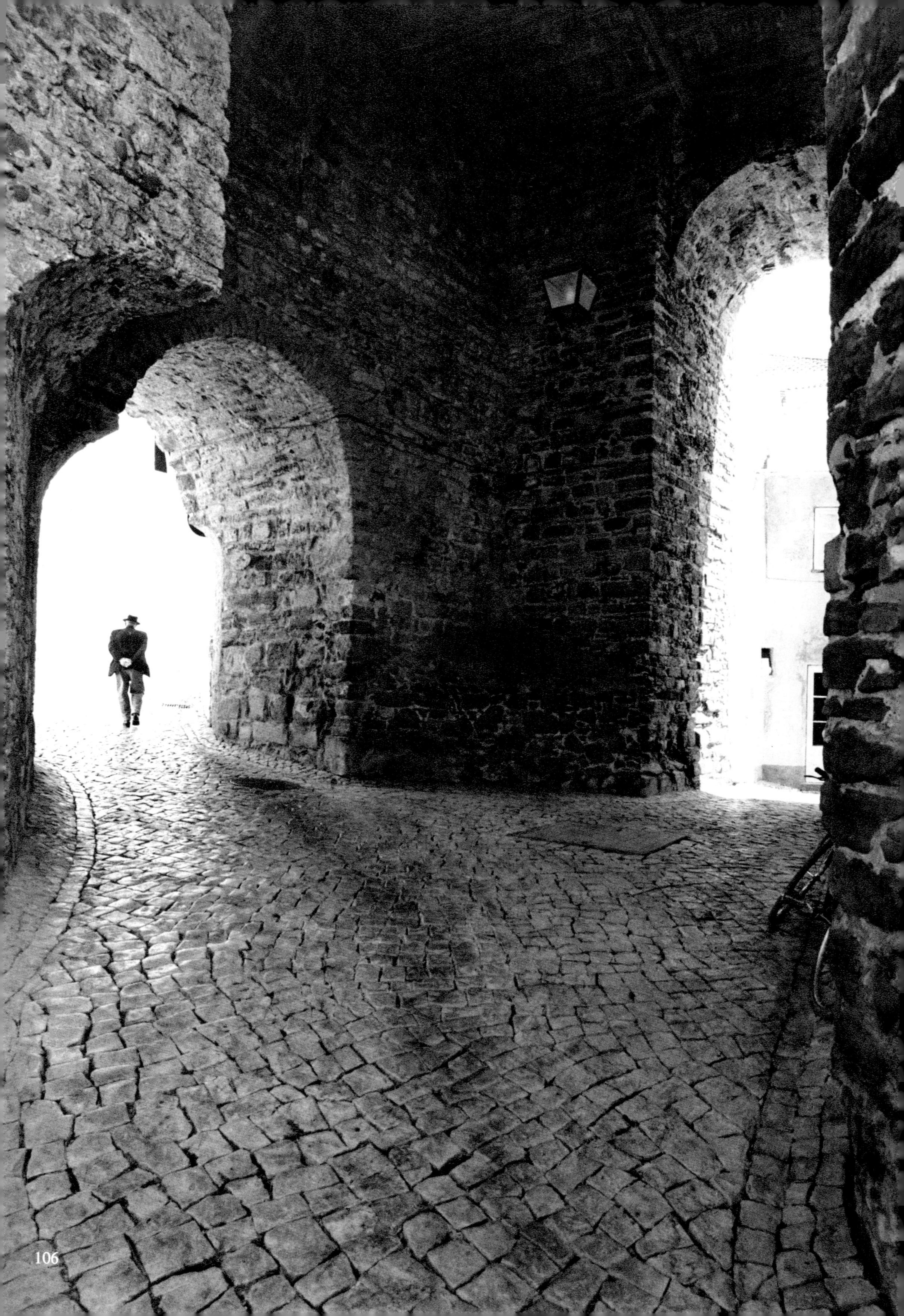

NOTES ON PLATES 81–106

81 A Peasant Couple in their Doorway, Algarve
The women in the Algarve wear head-scarves which often cover most of their faces. When they go out, this head-scarf is surmounted by a man's hat, usually black. The custom is believed to be a survival from Moorish times.

82 Earthenware Lobster Pots
At Cabanas, a small village near the Spanish frontier, a stack of the earthenware pots which are used for catching lobsters and crabs.

83 Potter at Estói
In the little town of Estói, a few miles north of Faro, a potter makes the brown, unglazed pots which are used for keeping water cool. His methods and equipment are unaffected by any modern innovations. The decoration on his pots is of a traditional simplicity: much the same ornamentation can be found all over the Mediterranean area, as far off as Greece.

84 Pierced Chimneys in the Algarve
These pierced chimneys, made of mortar or plaster, are one of the few solid memorials of the Moorish occupation of the Algarve, which came to an end with the capture of Faro in 1249. During the Spanish occupation, 1580–1640, the Algarve was often attacked by English raiders, and further damage was done in the earthquake of 1755. Architecturally, therefore, the Algarve has little to offer compared with other regions of Portugal.

The name Algarve derives from the Arabic Al-Gharb, meaning 'the western land'. This nomenclature was applied by the Moors both to the south-west of the Iberian Peninsula and to the district on the other side of the Straits of Gibraltar north and west of Fez. So when Afonso V (1438–81) captured Tangier and Arzila he adopted the title of 'King of Portugal and of the Algarves'.

Pierced chimneys, basically functional – to cope with strong winds – but treated decoratively are a special feature of southern Portugal, where it is natural that *mudéjar* (residual Moorish) architectural motifs should have persisted. Loulé (*see* plate 103) is particularly famous for the variety, caprice and fantasy of the forms employed for its chimneys and the patterns of their pierced smoke vents. The *Guia de Portugal* mentions shapes and patterns recalling sword hilts, snuff boxes, canisters, ears of corn, sugar shakers, dovecotes, sentry boxes, steeples, pepper grinders, minarets, chessmen, lanterns, candlesticks, obelisks, censers, cocked hats, decanters and turbans. However, even in 1927, when that volume of the *Guia* was published, the recent destruction of many of these delightful *mudéjar* chimneys was regretfully reported.

85 The Porch, Nossa Senhora das Rochas, Algarve

The chapel of Our Lady of the Rocks, near Armação de Pera in the Algarve, exemplifies the close connection between the everyday life of the fishing people and their religious faith. Here, the worn stones and smooth marble columns lead into a place apart, where nothing is altered in the ancient synthesis of danger, poverty and religious faith.

86 Nossa Senhora das Rochas

The sun beats down on the strangely shaped little whitewashed chapel on the cliff top; beyond, a warm sea glimmers. We are only a few miles from the raw concrete of new hotels, from the barren dunes divided into lots for summer villas.

The sanctuary chapel of the Senhora das Rochas is built on a tongue of rock, a hundred feet above the sea; not far away are the ruins of a Roman *castrum*. The hexagonal form of the chapel suggests that it dates from the seventeenth or eighteenth century, when polygonal and other centralized shapes were popular in Portugal, for chapels and even churches. The hexagonal chapel at Vila da Feira and the hexagonal church near Óbidos have already been mentioned in notes 16 and 64, and three of the octagonal chapels on the way up to the church of Bom Jesus do Monte near Braga are illustrated in plate 15. The close resemblance of the latter to the chapel of Our Lady of the Rocks is evident.

The Renaissance doctrine of the perfection of symmetrical shapes, and consequently the suitability of central plans for churches, had been publicized throughout Europe by means of Sebastiano Serlio's popular illustrated books on architecture, of which the fifth, devoted to churches, was first issued in 1547. Among other regular shapes, Serlio illustrated churches of hexagonal and octagonal plan with domed and pyramidal roofs; and it is from these examples that the Portuguese polygonal churches and chapels almost certainly derive.

87 VIRGIN AND CHILD, NOSSA SENHORA DAS ROCHAS
The statue of Our Lady and the Infant Jesus might be of almost any date, though She is adorned with bright new tinsel and a bunch of plastic lilies-of-the-valley.

88 EX-VOTOS, NOSSA SENHORA DAS ROCHAS
The walls of the church are hung with ex-votos, exact models of the tunny fishing boats which can be seen all along the coast of the Algarve.

89 BELFRY AT SAGRES
Two of the discordant, clattering bells which summon the faithful to church.

90 CHIMNEYS ON THE SCHOOL OF NAVIGATION, SAGRES
Massive chimneys like these are a common feature of this district of the Algarve, where the Atlantic gales blow for a large part of the year; this is the extreme south-western tip of Europe. For a similar chimney, *see* plate 49.

91 SAGRES
At Sagres (which derived its name from Cape St Vincent – the 'Promontorium Sacrum'), Prince Henry the Navigator established his school of navigation; here he received and correlated the scientific information from the various expeditions which he sent to explore the west coast of Africa and find the sea route to India.

'What is an Alexander crowned with trophies at the head of his army, compared with a Henry contemplating the ocean from his dwelling on the rock of Sagres? The one suggests the idea of a demon, the other of a tutelary angel,' wrote the eighteenth-century poet William Mickle, translator of Camões. Sagres was burned by Drake in 1597, during the Spanish occupation and was further ruined in the Great Earthquake. The headland itself is bare and bleak, buffeted by unending winds off the Atlantic.

92 PIG FARMER, ALGARVE
Portuguese pigs are long, lean and fierce in appearance. They live on the acorns which fall from the cork trees. Like most of his kind, the farmer carries an umbrella, wears a black felt hat, and shaves once a week.

93 VALE DO BURRINHO
Crenellated rooftops and white walls at Vale do Burrinho, which means 'the Valley of the Little Donkey'.

94 VILLAGE STREET, ALTE

Bright, dazzling walls and sober, black clothing provide an inevitable contrast in the village of Alte, on the way south. One of the overriding impressions of Portugal is the preference for black or dark colours – presumably because most clothes start off as Sunday best, and are later demoted to everyday wear.

95 CHURCH AT TAVIRA, ALGARVE

In Portugal even quite small parish churches have side chapels inside them, with reredoses donated by pious parishioners, either individually or as members of brotherhoods. When private resources permitted, or when religious manifestations enabled public subscriptions to be raised, separate chapels were built. The one in the background on the left of this photograph is an example of the simplest (and often the most charming) type of independent structure thus erected. The larger chapel in the foreground has by comparison a quite ambitious façade design (though the result is rather absurdly pompous and awkward), but it still belongs to the simplest architectural category of the chapel without towers, to which also belong the much more successful façades of the chapel of the Malheiro Reimão town house at Viana (plate 13) and the *ermida* of the Senhora das Salas near Sines (plate 102). These façades are related to the simplest kind of internal arrangement – a single nave.

More elaborate exteriors of course reflect greater internal complexity; and the degree of elaboration in turn reflects the ecclesiastical importance of the building and the wealth of the local community. At Sangalhos (plate 25), for example, the charming simplicity of the façade is overwhelmed by an imposing lateral tower displaying the ambitions of its rustic sponsors who have been able to afford at least one large bell, and a clock, housed under a baroque steeple surmounted by a weather-cock. At the *matriz* of Odeleite (plate 105) on the other hand, the resources available have been spent on the interior of the church, which is more complex architecturally and more elaborately decorated than the exterior would lead one to expect. The design to which all these chapels and minor churches ultimately aspired is demonstrated by the richest foundations, where money was no object, for example the great pilgrimage churches of Nossa Senhora de Mua (plate 52) and Bom Jesus do Monte (plate 15) with their twin towers flanking three-bay façades, to make a symmetrical composition of five bays in all. The great church of Mafra even has five full bays and eight half bays.

96 A SHOEBLACK AT TAVIRA

Highly polished shoes are a sign of respectability, and the traveller is soon shamed into conforming with the rules.

97 PINE-TREES TAPPED FOR RESIN
The production of resin is a major industry in Portugal. The trees are tapped twice a year, the resin running into a small earthenware cup (several of these can be seen on the ground). The resulting product contains 70 per cent solid resin (known as rosin), 20 per cent volatile essential oil (turpentine) and 10 per cent water and impurities. Rosin and turpentine are used in a wide variety of products. The pine here is *Pinus maritima* or *pinaster*, which is planted in enormous numbers all over Portugal.

98 PLOUGHING WITH MULES, VILA NOVA DE MILFONTES
The different parts of Portugal still retain different agricultural methods which they have inherited from the distant past. In the north, long-horned oxen are used with the heavy ploughs which are a Roman inheritance. In central Portugal, agriculture was much influenced by the Cistercians in their great monastery of Alcobaça. Here, near Vila Nova de Milfontes, we are on the road to the Algarve, the part of Portugal which assimilated the greatest Arab influence. In this area, mules are used for pulling the plough, which is lighter and more manageable than the northern type.

99 THE CROSS OF PORTUGAL, SILVES
Silves, then known as Kelb, was the Moorish capital of the province of Al-faghar, which later became the Kingdom of the Algarve. It was one of the last fortresses to be captured from the Moors by Afonso III, being taken by him in 1242. This crucifix, which is known as the Cross of Portugal, is situated near the Moorish castle. It is ten feet in height and, in addition to the image of the crucified Christ, bears a *pietà*, or Descent from the Cross, on its reverse side. The clothing worn by the Virgin, and the knobbly, late Gothic ornamentation, indicate that it dates from the Manueline period, the early years of the sixteenth century.

100 CHARNEL HOUSE, FARO
A Victorian account of the cemetery at Faro: 'The dead are here deposited in a very thick wall full of little arched openings, resembling a pigeon-house: each hole is just large enough to admit a body, and is afterwards closed up with masonry. After a certain number of years, when all the apartments are occupied, the oldest of the lodgers are turned out to make room for the newcomers; and as it frequently happens that the bones are still entire, the heads, arms and legs are made to serve as horrid ornaments. For this purpose thousands of skulls are seen fastened against the wall in cement, forming pilasters, or parts of a cornice; the other bones are distributed with equal attention to architectural arrangement, and the whole is then whitewashed' *(Murray's Guide,* 1875).

101 ROOFTOPS AT ODECEIXE

Odeceixe is a small village just south of the Seixe river, which here forms the boundary between the provinces of Alentejo and the Algarve. The Atlantic Ocean lies three or four kilometres to the west. The curious name of the village derives from the Arabic name of the river, Wadi Seixe. This small river was once navigable, but its bed was disturbed by the great earthquake of 1755, causing widespread flooding and stranding fish throughout the surrounding countryside.

102 NOSSA SENHORA DAS SALAS, SINES

On the western point of the bay of Sines, which projects into the Atlantic on the coast of the province of Estremadura, there stands this remote sanctuary chapel, or *ermida* (literally 'hermitage'). Inside it are *ex voto* paintings of shipwrecks presented by survivors in gratitude to the Senhora das Salas for saving them from drowning. The chapel dates from 1335, but it was reconstructed at the expense of Vasco da Gama (1469–1524), who was born at Sines. The Manueline doorway, its flanking pinnacles and the two carved and inscribed medallions (in square frames) on either side of the ogival doorhead date from Vasco da Gama's reconstruction, which was completed in 1529. In the eighteenth century the interior was decorated with *azulejos* and a baroque termination given to the façade.

Vasco da Gama's interest in the *ermida* of the Senhora das Salas is commemorated by a local story that when he passed the headland setting out or returning from oceanic voyages he always ordered his ship's guns to fire a salute.

103 STREET SIGN, LOULÉ

This sign, giving the name of the principal square in the Algarve town of Loulé, is made up of *azulejos,* sunk into a whitewashed wall. Afonso III was the king who, in the thirteenth century, completed the conquest of the Algarve from the Moors.

104 CASEMENT WINDOW, OLHÃO

In 1808 the newly built town of Olhão near Faro was given the official title of Vila Nova de Olhão. Its history goes back no further than the seventeenth century, when it started to be used by the fishermen of the Algarve as a haven for refitting and taking on fresh water supplies during the fishing season; straw huts were then put up for temporary accommodation. Gradually settled on a permanent basis, Olhão prospered as a result of the enterprise of its inhabitants who extended their fishing activities, in small caiques, far out into the Atlantic and down the west coast of Africa – even sailing, on one memorable occasion, to Brazil. When Gibraltar was besieged in 1779–82, and later when Cádiz was invested by the French during the Peninsular War, the bold sailors of Olhão made small fortunes by supplying both sides with victuals. These profits enabled them to rebuild their houses in stone and plaster. The present 'cubist town' of one-storey white houses was thus created.

The window illustrated here is probably of early nineteenth-century date (though preserving an eighteenth-century design).

The oldest building in Olhão is the parish church of Our Lady of the Rosary, which bears, on a corner stone, the inscription: '*A custa dos homens do mar deste povo se fes este templo novo no tempo que so havião huas palhotas em que vivião. Primeiro fundamento 1698.*' ('This new church was built at the expense of the seafarers of this community, at a time when they only had straw huts in which to live. First foundation 1698.')

The name Olhão (literally 'large eye') probably derives from an *olho de agua*, or spring, in the vicinity which must have provided an important reason for the original choice of the site.

105 Odeleite, a Village in the Algarve

Odeleite is situated on a tributary of the Guadiana river, which here forms the frontier between Portugal and Spain. Cultivation is concentrated along the flat ground near the stream; the hillsides, apart from a few olives and carob-trees, are given over to wild vegetation – gum cistus, wild lavender and yellow broom.

The parish church of Odeleite, prominent in the photograph on the right-hand side, is dedicated to Our Lady of the Visitation, and thanks partly to income bequeathed by an ancient benefactor, Prior José Martins Faleiro, has quite a fine interior. The bells hang in the simplest kind of open *campanário*, reminding us that the Algarve is particularly susceptible to earthquakes, which discourages the construction of towers, even when resources are available to build them.

106 Town Gate, Silves

Nearly everything that was of Arab origin in Silves has disappeared, except for the castle, now much restored, and its underground storage cisterns. The massive town walls are from a later date, when the city was threatened by attack from the sea, first by the Moors and later, when Portugal was occupied by Philip II of Spain, by English raiders.

Possibly dating from Roman times or even earlier, Silves developed under the rule of the Moors, between the eighth and twelfth centuries, into the chief city of their western province, Al-faghar. Estimated to have reached a population of thirty thousand, including many Arabs from the Yemen, it became famous as a centre of learning as well as for its fine buildings, gardens and orchards. Twice taken and sacked, by Fernando I of Castile in 1060 and by Sancho I of Portugal in 1189 (with the aid of a party of North

European crusaders on their way out to the Holy Land), it was on each occasion quickly recaptured by the Moors; and it was not until 1242 that they finally lost it to the legendary crusader Dom Paio Peres Correia (d. 1275), 'Captain-General of the frontiers of the Algarve', who later fought the Moors in Spain and became Master of the Hispanic Order of Santiago.

These wars destroyed the town's prosperity. It was made an episcopal see, but efforts to revive its economy failed. Its buildings were severely damaged by the great earthquakes of 1356 and 1531. By the mid-sixteenth century the population is said to have been reduced to 140 persons, and in 1577 the bishopric was transferred to Faro. Renewed attempts to rebuild were frustrated by the earthquake of 1722 (localized in the Algarve where it was very destructive) and the great earthquake of 1755, after which it is said that only ten houses remained intact. Consequently few buildings in the present town are of earlier than nineteenth-century date; and such is the inferior architectural character of the townscape that the writer in the *Guia de Portugal* of 1927 felt tempted, he tells us, to advise visitors to avert their eyes from the houses when walking through the streets.

INDEX

Numbers in italics refer to the plates, roman numerals to colour plates

AFONSO I 15, 19, 91
Afonso III 85, 158, 197, 198
Afonso IV 92, 158
Afonso V 194
Afonso, Jorge 155
Africa 21, 28, 38, 39, 198
Agriculture 20, 22, 53, 92, 98, 15, 16, 17, 19–20, 89, 195, 197
Albuquerque, Afonso de 25, 29
Alcáer do Sal 18
Alcazar Quibir, Battle of (1578) 28
Alcobaça monastery 24, 19–20, 91–3, 197
Alcochete VIII, 35
'Alentejo' 10–11
Alfonso IX of Leon 97
Algarve XI, 81, 84–92, 95, 11, 45, 142, 193–5, 197, 198, 199, 200
Aljubarrota, Battle of 21
Almeida, Dom Jorge de, bishop 94
Alte 94, 196
Álvares, Baltasar 7, 83
Amarante, Carlos Luis Ferraira 15, 87
Amélie, Ex-Queen 47, 149
Amorim, João Lopes de 11, 84
Angola 39
Anti-clericalism 26
António de São José 146
Aqueducts 75, 78, 157, 159
Arab culture see Islamic culture
Armação da Pera 85–8, 194
Arouca 96–7
Arrábida order 145–6
Arruda, Diego de 154, 160, 161
Arruda, Francisco de VII, 78, 32, 157, 159, 160, 161
Astorga 90
Aveiro, Duke of 146

Aviz, House of 21, 27, 155
Azores 22
Azulejos III, IV, 50, 103, 15, 22, 147, 149, 198

BACALHOA see Quinta da Bacalhoa
Batalha 69–73, 21, 152, 155–6
Beckford, William 10, 18, 20, 36, 41, 91, 151–2
Beira Alta 19–21, 89, 90
Beja 16, 90
Belém II, VII, 35, 36, 15, 18, 32, 147, 161
Bemposta Palace 143
Benevides family 146
Boitac, Diogo 50, 142, 146–7, 155
Bom Jesus do Monte 15, 86–7, 149, 194
Borrow, George 41–2, 151
Bos, Cornelis 86
Bracara Augusta 90
Braga 23, 17, 90–1
Braganza, House of 28, 32, 36, 37
Brazil 22, 28, 29, 30, 38, 198
Bristol, St Mary Redcliffe 156
Bull fighting IX, X, 35, 42
Burgundian monarchy 15, 19
Burton, Sir Richard 95
Bussaco 11, 25, 38

CABANAS 82, 193
Cabo de Espichel 52, 88, 148–9, 196
Cabral, Álvares 22
Camões, Luiz de 151, 157, 195
Canton 28
Cape St Vincent 12, 16
Cape sorrel 9
Capêlo, Brito 39

Carlos I 149
Castanheira, Count of 142
Castelo de Santa Maria 87
Castilho, João de 142, 155
Castro, Ferreira de 46
  Dona Inês de 20, 91–3
  Machada de 144
Catharina, Dona, wife of João III 150
Catherine of Braganza 143, 146
Celtic culture 15
Chanterène, Nicolas 55, 150
Charles II of England 143, 146
Christianization 17–19
Cistercian order 19, 91, 97, 197
Cistus plants 11
Citânias 15, 86
Citânia de Briteiros 18, 88–9
Coimbra 26, 34, 18, 19, 26, 28, 93–4, 97–8
Collin, Antoine I, 12
Colombo 22
Conimbriga 27–31, 15, 16, 94–5
Copabanca 143
Cork oak trees 6, 10, 11, 21, 195
Correia, Dom Paio Peres 200
Cosimo III, Grand Duke of Tuscany 146
Costa, Felix da 148
Courtesy 27
'Cross of Portugal' 99, 197
Crusades 19, 20, 21, 28, 199–200
Cruz, Agostinho do 146
Cueta, attack on 21
Cypresses 46, 145

DIAS, BARTOLOMEO 25
Dinis, King 9, 153
Domingues, Afonso 71, 155, 156
Douro 1, 10, 19, 81, 82
Dutra Banda 10

EARTHQUAKES 31, 32, 45, 142–3, 144, 145, 193, 198, 199, 200
Elvas Aqueduct 78, 157, 159
England, Portuguese relations with 21–2, 31, 37, 38, 39, 154
England, visitors from 10, 18, 20, 36, 37, 41, 42, 91, 151
Eschwege, Baron 56, 151
Estói 83, 193
Estoril 46–7
Eucalyptus trees 9, 37, 88
Évora 75, 76, 79, 80, 11, 16, 88, 157–8, 159–61
Exploration 21–2, 25, 30, 85, 199

FADO 9, 46
Faria Lobo, Silvestre de I, 12
Faro 100, 19, 197
Fatima 12
Ferdinand of Coburg, King Consort 38, 39, 150
Fernandes, Mateus 72, 73, 155, 156
Fernando I of Castile 199
Fernão, King 20
Fialho, Padre Manuel 158
Fielding, Henry 32, 37
Fishing VI, VIII, 9, 44, 45, 47, 60, 82, 88, 25, 35, 145, 148, 152, 193, 194, 195, 198–9
Flora XI, 9–12, 45
Florence 97, 149
Forests 17, 97, 11, 88, 197
France 158
Franciscan order 49, 80, 30, 145–6, 160
Francisco, Dom 148
Franco, Capt. Rodrigo 153

GAMA, VASCO DA 25, 150, 198
Gardens 54, 87, 149
Gilbert of Hastings, Abp. of Braga 19
Goa 22, 25, 39
Greenland 22
Guimarães 10–12, 84–5, 89

HENRIQUE, CARDINAL INFANTE 157, 159
Henry I of Castile 97

Henry, Count of Burgundy 15, 19, 85, 91
Henry the Navigator 22, 25, 156, 195
Herculano, Alexandre 19
Huguete 155

ILLITERACY 27
India 156; see also Goa
Inquisition 26
Islamic culture IV, VII, 12, 71, 84, 17–18, 22, 85, 145, 147, 149, 151, 153, 156, 193–4, 197, 199–200
Italy 87, 149
Ivens, Roberto 39

JAMES THE GREATER, ST 90
Japan 30
Jerónimos Convent, Belém 35, 36, 141–2
Jesuit order 79, 26, 30, 35, 93, 146, 159–60
Jews 16, 17, 18, 20, 26, 28, 29, 31, 85, 145
João I 21, 87, 151, 152, 155
João III 15, 26, 142, 150, 154, 157, 159
João IV 28, 146
João V 32, 39, 146, 153
João VI 37–8
John of Ypres 94
José I 35

KELB see Silves
Knights of Christ 153–4

LABRADOR 22
Language 16, 18, 41–2
Lees-Milne, James 39
Leixões 83
Lencastre, João de 146
Lima, River 85
Lisbon 35–48, 9, 19, 21, 26, 31, 32, 35–6, 37, 38, 39, 47, 83, 141–5, 149
London 146
Lopes, João 86
Lorvão 32, 33, 95–7
Loulé 103, 194, 198
Ludovic, J. F. 158
Lugo 90

Luis, Constable of Portugal 159
Lusiads 16, 27

MACÃO 30
Madeira 22
Mafra 32
Malheiros Reimões, Casa dos 13, 85
Manuel I 25, 86, 88, 141, 142, 144, 146, 147, 150, 151
Manueline style VII, 35, 36, 50, 58, 65–7, 69, 72, 73, 99, 102, 25–6, 32, 141–2, 146–8, 149, 150, 153, 154, 155–6, 160, 197, 198
Maquis 11
Maria I 12, 35, 36–7, 144, 149
Maria II 38, 150
Martin of Braga, St 17
Martinho de Santa Maria 145–6
Mati vegetation 11
Matilda, Dona 97
Maurice of Nassau 28
Medonça, Maria de 149
Mértola 16, 18, 151
Methuen Treaty 31, 82
Miguel, King 38
Mimosa 9, 10
Minho 84
Mombasa 22
Monasteries 24, 32, 35, 36, 49, 55, 65–73, 80, 19, 20, 91–3, 95–6, 141–2, 145–6, 150, 153–4, 155–6, 160–1, 197; see also Palace-monasteries
Monforte 62, 152–3
Moorish culture see Islamic culture
Mozambique 22, 39
Mozarabes 18, 19, 20
Mumadona, Lady 85

NASONI, NICCOLÒ 7, 8, 83, 84
Nazaré VI, 60, 61, 25, 152
Nossa Senhora de Mua 52, 88, 148–9, 196
Nossa Senhora des Rochas, Algarve 84–8, 194–5
Nossa Senhora das Salas 102, 196, 198
Nosso Senhor de Pedra Fria church 153

ÓBIDOS 63, 64, 20, 153
Odeceixe 101, 198
Odeleite 105, 196, 199
Oeiras Museum 40
Olhão 104, 198–9
Oliver of Ghent 94
Oporto 7–9, 19, 20, 31, 82–4, 85, 143
Ossonoba XI, 45
Ourique, Battle of 19

PAES, DOM DURANDO 158
Palace-monasteries 55, 56, 25, 32, 38, 150–1
Pedro I 24, 20, 91–3
Pedro II 31, 146
Pedro, Emperor of Brazil 38
Pedro, Dom, Consort of Maria I 12, 149
Pedro de Rates, St 90
Pena, Castelo de 56, 38, 39, 150–1
Pena, Convento da 55, 150
Peninsular Wars 37, 198
Pereira, Alvaro 87
    Diogo 88
    Fernão 87–8
    Rui 83, 88
Pessoa, Fernando 22
Peter of Alcántara, St 146
Philip II, King of Spain 28, 199
Philippa of Lancaster 21, 152, 155
Phylloxera vastatrix 82
Pine trees 17, 97, 9, 11, 88, 197
Pinto, Serpa 39
Pombal, Marquis de 26, 31, 35, 142, 144
Ponte Sálazar 43, 144–5
Port wine 4, 82
Portucale 19
Priscillianists 45

QUEIROZ, EÇA DE 9, 18, 26, 39
Queluz, Royal Palace of I, 54, 14, 149–50
Quinta da Bacalhoa III, IV, 53, 15, 22, 149

RASTRELLI 83
Rhodes, Cecil 39
Robert, Master 93
Robillon, Jean-Baptiste 54, 149–50
Roman culture XI, 27–31, 76, 15, 16, 45, 87, 89, 94–5, 158, 197

SABROSO 89
Sagres 89–91, 12, 195
Salamanca 143
Salazar, Dr António 9
Sancha, Dona 96
Sancho I 96, 199
Sangalhos 25, 93, 196
Santarém 18, 90
Santiago 90, 93, 94
Santos, Eugénio dos 144
São Tomé 22
Sarmento, Dr Martins 89
Scoville, Mrs 149
Sebastianismo 28
Sebastião, Dom 27–8, 38
Serlio, Sebastiano 153, 194–5
Serra da Arrábida 49, 10, 11, 145–6
Serra de Monchique 11
Serra del Sintra 57, 10, 11, 151
Sertorius, Quintus 157
Setúbal V, 50, 51, 25, 142
Sexuality, Portuguese attitude to 9, 18
Silva, André Ribeiro Soares de 85
Silva, Manuel Carneiro da 96
Silves 99, 106, 151, 197, 199–200
Sines 102, 196, 198
Sintra 58, 59, 18, 25, 37, 151, 152
Sousa, Dom Diogo de 91
Southey, Robert 10, 151, 152
Soveral, Marquis of 39
Spain 7–8, 38, 145, 158, 193, 195, 199
Spice trade 21, 25, 26
Storks 62, 152

Suevi 16, 87, 95

TAGUS VALLEY AND BRIDGE VIII, 43, 45, 47, 74, 10, 35, 144–5, 148, 157
Tavira 95, 96, 196
Teles, Dom Rodrigo de Moura, Abp. of Braga 87
Teresa, Countess of Portugal 91
Teresa, Dona (dau. of Sancho I) 32, 96, 97
Tomar 65–8, 26, 153–5, 161
Torralva, Diogo de 142
Trade 8, 20, 21, 22, 26, 28, 29, 31, 82, 86
Transport II, 10, 40, 15, 45–6
Trás-os-Montes 17, 88

VALE DO BURRINHO 93, 195
Viana do Castelo 13, 14, 85–6, 196
Vicente, Gil 151
    Mateus 54, 149–50
Vila da Feira 16, 87–8
Vila da Feira, Counts of 148
Vila Nogueira de Azeitão 89
Vila Nova de Gaia 7, 82–3
Vila Viçosa 77, 159
Vilar Formosa area 22, 90
Vines 2, 6, 10, 16, 81–2
Virathus 89
Visigoths 16, 17, 18, 87, 95
Voltaire 32, 35
Vries, Jan Vredemar de 86

WELLINGTON, 1ST DUKE OF 37
Windmills V, 25
Wine production and trade 2–7, 16, 21, 31, 81
Women, status of 29, 40–1

XAVIER, ST FRANCIS 25

YEMEN 199
Yevell, Henry 155

ZÊZERE, RIVER 74, 157